SENDEROS 1B

Spanish for a Connected World

VISTA®
HIGHER LEARNING

Boston, Massachusetts

On the cover: El Morro Fortress, Puerto Rico.

Publisher: José A. Blanco
Editorial Development: Armando Brito, Jhonny Alexander Calle, Deborah Coffey,
María Victoria Echeverri, Jo Hanna Kurth, Megan Moran, Jaime Patiño,
Raquel Rodríguez, Verónica Tejeda, Sharla Zwirek
Project Management: Sally Giangrande, Tiffany Kayes
Rights Management: Ashley Poreda, Annie Pickert Fuller
Technology Production: Egle Gutiérrez, Jamie Kostecki, Reginald Millington, Fabián Montoya, Paola Ríos Schaaf
Design: Radoslav Mateev, Gabriel Noreña, Andrés Vanegas
Production: Oscar Díez, Adriana Jaramillo

Student Text (Casebound-SIMRA) ISBN: 978-1-68005-629-7

Teacher's Edition ISBN: 978-1-68005-631-0

Library of Congress Control Number: 2017949634

1 2 3 4 5 6 7 8 9 TC 22 21 20 19 18 17

Printed in Canada.

SENDEROS 1B

Spanish for a Connected World

Table of Contents

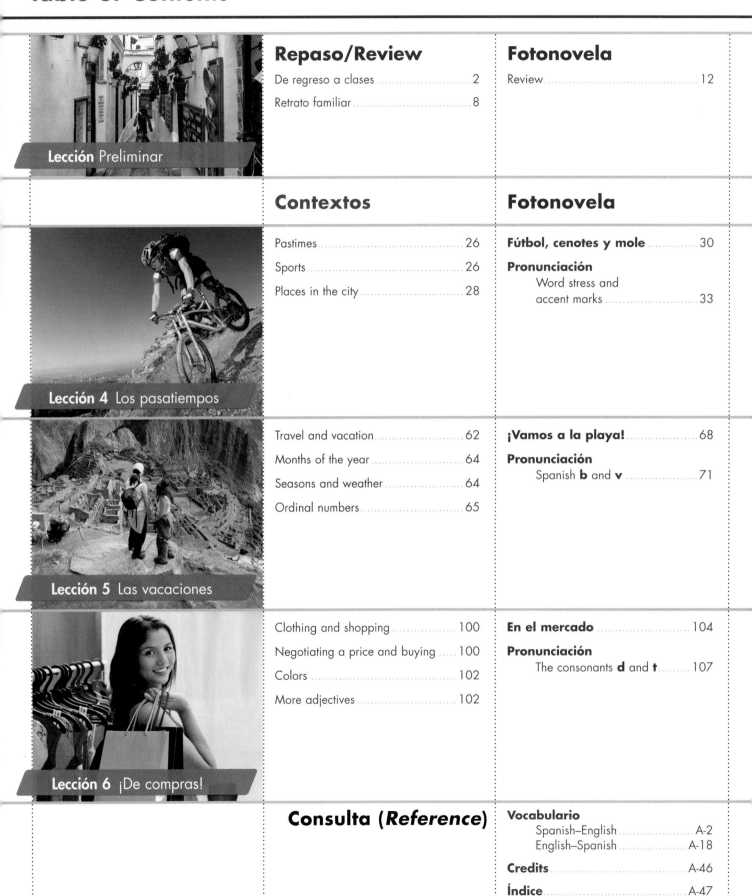

Icons

Familiarize yourself with these icons that
appear throughout **Senderos**.

◁))	Listening activity/section
👥	Pair activity
👥👥	Group activity

The Spanish-Speaking World

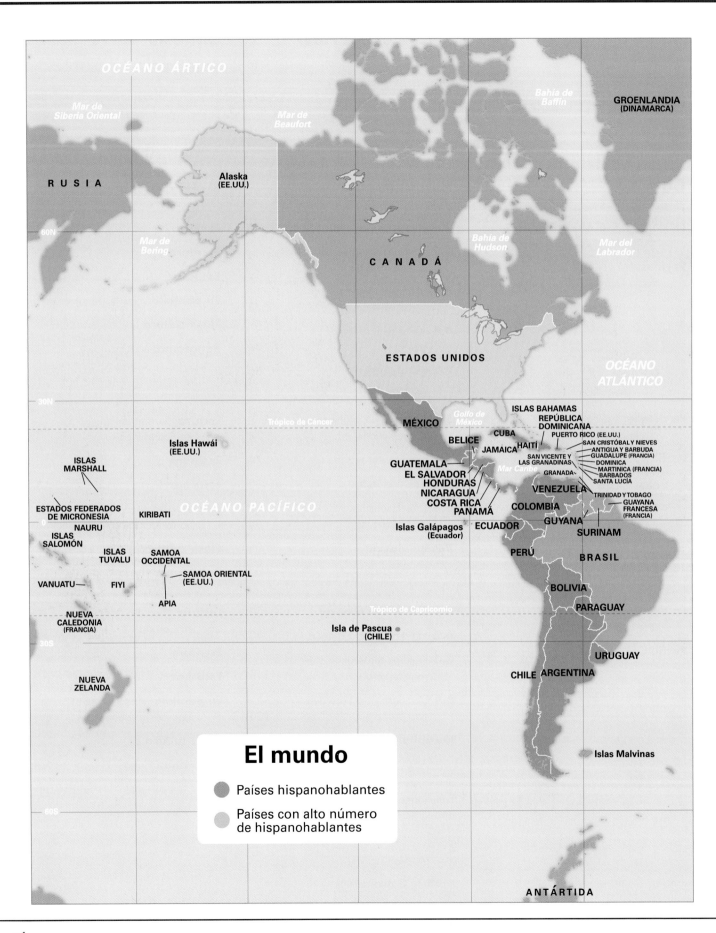

OCÉANO ÁRTICO

Mar de Siberia Oriental

Mar de Beaufort

Bahía de Baffin

GROENLANDIA (DINAMARCA)

RUSIA

Alaska (EE.UU.)

60N

Mar de Bering

Bahía de Hudson

Mar del Labrador

CANADÁ

ESTADOS UNIDOS

OCÉANO ATLÁNTICO

30N

Trópico de Cáncer

Golfo de México

ISLAS BAHAMAS

REPÚBLICA DOMINICANA

MÉXICO

CUBA

PUERTO RICO (EE.UU.)

BELICE

HAITÍ

SAN CRISTÓBAL Y NIEVES

Islas Hawái (EE.UU.)

JAMAICA

ANTIGUA Y BARBUDA

GUADALUPE (FRANCIA)

ISLAS MARSHALL

SAN VICENTE Y LAS GRANADINAS

DOMINICA

GUATEMALA

MARTINICA (FRANCIA)

EL SALVADOR

Mar Caribe

GRANADA

BARBADOS

SANTA LUCÍA

HONDURAS

ESTADOS FEDERADOS DE MICRONESIA

OCÉANO PACÍFICO

NICARAGUA

VENEZUELA

TRINIDAD Y TOBAGO

KIRIBATI

COSTA RICA

COLOMBIA

GUAYANA FRANCESA (FRANCIA)

PANAMÁ

NAURU

GUYANA

ISLAS SALOMÓN

ECUADOR

SURINAM

Islas Galápagos (Ecuador)

ISLAS TUVALU

PERÚ

SAMOA OCCIDENTAL

BRASIL

VANUATU

FIYI

SAMOA ORIENTAL (EE.UU.)

APIA

Trópico de Capricornio

BOLIVIA

NUEVA CALEDONIA (FRANCIA)

Isla de Pascua (CHILE)

PARAGUAY

30S

URUGUAY

NUEVA ZELANDA

CHILE ARGENTINA

Islas Malvinas

El mundo

● Países hispanohablantes

● Países con alto número de hispanohablantes

60S

ANTÁRTIDA

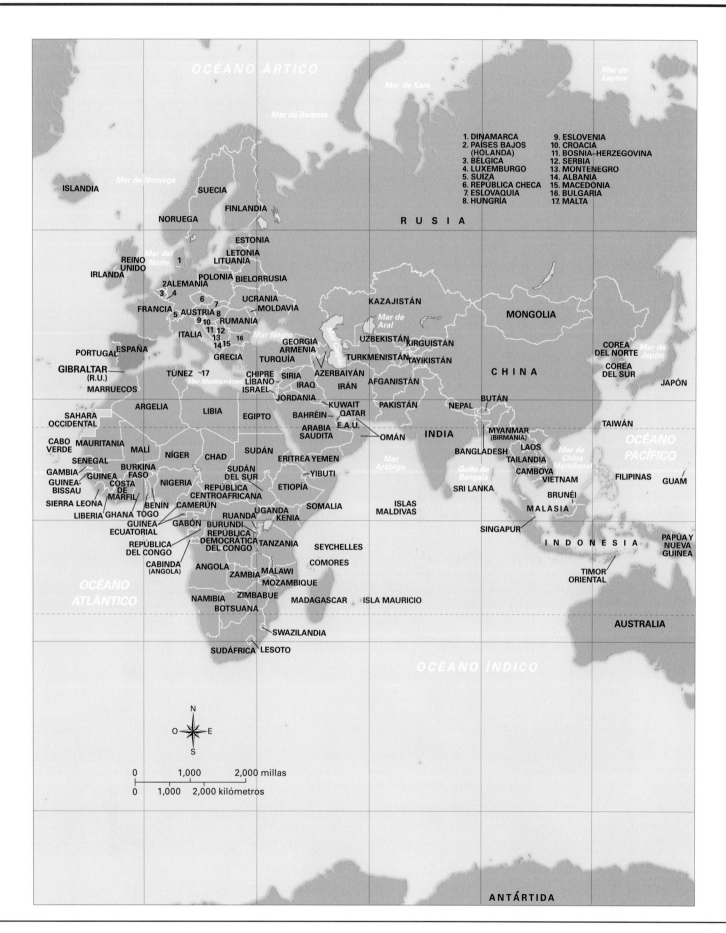

OCÉANO ÁRTICO

Mar de Kara

Mar de Laptev

Mar de Barents

Mar de Noruega

ISLANDIA

1. DINAMARCA
2. PAÍSES BAJOS (HOLANDA)
3. BÉLGICA
4. LUXEMBURGO
5. SUIZA
6. REPÚBLICA CHECA
7. ESLOVAQUIA
8. HUNGRÍA

9. ESLOVENIA
10. CROACIA
11. BOSNIA–HERZEGOVINA
12. SERBIA
13. MONTENEGRO
14. ALBANIA
15. MACEDONIA
16. BULGARIA
17. MALTA

SUECIA

FINLANDIA

RUSIA

NORUEGA

ESTONIA

Mar del Norte

LETONIA

REINO UNIDO

IRLANDA

1

LITUANIA

POLONIA BIELORRUSIA

KAZAJISTÁN

MONGOLIA

2 ALEMANIA

3 4

6

7

UCRANIA

Mar de Aral

FRANCIA

5 AUSTRIA 8

MOLDAVIA

UZBEKISTÁN

KIRGUISTÁN

9 10

RUMANIA

Mar Caspio

ITALIA

11 12

13

14 15

16

Mar Negro

GEORGIA

ARMENIA

TURKMENISTÁN

TAYIKISTÁN

COREA DEL NORTE

Mar de Japón

PORTUGAL

ESPAÑA

GRECIA

TURQUÍA

CHINA

COREA DEL SUR

GIBRALTAR (R.U.)

TÚNEZ 17

CHIPRE

LÍBANO

ISRAEL

SIRIA

IRAQ

AZERBAIYÁN

IRÁN

AFGANISTÁN

JAPÓN

MARRUECOS

Mar Mediterráneo

JORDANIA

ARGELIA

LIBIA

EGIPTO

KUWAIT

BAHRÉIN QATAR

PAKISTÁN

NEPAL

BUTÁN

TAIWÁN

SAHARA OCCIDENTAL

ARABIA SAUDITA

E.A.U.

OMÁN

INDIA

MYANMAR (BIRMANIA)

OCÉANO PACÍFICO

CABO VERDE

MAURITANIA

MALÍ

NÍGER

CHAD

SUDÁN

ERITREA YEMEN

Mar Arábigo

BANGLADESH

LAOS

Mar de China Meridional

SENEGAL

BURKINA FASO

SUDÁN DEL SUR

YIBUTI

Golfo de Bengala

TAILANDIA

CAMBOYA

FILIPINAS

GUAM

GAMBIA

GUINEA

GUINEA-BISSAU

COSTA DE MARFIL

NIGERIA

REPÚBLICA CENTROAFRICANA

ETIOPÍA

SRI LANKA

VIETNAM

BRUNÉI

SIERRA LEONA

BENÍN

CAMERÚN

SOMALIA

ISLAS MALDIVAS

MALASIA

LIBERIA GHANA TOGO

GUINEA ECUATORIAL

RUANDA

BURUNDI

GABÓN

REPÚBLICA DEMOCRÁTICA DEL CONGO

UGANDA

KENIA

SINGAPUR

INDONESIA

PAPÚA Y NUEVA GUINEA

REPÚBLICA DEL CONGO

TANZANIA

SEYCHELLES

CABINDA (ANGOLA)

ANGOLA

ZAMBIA

MALAWI

MOZAMBIQUE

COMORES

TIMOR ORIENTAL

OCÉANO ATLÁNTICO

NAMIBIA

ZIMBABUE

BOTSUANA

MADAGASCAR

ISLA MAURICIO

AUSTRALIA

SWAZILANDIA

SUDÁFRICA LESOTO

OCÉANO ÍNDICO

N

O E

S

0   1,000   2,000 millas

0   1,000   2,000 kilómetros

ANTÁRTIDA

Mexico

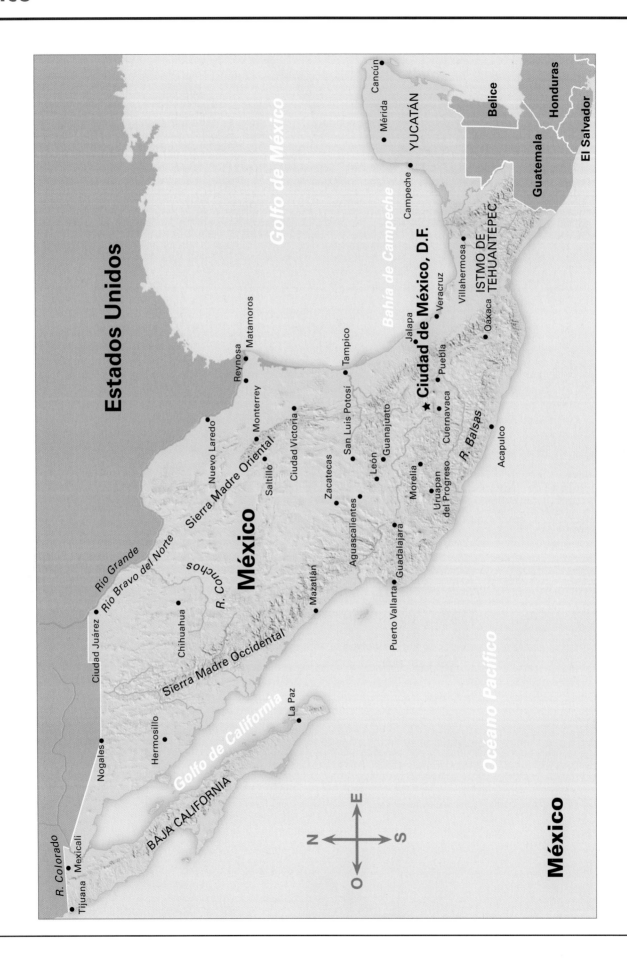

Central America and the Caribbean

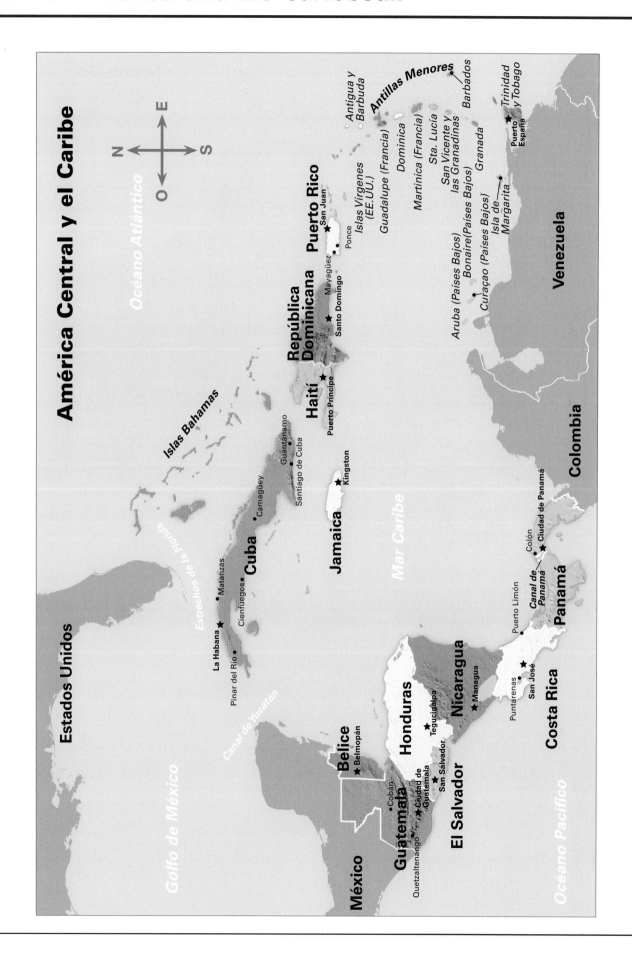

South America

Mar Caribe

Barranquilla
Maracaibo
Caracas ★
Venezuela
Puerto España
Trinidad y Tobago

Medellín
Colombia
Bogotá •
Cali •
Georgetown
Guyana
Paramaribo
Surinam
Cayena ★
Guayana Francesa

Pasto •
Quito ★
Ecuador
Guayaquil •
R. Orinoco

Iquitos •
Perú
R. Negro
R. Amazonas
Manaus •
Belém •

Lima ★
Cuzco •
Cordillera de los Andes
R. Madeira

Arequipa •
Lago Titicaca
La Paz ★
Bolivia
Sucre ★
Brasil
Brasilia ★
Recife •
Salvador •

Arica •
Iquique •
R. Paraguay

Antofagasta •
Salta •
R. Paraná
Belo Horizonte •
São Paulo •
Rio de Janeiro •
Santos •

Océano Pacífico

Paraguay
Asunción ★

Chile
Cordillera de los Andes

Córdoba •
R. Paraná
R. Uruguay
Pôrto Alegre •

Valparaíso •
Mendoza •
Rosario •
Santiago ★
Buenos Aires ★
Uruguay
Montevideo

Concepción •
Argentina
Océano Atlántico

Bahía Blanca •

Puerto Montt •

Estrecho de Magallanes
Punta Arenas •
Islas Malvinas

Tierra del Fuego

América del Sur

N
O ← → E
S

Islas Galápagos

Océano Pacífico

Isla Pinta
Isla Marchena
Isla Genovesa
Isla Isabela
Línea ecuatorial
Volcán Darwin
Isla Santiago (San Salvador)
Isla Fernandina
Puerto Ayora
Isla San Cristóbal
Isla Santa Cruz
Santo Tomás
Puerto Baquerizo Moreno
Isla Santa María
Isla Española

Spain

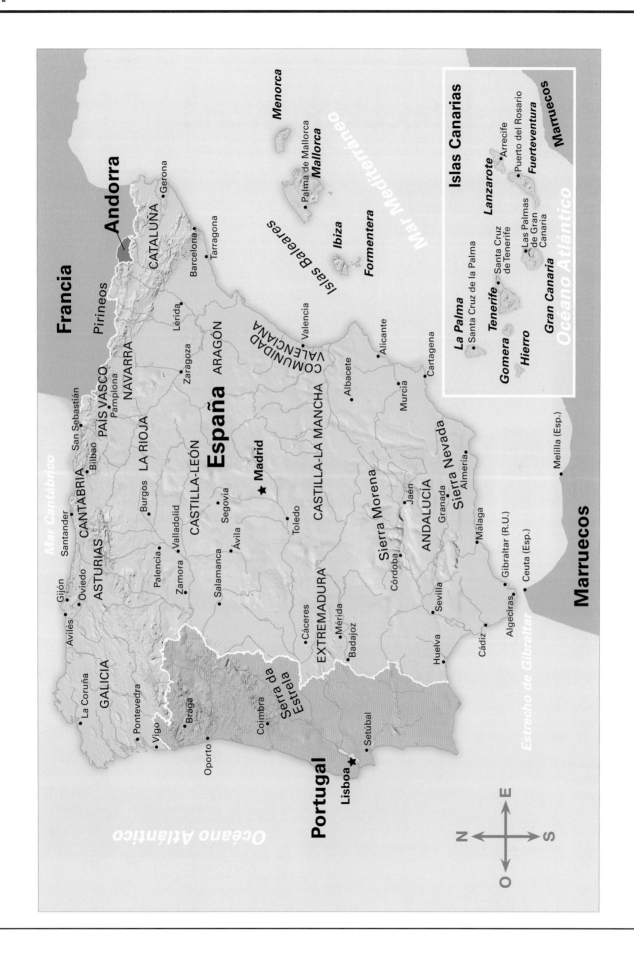

The Spanish-Speaking World

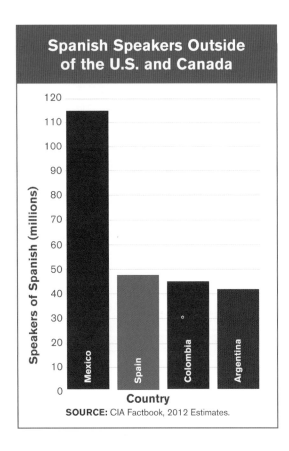

Spanish Speakers Outside of the U.S. and Canada

Speakers of Spanish (millions)

120
110
100
90
80
70
60
50
40
30
20
10
0

Mexico   Spain   Colombia   Argentina

Country

SOURCE: CIA Factbook, 2012 Estimates.

Do you know someone whose first language is Spanish? Chances are you do! More than approximately forty million people living in the U.S. speak Spanish; after English, it is the second most commonly spoken language in this country. It is the official language of twenty-two countries and an official language of the European Union and United Nations.

The Growth of Spanish

Have you ever heard of a language called Castilian? It's Spanish! The Spanish language as we know it today has its origins in a dialect called Castilian (castellano in Spanish). Castilian developed in the 9th century in north-central Spain, in a historic provincial region known as Old Castile. Castilian gradually spread towards the central region of New Castile, where it was adopted as the main language of commerce. By the 16th century, Spanish had become the official language of Spain and eventually, the country's role in exploration, colonization, and overseas trade led to its spread across Central and South America, North America, the Caribbean, parts of North Africa, the Canary Islands, and the Philippines.

Spanish in the United States

1500   1600   1700

16th Century
Spanish is the official language of Spain.

1565
The Spanish arrive in Florida and found St. Augustine.

PEDRO MENENDEZ DE AVILES.

1610
The Spanish found Santa Fe, today's capital of New Mexico, the state with the most Spanish speakers in the U.S.

Spanish in the United States

Spanish came to North America in the 16th century with the Spanish who settled in St. Augustine, Florida. Spanish-speaking communities flourished in several parts of the continent over the next few centuries. Then, in 1848, in the aftermath of the Mexican-American War, Mexico lost almost half its land to the United States, including portions of modern-day Texas, New Mexico, Arizona, Colorado, California, Wyoming, Nevada, and Utah. Overnight, hundreds of thousands of Mexicans became citizens of the United States, bringing with them their rich history, language, and traditions.

This heritage, combined with that of the other Hispanic populations that have immigrated to the United States over the years, has led to the remarkable growth of Spanish around the country. After English, it is the most commonly spoken language in 43 states. More than 12 million people in California alone claim Spanish as their first or "home" language.

You've made a popular choice by choosing to take Spanish in school. Not only is Spanish found and heard almost everywhere in the United States, but it is the most commonly taught foreign language in classrooms throughout the country! Have you heard people speaking Spanish in your community? Chances are that you've come across an advertisement, menu, or magazine that is in Spanish. If you look around, you'll find that Spanish can be found in some pretty common places. For example, most ATMs respond to users in both English and Spanish. News agencies and television stations such as CNN and Telemundo provide Spanish-language broadcasts. When you listen to the radio or download music from the Internet, some of the most popular choices are Latino artists who perform in Spanish. Federal government agencies such as the Internal Revenue Service and the Department of State provide services in both languages. Even the White House has an official Spanish-language webpage! Learning Spanish can create opportunities within your everyday life.

1800   1900   2015

1848
Mexicans who choose to stay in the U.S. after the Mexican-American War become U.S. citizens.

1959
After the Cuban Revolution, thousands of Cubans emigrate to the U.S.

2015
Spanish is the 2nd most commonly spoken language in the U.S., with more than approximately 52.5 million speakers.

Why Study Spanish?

Learn an International Language

There are many reasons to learn Spanish, a language that has spread to many parts of the world and has along the way embraced words and sounds of languages as diverse as Latin, Arabic, and Nahuatl. Spanish has evolved from a medieval dialect of north-central Spain into the fourth most commonly spoken language in the world. It is the second language of choice among the majority of people in North America.

Understand the World Around You

Knowing Spanish can also open doors to communities within the United States, and it can broaden your understanding of the nation's history and geography. The very names Colorado, Montana, Nevada, and Florida are Spanish in origin. Just knowing their meanings can give you some insight into the landscapes for which the states are renowned. Colorado means "colored red;" Montana means "mountain;" Nevada is derived from "snow-capped mountain;" and Florida means "flowered." You've already been speaking Spanish whenever you talk about some of these states!

State Name	Meaning in Spanish
Colorado	"colored red"
Florida	"flowered"
Montana	"mountain"
Nevada	"snow-capped mountain"

Connect with the World

Learning Spanish can change how you view the world. While you learn Spanish, you will also explore and learn about the origins, customs, art, music, and literature of people in close to two dozen countries. When you travel to a Spanish-speaking country, you'll be able to converse freely with the people you meet. And whether in the U.S., Canada, or abroad, you'll find that speaking to people in their native language is the best way to bridge any culture gap.

Why Study Spanish?

Expand Your Skills

Studying a foreign language can improve your ability to analyze and interpret information and help you succeed in many other subject areas. When you first begin learning Spanish, your studies will focus mainly on reading, writing, grammar, listening, and speaking skills. You'll be amazed at how the skills involved with learning how a language works can help you succeed in other areas of study. Many people who study a foreign language claim that they gained a better understanding of English. Spanish can even help you understand the origins of many English words and expand your own vocabulary in English. Knowing Spanish can also help you pick up other related languages, such as Italian, Portuguese, and French. Spanish can really open doors for learning many other skills in your school career.

Explore Your Future

How many of you are already planning your future careers? Employers in today's global economy look for workers who know different languages and understand other cultures. Your knowledge of Spanish will make you a valuable candidate for careers abroad as well as in the United States or Canada. Doctors, nurses, social workers, hotel managers, journalists, businessmen, pilots, flight attendants, and many other professionals need to know Spanish or another foreign language to do their jobs well.

How to Learn Spanish

Start with the Basics!

As with anything you want to learn, start with the basics and remember that learning takes time! The basics are vocabulary, grammar, and culture.

Vocabulary | Every new word you learn in Spanish will expand your vocabulary and ability to communicate. The more words you know, the better you can express yourself. Focus on sounds and think about ways to remember words. Use your knowledge of English and other languages to figure out the meaning of and memorize words like **conversación, teléfono, oficina, clase,** and **música**.

Grammar | Grammar helps you put your new vocabulary together. By learning the rules of grammar, you can use new words correctly and speak in complete sentences. As you learn verbs and tenses, you will be able to speak about the past, present, or future, express yourself with clarity, and be able to persuade others with your opinions. Pay attention to structures and use your knowledge of English grammar to make connections with Spanish grammar.

Culture | Culture provides you with a framework for what you may say or do. As you learn about the culture of Spanish-speaking communities, you'll improve your knowledge of Spanish. Think about a word like **salsa**, and how it connects to both food and music. Think about and explore customs observed on **Nochevieja** (New Year's Eve) or at a **fiesta de quince años** (a girl's fifteenth birthday party). Watch people greet each other or say good-bye. Listen for idioms and sayings that capture the spirit of what you want to communicate!

Teenagers celebrating at a **fiesta de quince años**.

Listen, Speak, Read, and Write

Listening | Listen for sounds and for words you can recognize. Listen for inflections and watch for key words that signal a question such as **cómo** (*how*), **dónde** (*where*), or **qué** (*what*). Get used to the sound of Spanish. Play Spanish pop songs or watch Spanish movies. Borrow audiobooks from your local library, or try to visit places in your community where Spanish is spoken. Don't worry if you don't understand every single word. If you focus on key words and phrases, you'll get the main idea. The more you listen, the more you'll understand!

Speaking | Practice speaking Spanish as often as you can. As you talk, work on your pronunciation, and read aloud texts so that words and sentences flow more easily. Don't worry if you don't sound like a native speaker, or if you make some mistakes. Time and practice will help you get there. Participate actively in Spanish class. Try to speak Spanish with classmates, especially native speakers (if you know any), as often as you can.

Reading | Pick up a Spanish-language newspaper or a pamphlet on your way to school, read the lyrics of a song as you listen to it, or read books you've already read in English translated into Spanish. Use reading strategies that you know to understand the meaning of a text that looks unfamiliar. Look for cognates, or words that are related in English and Spanish, to guess the meaning of some words. Read as often as you can, and remember to read for fun!

Writing | It's easy to write in Spanish if you put your mind to it. And remember that Spanish spelling is phonetic, which means that once you learn the basic rules of how letters and sounds are related, you can probably become an expert speller in Spanish! Write for fun—make up poems or songs, write e-mails or instant messages to friends, or start a journal or blog in Spanish.

Tips for Learning Spanish

Practice, practice, practice!

Seize every opportunity you find to listen, speak, read, or write Spanish. Think of it like a sport or learning a musical instrument—the more you practice, the more you will become comfortable with the language and how it works. You'll marvel at how quickly you can begin speaking Spanish and how the world that it transports you to can change your life forever!

- Listen to Spanish radio shows and podcasts. Write down words that you can't recognize or don't know and look up the meaning.

- Watch Spanish TV shows, movies, or YouTube clips. Read subtitles to help you grasp the content.

- Read Spanish-language newspapers, magazines, or blogs.

- Listen to Spanish songs that you like —anything from Shakira to a traditional mariachi melody. Sing along and concentrate on your pronunciation.

- Seek out Spanish speakers. Look for neighborhoods, markets, or cultural centers where Spanish might be spoken in your community. Greet people, ask for directions, or order from a menu at a Mexican restaurant in Spanish.

- Pursue language exchange opportunities (**intercambio cultural**) in your school or community. Try to join language clubs or cultural societies, and explore opportunities for studying abroad or hosting a student from a Spanish-speaking country in your home or school.

- Connect your learning to everyday experiences. Think about naming the ingredients of your favorite dish in Spanish. Think about the origins of Spanish place names in the U.S., like Cape Canaveral and Sacramento, or of common English words like *adobe, chocolate, mustang, tornado,* and *patio.*

- Use mnemonics, or a memorizing device, to help you remember words. Make up a saying in English to remember the order of the days of the week in Spanish (L, M, M, J, V, S, D).

- Visualize words. Try to associate words with images to help you remember meanings. For example, think of a **paella** as you learn the names of different types of seafood or meat. Imagine a national park and create mental pictures of the landscape as you learn names of animals, plants, and habitats.

- Enjoy yourself! Try to have as much fun as you can learning Spanish. Take your knowledge beyond the classroom and make the learning experience your own.

Useful Spanish Expressions

The following expressions will be very useful in getting you started learning Spanish. You can use them in class to check your understanding or to ask and answer questions about the lessons. Read En las **instrucciones** ahead of time to help you understand direction lines in Spanish, as well as your teacher's instructions. Remember to practice your Spanish as often as you can!

Expresiones útiles *Useful expressions*

¿Cómo se dice _____ en español?	How do you say _____ in Spanish?
¿Cómo se escribe _____?	How do you spell _____?
¿Comprende(n)?	Do you understand?
Con permiso.	Excuse me.
De acuerdo.	Okay.
De nada.	You're welcome.
¿De veras?	Really?
¿En qué página estamos?	What page are we on?
Enseguida.	Right away.
Más despacio, por favor.	Slower, please.
Muchas gracias.	Thanks a lot.
No entiendo.	I don't understand.
No sé.	I don't know.
Perdone.	Excuse me.
Pista	Clue
Por favor.	Please.
Por supuesto.	Of course.
¿Qué significa _____?	What does _____ mean?
Repite, por favor.	Please repeat.
Tengo una pregunta.	I have a question.
¿Tiene(n) alguna pregunta?	Do you have questions?
Vaya(n) a la página dos.	Go to page 2.

En las instrucciones *In direction lines*

Cierto o falso	True or false
Completa las oraciones de una manera lógica.	Complete the sentences logically.
Con un(a) compañero/a...	With a classmate...
Contesta las preguntas.	Answer the questions.
Corrige la información falsa.	Correct the false information.
Di/Digan...	Say...
En grupos...	In groups...
En parejas...	In pairs...
Entrevista...	Interview...
Forma oraciones completas.	Create/Make complete sentences.
Háganse preguntas.	Ask each other questions.
Haz el papel de...	Play the role of...
Haz los cambios necesarios.	Make the necessary changes.
Indica/Indiquen si las oraciones...	Indicate if the sentences...
Lee/Lean en voz alta.	Read aloud.
...que mejor completa...	...that best completes...
Toma nota...	Take note...
Tomen apuntes.	Take notes.
Túrnense...	Take turns...

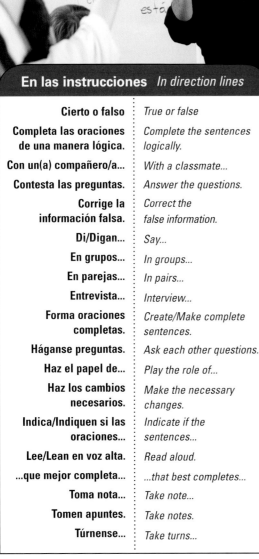

Common Names

Get started learning Spanish by using a Spanish name in class. You can choose from the lists on these pages, or you can find one yourself. How about learning the Spanish equivalent of your name? The most popular Spanish female names are Lucía, María, Paula, Sofía, and Valentina. The most popular male names in Spanish are Alejandro, Daniel, David, Mateo, and Santiago. Is your name, or that of someone you know, in the Spanish top five?

Más nombres masculinos	Más nombres femeninos
Alfonso	Alicia
Antonio (Toni)	Beatriz (Bea, Beti, Biata)
Carlos	Blanca
César	Carolina (Carol)
Diego	Claudia
Ernesto	Diana
Felipe	Emilia
Francisco (Paco)	Irene
Guillermo	Julia
Ignacio (Nacho)	Laura
Javier (Javi)	Leonor
Leonardo	Liliana
Luis	Lourdes
Manolo	Margarita (Marga)
Marcos	Marta
Oscar (Óscar)	Noelia
Rafael (Rafa)	Patricia
Sergio	Rocío
Vicente	Verónica

Los 5 nombres masculinos más populares	Los 5 nombres femeninos más populares
Alejandro	Lucía
Daniel	María
David	Paula
Mateo	Sofía
Santiago	Valentina

Lección preliminar

Conversaciones en la clase

Vocabulario

Hola.	Hi.
¿Cómo te llamas?	What's your name?
Encantado/a.	Pleased to meet you.
¿De dónde eres?	Where are you from?
la computación	computer science
el español	Spanish
la historia	history
el inglés	English
las matemáticas	mathematics
la música	music
enseñar	to teach
gustar	to like
estudiar	to study
preguntar	to ask
tomar (una clase)	to take (a class)

MARTÍN ¡Hola!
JESSICA ¡Hola! ¿Cómo te llamas?
MARTÍN Martín, ¿y tú?
JESSICA Jessica. Encantada.
MARTÍN Igualmente.
JESSICA ¿De dónde eres, Martín?
MARTÍN Soy de Argentina.

FELIPE ¡Hola, Andrés! ¿Cómo estás?
ANDRÉS Muy bien, ¿y tú?
FELIPE Bien, gracias. ¿Tienes clase de español a las ocho y cuarto?
ANDRÉS Sí, con la profesora Gómez.
FELIPE ¿Y te gusta la clase de español?
ANDRÉS Sí, me gusta mucho.

DIANA Ésa es la profesora Davis, y ésos son los profesores Pérez y Adams.
BEATRIZ ¿Qué enseña la profesora Pérez?
DIANA Ella enseña música, y el profesor Adams enseña computación.
BEATRIZ ¿Y te gustan esas clases?
DIANA La de computación sí, pero la de música no mucho.

Práctica

1 🔊 **Lee y escucha** Follow along while you listen to the dialogues on page 2. Listen for extra information at the end of each one. Then indicate whether the following conclusions are **falso** or **cierto**, based on what you heard.

1. Jessica es de los Estados Unidos, de California.

2. A Felipe le gusta la clase de español.

3. A Felipe no le gusta la clase de historia.

4. A Beatriz no le gusta la clase de música.

5. La profesora Davis enseña ciencias sociales.

Repaso: Present of -*ar* verbs

Juan Carlos estudia ciencias ambientales.

▶ Conjugate most regular **-ar** verbs in the present tense by dropping the **-ar** and adding the appropriate endings.

estudiar			preguntar	
yo	estudi**o**		yo	pregunt**o**
tú	estudi**as**		tú	pregunt**as**
Ud./él/ella	estudi**a**		Ud./él/ella	pregunt**a**
nosotros/as	estudi**amos**		nosotros/as	pregunt**amos**
vosotros/as	estudi**áis**		vosotros/as	pregunt**áis**
Uds./ellos/ellas	estudi**an**		Uds./ellos/ellas	pregunt**an**

▶ When two verbs are used together without a change in subject, the second verb is in the infinitive. To make the sentence negative, put **no** before the conjugated verbs.

Necesito comprar un libro.
I need to buy a book.

No necesito comprar un libro.
I don't need to buy a book.

Deseamos viajar hoy.
We want to travel today.

No deseamos viajar hoy.
We don't want to travel today.

The verb *gustar*

▶ To express your likes and dislikes, use:

(no) me gusta + [*singular nouns or infinitives*]
Me gust**a** el nuevo horario. No me gust**a** bailar.
I like the new schedule. I don't like to dance.

(no) me gustan + [*plural nouns*]
No me gust**an** las matemáticas.
I don't like mathematics.

▶ To ask a classmate about likes and dislikes, use **te**.
¿**Te** gusta la clase? ¿**Te** gustan las ciencias sociales?

2 **Completar** Complete the sentences with the correct forms of the verbs in parentheses.

1. Los profesores _____ (explicar) las lecciones.
2. Nosotras _____ (cenar) a las ocho.
3. Tú _____ (desayunar) en la cafetería.
4. ¿_____ (Trabajar) usted los viernes?
5. Me _____ (gustar) cantar y bailar.
6. Yo no _____ (desear) tomar limonada ahora.
7. Los chicos _____ (dibujar) con tiza.
8. Julio y yo _____ (escuchar) música rock.
9. ¿Te _____ (gustar) las lenguas extranjeras?
10. Ustedes esperan _____ (viajar) a Perú.

3 **Gustar** Luisa studies science. For each item, write what Luisa would say about his preferences, according to the cue. Follow the model.

modelo

trabajar en el laboratorio ☹
No me gusta trabajar en el laboratorio.

1. las ciencias marinas ☺
2. los exámenes de física ☹
3. escuchar la radio cuando estudio ☺
4. trabajar y conversar con los profesores ☺
5. la tarea de química ☹
6. la clase de biología ☺

4 **Escribir** Use words from each column to create complete sentences. Pay attention to conjugations.

1	2	3
Daniela	desear	a las doce
Sebastián	enseñar	en la cafetería
La clase de español	estudiar	estudiantes de secundaria
La profesora Cruz	ser	hablar con el profesor
Mis hermanos	terminar	la clase de biología
Nosotros	tomar	la tarea de matemáticas
Yo	trabajar	siete clases

modelo

Daniela toma siete clases.

Comunicación

5 **Contestar** Answer these questions.

1. ¿Cuántas clases tomas? ¿Cuál es tu clase favorita?

2. ¿Dónde estudias, en la biblioteca o en casa? ¿Escuchas música cuando estudias?

3. ¿A qué hora llegas a la escuela? ¿A qué hora regresas a casa?

4. ¿Con quién(es) cenas normalmente? ¿Quién prepara la comida (*food*)?

5. ¿Miras mucha televisión? ¿Qué programas te gustan?

6. ¿Te gusta viajar? ¿Qué países o culturas te gustan?

7. ¿Qué música escuchan tus amigos/as y tú? ¿Bailan ustedes? ¿Cantan?

8. ¿Qué te gusta hacer los fines de semana? ¿Descansas, preparas la tarea o pasas tiempo con tu familia?

6 **Actividades** With a partner, take turns asking each other if you do these activities. Also ask follow-up questions. Jot down your partner's answers and make note of which activities you both do.

modelo

desayunar en casa
Estudiante 1: ¿Desayunas en casa?
Estudiante 2: Sí, desayuno en casa.
Estudiante 1: ¿A qué hora desayunas los días de semana?
Estudiante 2: Desayuno a las siete de la mañana.
Estudiante 1: ¿Con quién desayunas?
Estudiante 2: Desayuno con mis padres.

bailar bien
comprar música en iTunes
estudiar geografía
mirar la televisión
practicar deportes
tomar clases después de la escuela
trabajar como voluntario(a)
viajar por el país
visitar museos de arte

7 **Escribir** Write an e-mail to a new friend. Introduce yourself, describe what classes you take, your studying habits, and what you do on school days and weekends. Talk about your likes and dislikes, and ask about your friend's.

modelo

Hola, Andrés:
Me llamo David y soy de Miami, Florida. Soy estudiante en una escuela secundaria. Tomo clases de historia, arte...

Repaso: Present of *estar*

Prepositions and adverbs often used with *estar*

al lado de	next to	**delante de**	in front of
a la derecha de	to the right of	**detrás de**	behind
a la izquierda de	to the left of	**en**	in; on
allá	over there	**encima de**	on top of
allí	there	**entre**	between
cerca de	near	**lejos de**	far from
con	with	**sin**	without
debajo de	below	**sobre**	on; over

COMPARE & CONTRAST

Compare the uses of the verb **estar** to those of the verb **ser**.

Uses of *estar*

Location
Estoy en casa.
I am at home.

Health
Juan Carlos **está** enfermo hoy.
Juan Carlos is sick today.

Well-being
—¿Cómo **estás**, Jimena?
How are you, Jimena?

—**Estoy** muy bien, gracias.
I'm very well, thank you.

Uses of *ser*

Identity
Hola, **soy** Maru.
Hello, I'm Maru.

Occupation
Soy estudiante.
I'm a student.

Origin
Ella **es** de México
She is from Mexico.

Telling time
Son las cuatro.
It's four o'clock.

Práctica

8

Completar There is a substitute teacher in Clara's class today. Complete the conversation with the correct forms of **ser** or **estar**.

SRA. GARCÍA   Buenos días. ¿Cómo (1)_____?

CLARA   Bien, gracias. ¿Cómo (2)_____ usted?

SRA. GARCÍA   (3)_____ muy bien. (4)_____ la señora García, la profesora de ciencias sociales. Y tú (5)_____ Clara Rivas, ¿verdad?

CLARA   Sí. Perdón, señora García pero, ¿dónde (6)_____ el profesor Duque?

SRA. GARCÍA   (7)_____ en una conferencia, pero regresa mañana. Clara, ¿en qué parte del libro (8)_____ ustedes?

CLARA   (Nosotros) (9)_____ en la lección 4.

SRA. GARCÍA   Muchas gracias, Clara. Ya (11)_____ las ocho, ¡es hora de comenzar la clase!

9 **Buscar** You are in a school supply store and can't find various items. Ask the clerk (your partner) about the location of five items in the drawing. Then switch roles.

> **modelo**
>
> **Estudiante 1:** ¿Dónde están los diccionarios?
> **Estudiante 2:** Los diccionarios están debajo de los libros de literatura.

10 **Entrevista** Take turns answering your classmate's questions.

1. ¿Cómo estás?

2. ¿Dónde estás ahora?

3. ¿Dónde está tu cuaderno de español?

4. ¿Dónde está tu diccionario de español?

5. ¿Dónde estás los sábados a las siete de la mañana?

6. ¿Dónde estás los miércoles a las ocho de la noche?

7. ¿Dónde están tus padres los lunes a las dos de la tarde?

11 **Escribir** A new student named Andrés just transferred into your Spanish class. With a partner, write a conversation where you greet each other, ask where you both are from, who the teacher is, and describe the location of items in the classroom. Use both **ser** and **estar**.

Te presento a mi familia

Vocabulario

los abuelos	*grandparents*
el/la hermano/a	*brother/sister*
los padres	*parents*
el/la primo/a	*cousin*
antipático/a	*unpleasant*
delgado/a	*thin*
gordo/a	*fat*
simpático/a	*nice; likeable*
el/la artista	*artist*
el/la doctor(a)	*doctor*
el/la periodista	*journalist*
el/la profesor(a)	*professor, teacher*

Me llamo Miguel, tengo 13 años y ésta es mi familia. Mi papá se llama Cristóbal, y es periodista y fotógrafo (*photographer*). Mi mamá se llama Anita y es artista. Tengo una hermana que se llama Valentina. Ella tiene 16 años y quiere ser artista como mi mamá y mi abuela. Mis abuelos se llaman Fernando y Sofía. Él tiene 61 años y ella 60. Ellos son los padres de mi mamá. ¿Y el perro? Se llama Rey y es un pastor alemán (*German Shepherd*). ¡Es el consentido (*spoiled one*) de la casa!

¡Hola! Mi nombre es Emily y vivo en Los Ángeles con mi familia. Mi mamá se llama Olivia y la quiero mucho. Ella tiene 50 años y es profesora de literatura latinoamericana en la universidad. El señor de lentes (*glasses*) es mi abuelo Michael. Él es muy inteligente y le gusta leer y escribir, y también le gusta correr en el parque y viajar por el mundo. La otra chica en la foto es mi prima Sara. Ella vive en Miami con su familia, pero le gusta visitarnos a menudo (*often*).

Práctica

1 **La foto de mi familia** Listen to Felipe talk about his family and complete the chart with the missing information according to what you hear.

NOMBRE	EDAD	OCUPACIÓN	RELACIÓN
FELIPE	12 años	estudiante de secundaria	hijo
MARGARITA		artista	
ALBERTO	36 años	fotógrafo	

Repaso: Descriptive adjectives

Felipe es gordo, antipático y muy feo.

▶ Adjectives are words that describe nouns. In Spanish, adjectives agree in both gender and number with the nouns they modify.

Forms and agreement of adjectives

Masculine		Feminine	
SINGULAR	PLURAL	SINGULAR	PLURAL
alt**o**	alt**os**	alt**a**	alt**as**
inteligent**e**	inteligent**es**	inteligent**e**	inteligent**es**
trabajad**or**	trabajad**ores**	trabajad**ora**	trabajad**oras**

▶ Descriptive adjectives, color words, and adjectives of nationality follow the noun:

el chico rubio, la mujer española, las sillas rojas

▶ Adjectives of quantity precede the noun:

muchos libros, dos turistas

▶ When placed before a singular masculine noun, the following adjectives are shortened:

bueno ⟶ buen; malo ⟶ mal
un buen día, un mal estudiante

▶ When placed before a singular noun, **grande** is shortened to **gran**, and the meaning changes to *great*.

una gran escuela

2   **Opuestos** For each adjective, give an adjective that is opposite in meaning. Keep the gender and number the same.

1. tonto
2. baja
3. gordo
4. viejos
5. simpáticas

6. bonito
7. difíciles
8. morena
9. malas
10. blanco

3   **Completar** Ernesto is talking about life at his new school. Complete the paragraph with the correct form of the adjectives from the list. Use each adjective only once. One adjective will not be used.

bueno	mismo
difícil	mucho
feo	simpático
inteligente	tonto
interesante	tres

En la escuela donde estudio tengo (1) _____ amigos: Ignacio, Carlos y Tomás. Son personas muy (2) _____; hablamos de todo. Ellos son (3) _____; reciben A en todos los exámenes. Yo no soy (4) _____, pero no tengo las (5) _____ notas. Las materias son (6) _____ y los profesores son (7) _____, pero en la clase de matemáticas hay (8) _____ tarea y la clase de química es (9) _____. Deseo tomar más clases de historia y de arte.

4   **Posesivos** Write the correct form of each possessive adjective.

1. _____ (*Your*, fam.) sobrino es muy joven.
2. _____ (*Her*) profesores son estrictos.
3. Olivia es _____ (*my*) hermana.
4. _____ (*Our*) casa es azul.
5. ¿Juliana es _____ (*your*, form.) esposa?
6. _____ (*His*) familia es pequeña.
7. Los libros viejos son de _____ (*our*) abuelos.
8. _____ (*My*) tíos son argentinos.

Comunicación

5   **Describe a tu familia** With a classmate, take turns asking each other questions about your families.

modelo
Estudiante 1: ¿Cómo es tu mamá?
Estudiante 2: Mi mamá es delgada. morena y muy simpática.

Repaso: Present of -er and -ir

▶ Create the present-tense forms of most regular verbs by dropping the -**er** or -**ir** and adding the appropriate endings.

comer		escribir	
com**o**	com**emos**	escrib**o**	escrib**imos**
com**es**	com**éis**	escrib**es**	escrib**ís**
com**e**	com**en**	escrib**e**	escrib**en**

Jimena lee.

Repaso: Present of *tener* and *venir*

Tengo una familia pequeña.

tener		venir	
ten**go**	tenemos	ven**go**	venimos
ti**e**nes	tenéis	vi**e**nes	venís
ti**e**ne	ti**e**nen	vi**e**ne	vi**e**nen

Práctica

6

🔊

Conversación Complete the conversation with the correct form of the appropriate verb. Then, act it out with a partner.

—Hola, Raquel. ¿Qué (1) _____ (escribir/comprender) en el teléfono?

—Hola, Simón. (2) _____ (Comer/Escribir) un mensaje de texto (*text message*) para mi amiga Inés.

—¿Inés? Ella (3) _____ (abrir/vivir) cerca del parque, ¿verdad?

—Sí, exactamente. Por las tardes ella y yo (4) _____ (correr/decidir) en el parque.

—¡Qué bien! A mí también me gusta (5) _____ (correr/leer).

—¿Ah, sí? ¿Por qué no (6) _____ (tener/venir) con nosotras? Corremos y después (7) _____ (beber/creer) un batido.

—Em… no, gracias. (8) _____ (Recibir/Tener) que terminar la tarea y a las cinco (9) _____ (describir/asistir) a una lección de piano.

—Ay, Simón. De verdad (10) _____ (deber/compartir) practicar más deportes.

Comunicación

7

Un día común y corriente Write a paragraph describing a typical day in your life. Include as many verbs ending in -**er** and -**ir** as possible.

Fotonovela Review

En los tres primeros episodios de la Fotonovela, Marissa viaja a México y conoce a la familia Díaz.

PERSONAJES

MARISSA

SRA. DÍAZ

SR. DÍAZ

FELIPE

JIMENA

MIGUEL

JUAN CARLOS

MARISSA ¿Quiénes son los dos chicos de las fotos? ¿Jimena y Felipe?

SRA. DÍAZ Sí. Ellos son estudiantes.

FELIPE Estás en México, ¿verdad? Nosotros somos tu diccionario.

FELIPE Oye, Marissa, ¿cuántas clases tomas?

MARISSA Tomo cuatro clases: ... español, historia, literatura... y también geografía. Me gusta mucho la cultura mexicana.

MARISSA ¡Qué bonitas son tus hijas! Y ¡qué simpáticas!

SRA. DÍAZ Chicas, ¿compartimos una trajinera?

MARISSA ¡Claro que sí! ¡Qué bonitas son!

En los próximos episodios, Marissa y sus nuevos amigos viajarán (*will travel*) a la Península de Yucatán para divertirse (*have fun*) y explorar lugares hermosos.

¿Qué pasó?

1 **Organizar** Organize the following events in chronological order.

_____ Marissa conoce a Felipe y a Jimena.

_____ Marissa pasea en una trajinera.

_____ Marissa llega a México.

_____ Marissa conoce a Juan Carlos y a Miguel.

_____ Marissa y la familia Díaz visitan a Xochimilco.

_____ Marissa conoce a la Sra. Díaz.

2 **¿Cierto o falso?** Indicate if each statement is **cierto** or **falso**. Then, correct the false statements.

1. El Sr. Díaz y la Sra. Díaz son de Cuba.

2. Marissa no necesita su diccionario en México, según Felipe.

3. Marissa toma inglés, historia, arte y geografía.

4. Marissa tiene tres hermanos: Zack, Jennifer y Adam.

5. La Sra. Díaz tiene dos hermanos: Roberto y Ramón.

6. Ana María es la tía de Felipe y Jimena.

3 **Identificar** Indicate which person would make each statement. One name will be used twice, and one won't be used at all.

1. Ésta es la Ciudad de México.

2. Sí, de La Habana, y Roberto es de Mérida.

3. La verdad, mi familia es pequeña.

4. ¡Debes viajar a Mérida!

5. No, gracias. Tengo que leer.

SRA. DÍAZ

FELIPE

MARISSA

JIMENA

SR. DÍAZ

EN DETALLE

El español
en Latinoamérica

As a Spanish language learner, you are on your way to being able to communicate with a vast number of people from diverse regions, backgrounds, and cultures. There are about 500 million Spanish-speakers in the world, but less than 600 years ago, Spanish was used only in the northern and central regions of the Iberian Peninsula. In 1492, the **Reyes Católicos°** unified Spain under Christian rule and the Spanish language. In that same year, they commissioned **Cristóbal Colón°** to search for a new trade route to India, on which he carried the Spanish language to the Americas.

Although Columbus initially sought to explore and establish trade routes, a principal goal of the Spaniards in the Americas quickly became conquest and evangelism—spreading the Catholic faith. The Spanish encountered millions of indigenous people who spoke a vast number of languages and dialects. The Spanish **conquistadores** used various indigenous languages to communicate their religious message, and several were preserved this way throughout colonial times. For example, **quechua** was the main means of communication in the central Andean region between the Spaniards and the indigenous population. Over time, the geographic reach of quechua continued to expand, and words from many different indigenous languages were incorporated into Spanish. **Papa°** and **jaguar°** are just two examples.

Over the following few centuries of colonial rule, descendants of the Spanish and majority **mestizo°** population perpetuated the use of Spanish. After the wars of independence, most nations opted to have Spanish as their official language. However, millions of Latin Americans continue to speak a multitude of indigenous languages, especially in rural areas. And in several Latin American countries, indigenous languages have co-official status: Bolivia (**quechua, aimará**), Ecuador (**quechua, aimará**), Paraguay (**guaraní**), and Peru (**quechua, aimará**).

Otras° lenguas indígenas

Lengua	Donde se habla	Más información
náhuatl	México	lengua de los aztecas
chibcha	(lengua extinta)	lengua dominante en Colombia y Panamá en tiempos precolombinos°
maya	Guatemala, México, Honduras	en tiempos precolombinos usan un sistema jeroglífico°
taíno	(lengua extinta)	lengua más dominante en la región del Caribe en tiempos precolombinos
mapuche	Chile	no tiene relación con otras lenguas indígenas

Reyes Católicos *the Catholic King Fernando of Aragón and Queen Isabel of Castilla* **Cristóbal Colón** *Christopher Columbus* **Papa** *Potato (from Quechua)* **jaguar** *jaguar (from Guarani)* **mestizo** *mixed Spanish and indigenous ancestry* **Otras** *Other* **precolombinos** *pre-Columbian* **jeroglífico** *hieroglyphic*

ACTIVIDADES

1 **Cierto o falso?** Indicate whether each statement is **cierto** or **falso**. Correct the false statements.

1. About 500,000 people speak Spanish worldwide.

2. The Spanish **conquistadores** often communicated Catholic teachings in indigenous languages.

3. Indigenous languages did not survive the Spanish conquest.

4. **Quechua** originated in the Caribbean.

5. Many Spanish words have indigenous origins.

6. Today, indigenous languages are not widely spoken in Latin America.

7. **Aimará** is spoken in Paraguay.

8. **Taíno** and **chibcha** are extinct languages.

9. The Aztecs spoke **maya**.

10. **Mapuche** and **quechua** belong to the same linguistic family.

Palabras de origen indígena

el aguacate (náhuatl)	avocado
la barbacoa (taíno)	barbecue
la cancha (quechua)	field, court
el chile (náhuatl)	chili (pepper)
el coyote (náhuatl)	coyote
el huracán (taíno)	hurricane
la maraca (guaraní)	maraca
la palta (quechua)	avocado
el puma (quechua)	puma

Civilizaciones precolombinas

La civilización maya This civilization is known for its art, architecture, mathematics, and astronomy. The Maya developed a counting system based on 20 and the concept of zero. Remains of Maya temples, such as **Tikal** in Guatemala and **Chichén Itzá** on the Yucatan Peninsula, are now popular tourist attractions.

El imperio azteca This civilization, based in Mexico's central valley, greatly expanded its domain through military conquest and alliances. The Aztecs founded their capital, **Tenochtitlán**, in 1325; by the time the Spanish arrived in 1519, it was one of the largest cities in the world.

El imperio incaico The Incas developed an innovative agricultural system of terraces and constructed a vast network of roads with the capital, Cusco, at its center. One of the most famous legacies of the Incan Empire is the mountaintop ruins of **Machu Picchu**.

Día de la Independencia

During the early morning hours of September 16, 1810, a Mexican priest rang his church bell in the town of Dolores and gave a rousing call for a free, independent Mexico: **¡Viva° la Independencia! ¡Muera el mal gobierno°!** After 11 years of war, Mexico won its independence from Spain, which it commemorates on the 16th of September. Although Mexico's **Día de la Independencia** is officially September 16th, the celebrations begin the night before. Father Miguel Hidalgo's act, now known as **el Grito° de Dolores**, is reenacted every year in **zócalos°** across Mexico, accompanied by fireworks, music, and revelers dressed in the colors of the Mexican flag.

Beginning in 1811, similar movements for freedom ignited all over Central America. Finally, on September 15, 1821, Costa Rica, El Salvador, Guatemala, Honduras, and Nicaragua signed the **Acta de Independencia de Centroamérica**, thus proclaiming their autonomy from Spain. These five countries all celebrate their independence on September 15th.

Viva *Long live* Muera el mal gobierno *Down with bad government* Grito *Shout* zócalos *plazas*

Conexión Internet

When did Colombia, Ecuador, Perú, and Bolivia win their independence from Spain?	Use the web to find more cultural information related to this **Cultura** section.

2 **Comprensión** Complete these sentences.

1. Mexicans reenact _____ as part of Independence Day.
2. The capital of the _____ Empire was one of the largest cities in the world.
3. **Palta** and _____ both mean avocado.
4. Honduras and Nicaragua celebrate their independence on _____.
5. _____ is a Nahuatl word referring to an animal.

3 **Los indígenas** With a classmate, research one of the indigenous groups mentioned on these pages, or another pre-Columbian civilization in Latin America. Prepare a brief oral presentation about the group's culture, language, customs, and place in history.

¿Cuál es el nombre de los siguientes lugares?

Vocabulario	
la agencia de viajes	*travel agency*
el almacén	*department store*
el centro comercial	*shopping mall*
el cine	*cinema*
la estación de autobuses	*bus station*
el estadio	*stadium*
el gimnasio	*gym*
el hotel	*hotel*
la librería	*book store*
el mercado	*market*
el museo	*museum*
el parque	*park*
el restaurante	*restaurant*
la tienda	*store*

1

2

3

4

5

6

7

8

Preview: Present of *ir*

Él va a los museos.

Ellos van a parque.

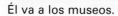

ir	
yo	**voy**
tú	**vas**
Ud./él/ella	**va**
nosotros/as	**vamos**
vosotros/as	**vais**
Uds./ellos/ellas	**van**

▶ **Ir** is often used with the preposition **a**; if **a** is followed by the definite article **el**, they form a contraction: **a + el = al.**

Vamos al [a + el] parque.

▶ **Ir** has many everyday uses, including expressing future plans:

ir a + [*infinitive*] = *to be going to* + [*infinitive*]
ir a nadar, ir a correr

vamos a [*infinitive*] = *let's* [*infinitive*]
¡Vamos a nadar a la piscina! - *Let's swim in the pool.*
Vamos a correr al parque. - *Let's run in the park.*
Vamos a ver un partido de fútbol en el estadio. - *Let's watch a soccer game in the stadium.*

Práctica

1 **¡Vamos!** Complete the following sentences using the vocabulary on the previous page.

> **modelo**
>
> **Para planear un viaje, vamos** a la agencia de viajes.

1. Para tomar un autobús, vas _____.

2. Para correr, vamos _____.

3. Para aprender sobre historia y arte, vas _____.

4. Para comprar ropa (*clothes*), vas _____.

5. Para ver una película, vamos _____.

6. Para ver un partido de fútbol americano, vamos _____.

7. Para comprar comida (*food*), vas _____.

2   **El verbo *ir*** Complete the sentences with the correct form of the verb **ir** and **a**, **al**, or **a la**.

1. Los jóvenes _____ _____ plaza.
2. ¿Ustedes _____ _____ estadio?
3. Mi abuela _____ _____ iglesia.
4. Tú _____ _____ restaurante.
5. Yo _____ _____ gimnasio.
6. Fernanda y yo _____ _____ cine.

3   **¿Adónde?** With a partner, take turns asking and answering questions about where these people are going and what they are going to do there.

> **modelo**
>
> **Estudiante 1:** ¿Adónde va Estela?
> **Estudiante 2:** Va a la Librería Sol.
>   ¿Qué va a comprar allí?
> **Estudiante 1:** Va a comprar un libro.

Estela

1. Álex y Miguel

2. mi amigo

3. tú

4. los estudiantes

5. la profesora Torres

6. ustedes

Comunicación

4   **El fin de semana** Write a short text about your schedule and the places you visit on Saturdays and Sundays. Don't forget to use **ir a**.

> **modelo**
>
> Todos los sábados a las nueve de la mañana voy a
> clases de piano. Luego, a las doce, voy a un restaurante
> con mi familia...

Mi deporte favorito

Vocabulario

la piscina	the swimming pool
un partido de fútbol	a soccer match
jugar al baloncesto	to play basketball
jugar al béisbol	to play baseball
jugar al fútbol	to play soccer
jugar al tenis	to play tennis
jugar al vóleibol	to play volleyball
montar en bicicleta	to ride a bike
nadar	to swim
patinar	to skate
practicar un deporte	to practice a sport
preferir	to prefer
surfear	to surf

1 ¿Qué hacen estos chicos?
Juegan al fútbol.

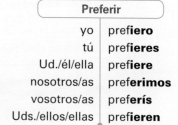

2 ¿Cuál es tu deporte favorito?
El baloncesto.

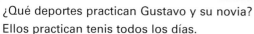
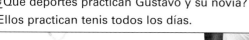

3 ¿Qué deportes practican Gustavo y su novia?
Ellos practican tenis todos los días.

4 ¿Te gusta nadar?
Sí, me encanta la natación.

Preferir

yo	prefiero
tú	prefieres
Ud./él/ella	prefiere
nosotros/as	preferimos
vosotros/as	preferís
Uds./ellos/ellas	prefieren

Jugar

yo	juego
tú	juegas
Ud./él/ella	juega
nosotros/as	jugamos
vosotros/as	jugáis
Uds./ellos/ellas	juegan

5 ¿Te gusta el surf?
No mucho. Prefiero el vóleibol.

Práctica

¡Fútbol! Read the following paragraph. Then, work with a classmate to answer the questions based on the reading.

¿Cómo traduces la palabra *football* al español? Ten cuidado y no te confundas (*don't make a mistake*). El deporte que en los Estados Unidos llaman *soccer*, en el mundo hispano se llama fútbol. Y el deporte que los estadounidenses llaman *football*, los hispanohablantes lo llaman fútbol americano. Son deportes diferentes, pero tienen también muchas similitudes: los dos se juegan con once jugadores, utilizan balones o pelotas (*balls*) y son deportes de contacto. Además, millones de personas celebran y ven los partidos de ambos (*both*) deportes en la televisión y en los estadios. Pero, ¿sabes por qué a diferencia del resto del mundo el fútbol se llama *soccer* en los Estados Unidos?

1. ¿Cómo se dice *soccer* en los países hispanohablantes?

2. ¿Cuáles son las similitudes entre el fútbol y el fútbol americano?

3. ¿Practicas fútbol o fútbol americano? ¿Cuál de los dos prefieres?

4. ¿Qué otros deportes practicas?

5. ¿Prefieres practicar deportes, o verlos en la televisión? ¿Por qué?

Repaso: Numbers 31 and higher

Hay cuarenta y siete estudiantes en la clase de geografía.

31	**treinta y uno**	101	**ciento uno**
32	**treinta y dos**	200	**doscientos/as**
	(*and so on*)	500	**quinientos/as**
40	**cuarenta**	700	**setecientos/as**
50	**cincuenta**	900	**novecientos/as**
60	**sesenta**	1.000	**mil**
70	**setenta**	2.000	**dos mil**
80	**ochenta**	5.100	**cinco mil cien**
90	**noventa**	100.000	**cien mil**
100	**cien, ciento**	1.000.000	**un millón (de)**

▶ The numbers 200 through 999 agree in gender with the nouns they modify.

324 plum**as** ⟶ trescient**as** veinticuatro plum**as**

500 flor**es** ⟶ quinient**as** flor**es**

2 **Resultados** Provide these basketball scores in Spanish.

1. _____

2. _____

3. _____

4. _____

5. _____

6. _____

3 **Matemáticas básicas** Solve the following math problems. Write out the numbers in Spanish.

modelo

150 + 20 = *ciento setenta*

1. 325 + 189 =

2. 500 – 222 =

3. 101 + 32 + 13 =

4. 410 + 509 + 678 =

5. 800 + 500 + 1.050 =

6. 1.900 + 2.019 =

7. 5.421 + 7.693 =

8. 90.000 – 80.300 =

9. 25.000 + 168.005 =

10. 205.000 – 178.040 =

1 **Emparejar** Match each question or expression in the first column with an answer in the second.

1. ¿Cómo se llama usted? _____ Soy de Mérida.

2. ¿De dónde es usted? _____ No, tengo clase de biología.

3. ¿Cuántos años tienes? _____ A las ocho y cuarto.

4. ¿Cuántos años tiene Jimena? _____ Francisco, mucho gusto.

5. Muchas gracias. _____ Tengo 14 años, ¿y tú?

6. ¿A qué hora es la clase de español? _____ No hay de qué.

7. ¿Tienes clase de historia a las diez y media? _____ Ella tiene 19 años.

2 **Analogías** Complete the following analogies.

1. maleta ⟶ pasajero = mochila ⟶ estudiante

2. Cristina ⟶ chica = Felipe ⟶ _____

3. once ⟶ doce = jueves ⟶ _____

4. abuela ⟶ abuelo = padre ⟶ _____

5. biología ⟶ materia = martes ⟶ _____

6. Miguel ⟶ nombre = Díaz ⟶ _____

7. papel ⟶ cuaderno = miércoles ⟶ _____

8. Argentina ⟶ Buenos Aires = Estados Unidos ⟶ _____

9. Picasso ⟶ arte = Cervantes ⟶ _____

3 **Adjetivos** Complete each phrase with the appropriate adjective from the list. Each adjective can only be used once.

alemán	gordo
altas	interesante
difícil	jóvenes
española	simpáticos

◀ **Adjetivos calificativos**
p. 9

1. El novio de mi prima es _____. Vive en Berlín.

2. Mis abuelos no son _____, pero tampoco son viejos.

3. Jimena y Francisco son jóvenes y muy _____.

4. La tarea de biología es _____. No la entiendo.

5. Esta novela es muy _____. Me gusta mucho.

6. Mis primas Ana y Cecilia son dos chicas muy _____.

7. Mi papá come mucho y es muy _____.

8. Mi nueva profesora de literatura es _____.

4   **Números** Write these numbers in Spanish.

Los números
p. 20

1. 751 _____

2. 99 _____

3. 4.010 _____

4. 844 _____

5. 738.266 _____

6. 23.110.680 _____

7. 1.033 _____

8. 1.500.307 _____

5   **Identificar** Find the word that does not belong.

1. profesor – padre – nieto – sobrino
2. literatura – español – historia – miércoles
3. martes – sábado – semana – lunes
4. baloncesto – natación – fútbol – vóleibol
5. prima – sobrino – mamá – tía
6. museo – almacén – centro comercial – mercado
7. escuela – matemáticas – biblioteca - librería
8. piscina – gimnasio – restaurante - estadio

6   **Verbos** Provide the appropriate present tense form of each verb.

Tener and **venir**
p. 11

1. Los gemelos Ana María y Carlos _____ (tener) 13 años.

2. Todos los días a las seis (yo) _____ (correr) en el parque.

3. (Yo) _____ (vivir) en un apartamento con mis padres y mi abuela.

4. Los chicos _____ (abrir) sus libros de historia.

5. Mi hermana _____ (aprender) a nadar los sábados en la piscina de la escuela.

Ir
p. 17

6. ¿Adónde _____ (ir) tu hermano con tanta prisa (in such a hurry)?

Jugar
p. 19

7. ¿Ustedes _____ (jugar) al fútbol y _____ (montar) en bicicleta todos los días?

8. ¿De dónde _____ (venir) tú? (Yo) _____ (venir) del museo.

9. Mañana (yo) _____ (ir) a leer un buen libro toda la tarde.

-er verbs comer	
yo	com**o**
tú	com**es**
Ud./él/ella	com**e**
nosotros/as	com**emos**
vosotros/as	com**éis**
Uds./ellos/ellas	com**en**

-ir verbs escribir	
yo	escrib**o**
tú	escrib**es**
Ud./él/ella	escrib**e**
nosotros/as	escrib**imos**
vosotros/as	escrib**ís**
Uds./ellos/ellas	escrib**en**

1 **Mi personaje favorito** Pick two of the **Fotonovela** characters and write a paragraph describing them. Don't forget to mention their family members and their likes and dislikes.

2 **Mi escena favorita** In groups of three or four, choose one or two of the **Fotonovela** scenes you have liked the most, and recreate them. Plan a dialogue based on the scenes below, or choose another scene that you liked from the **Fotonovela**.

1. Marissa conoce a la familia Díaz.

2. Marissa conoce a nuevos amigos y habla sobre las clases.

3. Un picnic en un lugar muy especial.

Los pasatiempos

4

Communicative Goals

You will learn how to:

- Talk about pastimes, weekend activities, and sports
- Make plans and invitations

A PRIMERA VISTA
- ¿Es esta persona un atleta o un artista?
- ¿En qué tiene interés, en el ciclismo o en el tenis?
- ¿Es viejo? ¿Es delgado?
- ¿Tiene frío o calor?

Los pasatiempos

Más vocabulario

el béisbol	baseball
el ciclismo	cycling
el esquí (acuático)	(water) skiing
el fútbol americano	football
el golf	golf
el hockey	hockey
la natación	swimming
el tenis	tennis
el vóleibol	volleyball
el equipo	team
el parque	park
el partido	game; match
la plaza	city or town square
andar en patineta	to skateboard
bucear	to scuba dive
escalar montañas (f., pl.)	to climb mountains
esquiar	to ski
ganar	to win
ir de excursión	to go on a hike
practicar deportes (m., pl.)	to play sports
escribir una carta/ un mensaje electrónico	to write a letter/ an e-mail
leer el correo electrónico	to read e-mail
leer una revista	to read a magazine
deportivo/a	sports-related

Variación léxica

piscina ←→	pileta (Arg.); alberca (Méx.)
baloncesto ←→	básquetbol (Amér. L.)
béisbol ←→	pelota (P. Rico, Rep. Dom.)

PARQUE MUNICIPAL

Lee el periódico. (leer)

Pasea en bicicleta. (pasear)

la pelota

el fútbol

la jugadora

Visitan el monumento. (visitar)

Pasean. (pasear)

Toma el sol. (tomar)

Nada. (nadar)

la piscina

Práctica

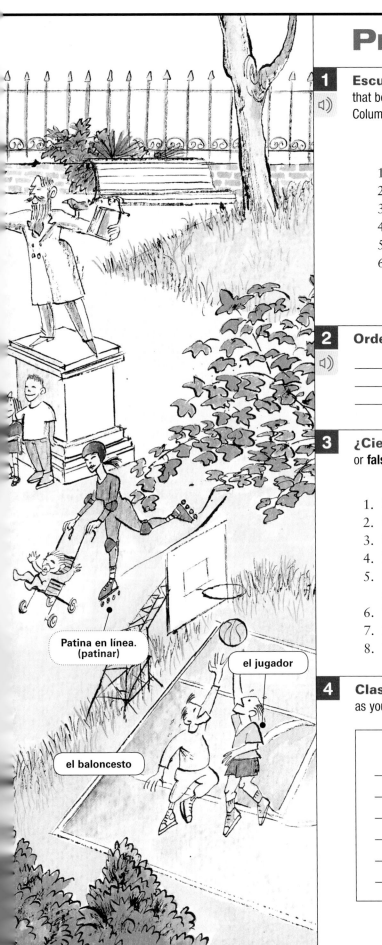

Patina en línea.
(patinar)

el jugador

el baloncesto

1 **Escuchar** Indicate the letter of the activity in Column B that best corresponds to each statement you hear. Two items in Column B will not be used.

A   B

1. _____   a. leer el correo electrónico
2. _____   b. tomar el sol
3. _____   c. pasear en bicicleta
4. _____   d. ir a un partido de fútbol americano
5. _____   e. escribir una carta
6. _____   f. practicar muchos deportes
             g. nadar
             h. ir de excursión

2 **Ordenar** Order these activities according to what you hear in the narration.

_____ a. pasear en bicicleta   _____ d. tomar el sol
_____ b. nadar   _____ e. practicar deportes
_____ c. leer una revista   _____ f. patinar en línea

3 **¿Cierto o falso?** Indicate whether each statement is **cierto** or **falso** based on the illustration.

	Cierto	Falso
1. Un hombre nada en la piscina.	O	O
2. Un hombre lee una revista.	O	O
3. Un chico pasea en bicicleta.	O	O
4. Dos muchachos esquían.	O	O
5. Una mujer y dos niños visitan un monumento.	O	O
6. Un hombre bucea.	O	O
7. Hay un equipo de hockey.	O	O
8. Una mujer toma el sol.	O	O

4 **Clasificar** Fill in the chart below with as many terms from **Contextos** as you can.

Actividades	Deportes	Personas

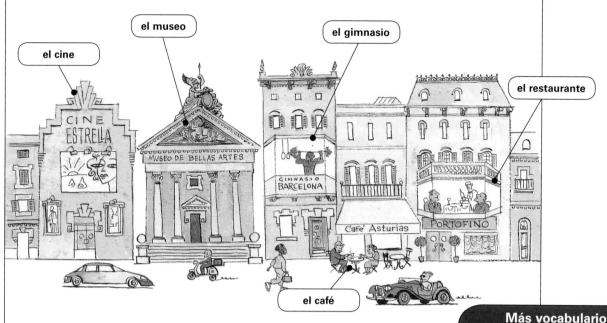

el cine · el museo · el gimnasio · el restaurante · el café

En el centro

Más vocabulario

la diversión	fun activity; entertainment; recreation
el fin de semana	weekend
el pasatiempo	pastime; hobby
los ratos libres	spare (free) time
el videojuego	video game
la iglesia	church
el lugar	place
ver películas (f., pl.)	to watch movies
favorito/a	favorite

5   **Identificar** Identify the place where these activities would take place.

> **modelo**
> Esquiamos. Es una montaña.

1. Tomamos una limonada.
2. Vemos una película.
3. Nadamos y tomamos el sol.
4. Hay muchos monumentos.
5. Comemos tacos y fajitas.
6. Miramos pinturas (*paintings*) de Diego Rivera y Frida Kahlo.
7. Hay mucho tráfico.
8. Practicamos deportes.

6   **Lugares** Indicate what you do in the places mentioned below.

> **modelo**
> una plaza
> Camino por la plaza y miro a las personas.

beber	escalar	mirar	practicar
caminar	escribir	nadar	tomar
correr	leer	patinar	visitar

1. una biblioteca
2. un estadio
3. una plaza
4. una piscina
5. las montañas
6. un parque
7. un café
8. un museo

Comunicación

7 **Guadalajara** Read this description of Guadalajara. Then indicate whether the following conclusions are **lógico** or **ilógico**, based on what you read.

> Guadalajara es una gran ciudad del estado de Jalisco, México. ¿Te gustan los parques? El Parque Mirador Independencia es un buen lugar para pasear en bicicleta, andar en patineta o tomar el sol. ¿Te gusta el cine? Guadalajara es un importante centro cultural, famosa por el Festival de Cine de Guadalajara. ¿Tienes hambre? Hay fabulosos restaurantes por toda la ciudad. ¿Te gustan los deportes? Debes asistir a un partido del Club Deportivo Guadalajara, uno de los equipos de fútbol más populares de México. ¿Te gusta el arte? Guadalajara es también muy famosa por sus museos y sus monumentos.

	Lógico	Ilógico
1. En el Parque Mirador Independencia, hay lugar para la diversión.	○	○
2. Asistes al Festival de Cine de Guadalajara para ver películas.	○	○
3. En Guadalajara, la gente come bien.	○	○
4. No hay estadios de fútbol en Guadalajara.	○	○
5. En Guadalajara, los turistas visitan monumentos.	○	○

8 **Entrevista** Answer your partner's questions.

1. ¿Hay un café cerca de tu casa?
2. ¿Cuál es tu restaurante favorito?
3. ¿Te gusta viajar y visitar monumentos?
4. ¿Te gusta ir al cine los fines de semana?
5. ¿Cuáles son tus películas favoritas?
6. ¿Te gusta practicar deportes?
7. ¿Cuáles son tus deportes favoritos?
8. ¿Cuáles son tus pasatiempos favoritos?

CONSULTA

To review expressions with **gustar**, see **Senderos 1A, Estructura 2.1**, p. 76.

9 **Pasatiempos** Write a paragraph about the pastimes three of your friends and family members enjoy.

> *modelo*
> Mi hermana pasea mucho en bicicleta, pero mis padres practican la natación. Mi hermano no nada, pero visita muchos museos.

10 **Conversación** Using the words and expressions provided, work with a partner to prepare a short conversation about pastimes.

¿a qué hora?	¿con quién(es)?	¿dónde?
¿cómo?	¿cuándo?	¿qué?

> *modelo*
> **Estudiante 1:** ¿Cuándo patinas en línea?
> **Estudiante 2:** Patino en línea los domingos. Y tú, ¿patinas en línea?
> **Estudiante 1:** No, no me gusta patinar en línea. Me gusta practicar el béisbol.

Fútbol, cenotes y mole

Maru, Miguel, Jimena y Marissa visitan un cenote, mientras
Felipe y Juan Carlos van a un partido de fútbol.

PERSONAJES

 MIGUEL

 PABLO

MIGUEL Buenos días a todos.

TÍA ANA MARÍA Hola, Miguel.
Maru, ¿qué van a hacer hoy?

MARU Miguel y yo vamos a
llevar a Marissa a un cenote.

MARISSA ¿No vamos a nadar?
¿Qué es un cenote?

MIGUEL Sí, sí vamos a nadar.
Un cenote... difícil de
explicar. Es una piscina
natural en un hueco profundo.

MARU ¡Ya vas a ver! Seguro
que te va a gustar.

(unos minutos después)

EDUARDO Hay un partido de fútbol
en el parque. ¿Quieren ir conmigo?

PABLO Y conmigo. Si no consigo
más jugadores, nuestro equipo
va a perder.

ANA MARÍA Marissa, ¿qué
te gusta hacer? ¿Escalar
montañas? ¿Ir de excursión?

MARISSA Sí, me gusta ir de
excursión y practicar el esquí
acuático. Y usted, ¿qué prefiere
hacer en sus ratos libres?

PABLO Mi mamá tiene muchos
pasatiempos y actividades.

EDUARDO Sí. Ella nada y juega
al tenis y al golf.

PABLO Va al cine y a los museos.

ANA MARÍA Sí, salgo mucho los
fines de semana

FELIPE ¿Recuerdas el restaurante
del mole?

EDUARDO ¿Qué restaurante?

JIMENA El mole de mi tía
Ana María es mi favorito.

MARU Chicos, ya es hora. ¡Vamos!

ANA MARÍA
 MARU
 MARISSA
 EDUARDO
 FELIPE
 JUAN CARLOS
 JIMENA
 DON GUILLERMO

7

(*más tarde, en el parque*)

PABLO No puede ser. ¡Cinco a uno!

FELIPE ¡Vamos a jugar! Si perdemos, compramos el almuerzo. Y si ganamos...

EDUARDO ¡Empezamos!

8

(*mientras tanto, en el cenote*)

MARISSA ¿Hay muchos cenotes en México?

MIGUEL Sólo en la península de Yucatán.

MARISSA ¡Vamos a nadar!

9

(*Los chicos visitan a don Guillermo, un vendedor de paletas heladas.*)

JUAN CARLOS Don Guillermo, ¿dónde podemos conseguir un buen mole?

FELIPE Eduardo y Pablo van a pagar el almuerzo. Y yo voy a pedir un montón de comida.

10

FELIPE Sí, éste es el restaurante. Recuerdo la comida.

EDUARDO Oye, Pablo... No tengo...

PABLO No te preocupes, hermanito.

FELIPE ¿Qué buscas? (*muestra la cartera de Pablo*) ¿Esto?

Expresiones útiles

Making invitations

Hay un partido de fútbol en el parque. ¿Quieren ir conmigo?
There's a soccer game in the park. Do you want to come with me?

¡Yo puedo jugar!
I can play!

Mmm... no quiero.
Hmm... I don't want to.

Lo siento, pero no puedo.
I'm sorry, but I can't.

¡Vamos a nadar!
Let's go swimming!

Sí, vamos.
Yes, let's go.

Making plans

¿Qué van a hacer hoy?
What are you going to do today?

Vamos a llevar a Marissa a un cenote.
We are taking Marissa to a cenote.

Vamos a comprar unas paletas heladas.
We're going to buy some popsicles.

Vamos a jugar. Si perdemos, compramos el almuerzo.
Let's play. If we lose, we'll buy lunch.

Talking about pastimes

¿Qué te gusta hacer? ¿Escalar montañas? ¿Ir de excursión?
What do you like to do? Mountain climbing? Hiking?

Sí, me gusta ir de excursión y practicar esquí acuático.
Yes, I like hiking and water skiing.

Y usted, ¿qué prefiere hacer en sus ratos libres?
And you, what do you like to do in your free time?

Salgo mucho los fines de semana.
I go out a lot on the weekends.

Voy al cine y a los museos.
I go to the movies and to museums.

Additional vocabulary

el/la aficionado/a *fan*
la cartera *wallet*　　**el hueco** *hole*
un montón de *a lot of*

¿Qué pasó?

1 Escoger Choose the answer that best completes each sentence.

1. Marissa, Maru y Miguel desean _____.
   a. nadar
   b. correr por el parque
   c. leer el periódico

2. A Marissa le gusta _____.
   a. el tenis
   b. el vóleibol
   c. ir de excursión y practicar esquí acuático

3. A la tía Ana María le gusta _____.
   a. jugar al hockey
   b. nadar y jugar al tenis y al golf
   c. hacer ciclismo

4. Pablo y Eduardo pierden el partido de _____.
   a. fútbol
   b. béisbol
   c. baloncesto

5. Juan Carlos y Felipe desean _____.
   a. patinar
   b. esquiar
   c. comer mole

2 Identificar Identify the person who would make each statement.

1. A mí me gusta nadar, pero no sé qué es un cenote. _____
2. Mamá va al cine y al museo en sus ratos libres. _____
3. Yo voy a pedir mucha comida. _____
4. ¿Quieren ir a jugar al fútbol con nosotros en el parque? _____
5. Me gusta salir los fines de semana. _____

MARISSA
FELIPE
EDUARDO
PABLO
TÍA ANA MARÍA

3 Preguntas Answer the questions using the information from the **Fotonovela.**

1. ¿Qué van a hacer Miguel y Maru?
2. ¿Adónde van Felipe y Juan Carlos mientras sus amigos van al cenote?
3. ¿Quién gana el partido de fútbol?
4. ¿Quiénes van al cenote con Maru y Miguel?

4 Conversación With a partner, prepare a conversation in which you talk about pastimes and invite each other to do some activity together. Use these expressions and also look at **Expresiones útiles** on the previous page.

¿A qué hora? *(At) What time?* **contigo** *with you*	**¿Dónde?** *Where?* **No puedo porque...** *I can't because...*	**Nos vemos a las siete.** *See you at seven.*

▶ ¿Eres aficionado/a a...?
▶ ¿Te gusta...?
▶ ¿Por qué no...?
▶ ¿Quieres... conmigo?
▶ ¿Qué vas a hacer esta noche?

Pronunciación
Word stress and accent marks

pe-lí-cu-la **e-di-fi-cio** **ver** **yo**

Every Spanish syllable contains at least one vowel. When two vowels are joined in the same syllable they form a **diphthong***. A **monosyllable** is a word formed by a single syllable.

bi-blio-te-ca **vi-si-tar** **par-que** **fút-bol**

The syllable of a Spanish word that is pronounced most emphatically is the "stressed" syllable.

pe-lo-ta **pis-ci-na** **ra-tos** **ha-blan**

Words that end in **n**, **s**, or a **vowel** are usually stressed on the next-to-last syllable.

na-ta-ción **pa-pá** **in-glés** **Jo-sé**

If words that end in **n**, **s**, or a **vowel** are stressed on the last syllable, they must carry an accent mark on the stressed syllable.

bai-lar **es-pa-ñol** **u-ni-ver-si-dad** **tra-ba-ja-dor**

Words that do not end in **n**, **s**, or a **vowel** are usually stressed on the last syllable.

béis-bol **lá-piz** **ár-bol** **Gó-mez**

If words that do not end in **n**, **s**, or a **vowel** are stressed on the next-to-last syllable, they must carry an accent mark on the stressed syllable.

*The two vowels that form a diphthong are either both weak or one is weak and the other is strong.

En la unión está la fuerza.[2]

Práctica Pronounce each word, stressing the correct syllable. Then give the word stress rule for each word.

1. profesor
2. Puebla
3. ¿Cuántos?
4. Mazatlán
5. examen
6. ¿Cómo?
7. niños
8. Guadalajara
9. programador
10. México
11. están
12. geografía

Oraciones Read the conversation aloud to practice word stress.

MARINA Hola, Carlos. ¿Qué tal?
CARLOS Bien. Oye, ¿a qué hora es el partido de fútbol?
MARINA Creo que es a las siete.
CARLOS ¿Quieres ir?
MARINA Lo siento, pero no puedo. Tengo que estudiar biología.

Quien ríe de último, ríe mejor.[1]

Refranes Read these sayings aloud to practice word stress.

1 He who laughs last, laughs best.
2 United we stand.

EN DETALLE

Real Madrid y Barça:
rivalidad total

Soccer in Spain is a force to be reckoned with, and no two teams draw more attention than **Real Madrid** and the **Fútbol Club Barcelona**. Whether the venue is Madrid's **Santiago Bernabéu** or Barcelona's **Camp Nou**, the two cities shut down for the showdown, paralyzed by **fútbol** fever. A ticket to the actual game is always the hottest ticket in town.

The rivalry between **Real Madrid** and **Barça** is about more than soccer. As the two biggest, most powerful cities in Spain, Barcelona and Madrid are constantly compared to one another and have a natural rivalry. There is also a political component to the dynamic. Barcelona, with its distinct language and culture, has long struggled for increased autonomy from Madrid's centralized government. Under Francisco Franco's rule (1939–1975), when repression of the Catalan identity was at its height, a game between **Real Madrid** and **FC Barcelona** was wrapped up with all the symbolism of the regime versus the resistance, even though both teams suffered casualties in Spain's civil war and the subsequent Franco dictatorship.

Although the dictatorship is long over, the momentum of all those decades of competition still transforms both cities into a frenzied, tense panic leading up to the game. Once the final score is announced, one of those cities is transformed again, this time into the best party in the country.

Rivalidades del fútbol

Argentina: Boca Juniors vs River Plate

México: Águilas del América vs Chivas del Guadalajara

Chile: Colo Colo vs Universidad de Chile

Guatemala: Comunicaciones vs Municipal

Uruguay: Peñarol vs Nacional

Colombia: Millonarios vs Independiente Santa Fe

ACTIVIDADES

1 **¿Cierto o falso?** Indicate whether each statement is **cierto** or **falso**. Correct the false statements.

1. People from Spain don't like soccer.
2. Madrid and Barcelona are the most important cities in Spain.
3. Santiago Bernabéu is a stadium in Barcelona.
4. The rivalry between Real Madrid and FC Barcelona is not only in soccer.
5. Barcelona has resisted Madrid's centralized government.
6. Only the FC Barcelona team was affected by the civil war.
7. During Franco's regime, the Catalan culture thrived.
8. There are many famous rivalries between soccer teams in the Spanish-speaking world.
9. River Plate is a popular team from Argentina.
10. Comunicaciones and Peñarol are famous rivals in Guatemala.

ASÍ SE DICE

Los deportes

el/la árbitro/a	*referee*
el/la atleta	*athlete*
la bola; el balón	**la pelota**
el campeón/ la campeona	*champion*
la carrera	*race*
competir	*to compete*
empatar	*to tie*
la medalla	*medal*
el/la mejor	*the best*
mundial	*worldwide*
el torneo	*tournament*

EL MUNDO HISPANO

Atletas importantes

World-renowned Hispanic athletes:

- **Rafael Nadal** (España) has won 14 Grand Slam singles titles and the 2008 Olympic gold medal in singles tennis.

- **Lionel Andrés Messi** (Argentina) is one of the world's top soccer players. He plays for **FC Barcelona** and for the Argentine national team.

- **Mireia Belmonte García** (España) won two silver medals in swimming at the 2012 Olympics.

- **Lorena Ochoa** (México) was the top-ranked female golfer in the world when she retired in 2010 at the age of 28. She still hosts an LPGA golf tournament, the Lorena Ochoa Invitational, every year.

PERFILES

Miguel Cabrera y Paola Espinosa

Miguel Cabrera, considered one of the best hitters in baseball, now plays first base for the Detroit Tigers. Born in Venezuela in 1983, he made his Major League debut at the age of 20. Cabrera has been selected for both the National League and American League All-Star Teams. In 2012, he became the first player since 1967 to win the Triple Crown.

Mexican diver **Paola Milagros Espinosa Sánchez**, born in 1986, has competed in three Olympics (2004, 2008, and 2012). She and her partner Tatiana Ortiz took home a bronze medal in 2008. In 2012, she won a silver medal with partner Alejandra Orozco. She won three gold medals at the Pan American Games in 2007 and again in 2011.

Conexión Internet

¿Qué deportes son populares en los países hispanos?

Use the Web to find more cultural information related to this **Cultura** section.

ACTIVIDADES

2 **Comprensión** Write the name of the athlete described in each sentence.

1. Es un jugador de fútbol de Argentina. _____

2. Es una mujer que practica el golf. _____

3. Es un jugador de béisbol de Venezuela. _____

4. Es una mujer mexicana que practica un deporte en la piscina. _____

3 **¿Quién es?** Write a short paragraph describing an athlete that you like. What does he/she look like? What sport does he/she play? Where does he/she live?

4.1 Present tense of **ir**

ANTE TODO The verb **ir** (*to go*) is irregular in the present tense. Note that, except for the **yo** form (**voy**) and the lack of a written accent on the **vosotros** form (**vais**), the endings are the same as those for regular present tense **-ar** verbs.

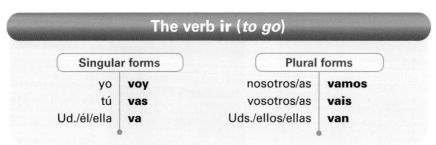

The verb ir (*to go*)

Singular forms		Plural forms	
yo	**voy**	nosotros/as	**vamos**
tú	**vas**	vosotros/as	**vais**
Ud./él/ella	**va**	Uds./ellos/ellas	**van**

▶ **Ir** is often used with the preposition **a** (*to*). If **a** is followed by the definite article **el**, they combine to form the contraction **al**. If **a** is followed by the other definite articles (**la, las, los**), there is no contraction.

$$a + el = al$$

Voy **al** parque con Juan.
I'm going to the park with Juan.

Mis amigos van **a las** montañas.
My friends are going to the mountains.

▶ The construction **ir a** + [*infinitive*] is used to talk about actions that are going to happen in the future. It is equivalent to the English *to be going* + [*infinitive*].

Va a leer el periódico.
He is going to read the newspaper.

Van a pasear por el pueblo.
They are going to walk around town.

AYUDA

When asking a question that contains a form of the verb **ir**, remember to use **adónde**:

¿Adónde vas?
(To) Where are you going?

¡Voy a ir con ellos!

Ella va al cine y a los museos.

▶ **Vamos a** + [*infinitive*] can also express the idea of *let's (do something)*.

Vamos a pasear.
Let's take a walk.

¡Vamos a comer!
Let's eat!

¡INTÉNTALO! Provide the present tense forms of **ir**.

1. Ellos ___*van*___.
2. Yo _____.
3. Tu amigo _____.
4. Adela _____.
5. Mi prima y yo _____.
6. Tú _____.
7. Ustedes _____.
8. Nosotros _____.
9. Usted _____.
10. Nosotras _____.
11. Miguel _____.
12. Ellas _____.

Práctica

1 **¿Adónde van?** Everyone in your neighborhood is dashing off to various places.
Say where they are going.

1. la señora Castillo / el centro
2. las hermanas Gómez / la piscina
3. tu tío y tu papá / el partido de fútbol
4. yo / el Museo de Arte Moderno
5. nosotros / el restaurante Miramar

2 **¿Qué van a hacer?** These sentences describe what several students in a college
hiking club are doing today. Use **ir a** + [*infinitive*] to say that they are also going to do the
same activities tomorrow.

> *modelo*
>
> Martín y Rodolfo nadan en la piscina.
> Van a nadar en la piscina mañana también.

1. Sara lee una revista.
2. Yo practico deportes.
3. Ustedes van de excursión.
4. El presidente del club patina.
5. Tú tomas el sol.
6. Paseamos con nuestros amigos.

3 **Actividades** Indicate where the people are going and what they are going to do there.

> *modelo*
>
> Estela va a la Librería Sol.
> Va a comprar un libro.

Estela

1. Álex y Miguel

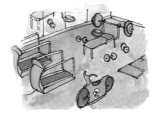

2. mi amigo

3. tú

4. los estudiantes

5. la profesora Torres

6. ustedes

Comunicación

4

Esta noche Listen to the conversation between Enrique and Rosa. Then indicate whether the following conclusions are **lógico** or **ilógico**, based on what you heard.

	Lógico	Ilógico
1. Rosa y Mercedes van a ver una película esta noche.	○	○
2. A Enrique le gustan los deportes.	○	○
3. Enrique va a ir al estadio esta noche.	○	○
4. Enrique y Pedro van a cenar mientras (*while*) miran el partido.	○	○
5. A Rosa no le gustan los restaurantes japoneses.	○	○
6. Rosa y Enrique conversan en el cine.	○	○

5

Situaciones Work with a partner and say where you and your friends go in these situations.

1. Cuando deseo descansar…
2. Cuando mi mejor amigo/a tiene que estudiar…
3. Si deseo hablar con mis amigos…
4. Cuando mis amigos y yo tenemos hambre…
5. En mis ratos libres…
6. Cuando mis amigos desean esquiar…
7. Si estoy de vacaciones…
8. Si tengo ganas de leer…

6

Entrevista With a partner, take turns asking each other where you are going and what you are going to do on your next vacation.

> **modelo**
>
> **Estudiante 1:** ¿Adónde vas de vacaciones (*on vacation*)?
> **Estudiante 2:** Voy a Guadalajara con mi familia.
> **Estudiante 1:** ¿Y qué van a hacer (*to do*) ustedes en Guadalajara?
> **Estudiante 2:** Vamos a visitar unos monumentos y museos. ¿Y tú?

Síntesis

7

Planes Make a schedule of your activities for the weekend.

▶ For each day, list at least three things you have to do.
▶ For each day, list at least two things you will do for fun.

CONSULTA

To review the present tense of regular **-ar** verbs, see **Senderos 1A, Estructura 2.1**, p. 74.

• • •

To review the present tense of regular **-er** and **-ir** verbs, see **Senderos 1A, Estructura 3.3**, p. 120.

4.2 Stem-changing verbs: e→ie, o→ue

ANTE TODO Stem-changing verbs deviate from the normal pattern of regular verbs. When stem-changing verbs are conjugated, they have a vowel change in the last syllable of the stem.

INFINITIVE		VERB STEM		STEM CHANGE		CONJUGATED FORM
empezar	▶	emp**ez**-	▶	emp**iez**-	▶	emp**ie**zo
volver		v**o**lv-		v**ue**lv-		v**ue**lvo

▶ In many verbs, such as **empezar** (*to begin*), the stem vowel changes from **e** to **ie**. Note that the **nosotros/as** and **vosotros/as** forms don't have a stem change.

The verb empezar (e:ie) (*to begin*)

Singular forms		Plural forms	
yo	emp**ie**zo	nosotros/as	empezamos
tú	emp**ie**zas	vosotros/as	empezáis
Ud./él/ella	emp**ie**za	Uds./ellos/ellas	emp**ie**zan

Los chicos empiezan a hablar de su visita al cenote.

Ellos vuelven a comer en el restaurante.

▶ In many other verbs, such as **volver** (*to return*), the stem vowel changes from **o** to **ue**. The **nosotros/as** and **vosotros/as** forms have no stem change.

The verb volver (o:ue) (*to return*)

Singular forms		Plural forms	
yo	v**ue**lvo	nosotros/as	volvemos
tú	v**ue**lves	vosotros/as	volvéis
Ud./él/ella	v**ue**lve	Uds./ellos/ellas	v**ue**lven

▶ To help you identify stem-changing verbs, they will appear as follows throughout the text:

empezar (e:ie), volver (o:ue)

Common stem-changing verbs

e:ie		o:ue	
cerrar	to close	**almorzar**	to have lunch
comenzar (a + inf.)	to begin	**contar**	to count; to tell
empezar (a + inf.)	to begin	**dormir**	to sleep
entender	to understand	**encontrar**	to find
pensar	to think	**mostrar**	to show
perder	to lose; to miss	**poder (+ inf.)**	to be able to; can
preferir (+ inf.)	to prefer	**recordar**	to remember
querer (+ inf.)	to want; to love	**volver**	to return

¡LENGUA VIVA!

The verb **perder** can mean *to lose* or *to miss*, in the sense of "to miss a train."

Siempre pierdo mis llaves.
I always lose my keys.

Es importante no perder el autobús.
It's important not to miss the bus.

▶ **Jugar** (*to play a sport or a game*) is the only Spanish verb that has a **u:ue** stem change. **Jugar** is followed by **a** + [*definite article*] when the name of a sport or game is mentioned.

Ella juega al tenis y al golf.

Los chicos juegan al fútbol.

▶ **Comenzar** and **empezar** require the preposition **a** when they are followed by an infinitive.

Comienzan a jugar a las siete.
They begin playing at seven.

Ana **empieza a** escribir una postal.
Ana is starting to write a postcard.

▶ **Pensar** + [*infinitive*] means *to plan* or *to intend to do something*. **Pensar en** means *to think about someone* or *something*.

¿**Piensan** ir al gimnasio?
Are you planning to go to the gym?

¿**En** qué **piensas**?
What are you thinking about?

¡INTÉNTALO!   Provide the present tense forms of these verbs.

cerrar (e:ie)

1. Ustedes ___cierran___.
2. Tú _____.
3. Nosotras _____.
4. Mi hermano _____.
5. Yo _____.
6. Usted _____.
7. Los chicos _____.
8. Ella _____.

dormir (o:ue)

1. Mi abuela no ___duerme___.
2. Yo no _____.
3. Tú no _____.
4. Mis hijos no _____.
5. Usted no _____.
6. Nosotros no _____.
7. Él no _____.
8. Ustedes no _____.

Práctica

1 **Completar** Complete this conversation with the appropriate forms of the verbs.

PABLO Óscar, voy al centro ahora.

ÓSCAR ¿A qué hora (1)_____ (pensar) volver? El partido de fútbol (2)_____ (empezar) a las dos.

PABLO (3)_____ (Volver) a la una. (4)_____ (Querer) ver el partido.

ÓSCAR (5)¿_____ (Recordar) que (*that*) nuestro equipo es muy bueno? (6)¡_____ (Poder) ganar!

PABLO No, (7)_____ (pensar) que va a (8)_____ (perder). Los jugadores de Guadalajara son salvajes (*wild*) cuando (9)_____ (jugar).

2 **Preferencias** Indicate what these people want to do, using the cues provided.

modelo

Guillermo: estudiar / pasear en bicicleta
Guillermo no quiere estudiar. Prefiere pasear en bicicleta.

1. tú: trabajar / dormir
2. ustedes: mirar la televisión / jugar al dominó
3. tus amigos: ir de excursión / descansar
4. tú: comer en la cafetería / ir a un restaurante
5. Elisa: ver una película / leer una revista
6. María y su hermana: tomar el sol / practicar el esquí acuático

3 **Describir** Use a verb from the list to describe what these people are doing.

almorzar   cerrar   contar   dormir   encontrar   mostrar

1. las niñas   2. yo   3. nosotros

4. tú   5. Pedro   6. Teresa

Comunicación

4 **Frecuencia** Use the verbs from the list and other stem-changing verbs you know to explain which activities you do daily (**todos los días**), which you do once a month (**una vez al mes**), and which you do once a year (**una vez al año**).

> *modelo*
>
> Yo recuerdo a mi familia todos los días. Yo pierdo uno de
> mis libros una vez al año...

cerrar	encontrar	poder	recordar
dormir	jugar	preferir	¿?
empezar	perder	querer	

5 **En la televisión** Read the television listings for Saturday. With a partner, role-play a conversation between two siblings arguing about what to watch.

> *modelo*
>
> **Hermano:** *Podemos ver la Copa Mundial.*
> **Hermana:** *¡No, no quiero ver la Copa Mundial! Prefiero ver...*

	13:00	14:00	15:00	16:00	17:00	18:00	19:00	20:00	21:00	22:00	23:00
7	Copa Mundial (*World Cup*) de fútbol				República Deportiva	Campeonato (*Championship*) Mundial de Vóleibol: México-Argentina				Torneo de Natación	
8	Abierto (*Open*) Mexicano de Tenis: Santiago González (México) vs. Nicolás Almagro (España). Semifinales			Campeonato de baloncesto: Los Correcaminos de Tampico vs. los Santos de San Luis				Aficionados al buceo		Cozumel: Aventuras	
12	Yo soy Betty, la fea		Héroes		Hermanos y hermanas			Película: **Sin nombre**		Película: **El coronel no tiene quien le escriba**	
13	El padrastro		60 Minutos				El esquí acuático			Patinaje artístico	
17	Biografías: La artista Frida Kahlo			Música de la semana			Entrevista del día: Iker Casillas y su pasión por el fútbol			Cine de la noche: **Elsa y Fred**	

NOTA CULTURAL

Iker Casillas Fernández is a famous goalkeeper for **Real Madrid**. A native of Madrid, he is among the best goalkeepers of his generation.

Síntesis

6 **Deportes** Write a paragraph about your favorite sport. Mention why you like it, and whether you practice it or watch it on TV. Include some facts you know about the sport. Use at least three stem-changing verbs.

> *modelo*
>
> Mi deporte favorito es el béisbol porque es un deporte interesante.
> Esta noche pienso ver el partido de los Padres en la televisión.
> Empieza a las siete...

4.3 Stem-changing verbs: e→i

ANTE TODO You've already seen that many verbs in Spanish change their stem vowel when conjugated. There is a third kind of stem-vowel change in some verbs, such as **pedir** (*to ask for; to request*). In these verbs, the stressed vowel in the stem changes from **e** to **i**, as shown in the diagram.

INFINITIVE		VERB STEM		STEM CHANGE		CONJUGATED FORM
pedir	▶	p**e**d-	▶	p**i**d-	▶	p**i**do

▶ As with other stem-changing verbs you have learned, there is no stem change in the **nosotros/as** or **vosotros/as** forms in the present tense.

The verb pedir (e:i) (*to ask for; to request*)

Singular forms		Plural forms	
yo	p**i**do	nosotros/as	pedimos
tú	p**i**des	vosotros/as	pedís
Ud./él/ella	p**i**de	Uds./ellos/ellas	p**i**den

▶ To help you identify verbs with the **e:i** stem change, they will appear as follows throughout the text:

pedir (e:i)

▶ These are the most common **e:i** stem-changing verbs:

conseguir	**decir**	**repetir**	**seguir**
to get; to obtain	*to say; to tell*	*to repeat*	*to follow; to continue; to keep (doing something)*

Pido favores cuando es necesario.
I ask for favors when it's necessary.

Javier **dice** la verdad.
Javier is telling the truth.

Sigue con su tarea.
He continues with his homework.

Consiguen ver buenas películas.
They get to see good movies.

▶ **¡Atención!** The verb **decir** is irregular in its **yo** form: **yo digo.**

▶ The **yo** forms of **seguir** and **conseguir** have a spelling change in addition to the stem change **e:i.**

Sigo su plan.
I'm following their plan.

Consigo novelas en la librería.
I get novels at the bookstore.

¡INTÉNTALO! Provide the correct forms of the verbs.

repetir (e:i)	**decir (e:i)**	**seguir (e:i)**
1. Arturo y Eva _repiten_.	1. Yo _digo_.	1. Yo _sigo_.
2. Yo _____.	2. Él _____.	2. Nosotros _____.
3. Nosotros _____.	3. Tú _____.	3. Tú _____.
4. Julia _____.	4. Usted _____.	4. Los chicos _____.
5. Sofía y yo _____.	5. Ellas _____.	5. Usted _____.

Práctica

1 **Completar** Complete these sentences with the correct form of the verb provided.

1. Cuando mi familia pasea por la ciudad, mi madre siempre (*always*) va a un café y _____ (pedir) una soda.
2. Pero mi padre _____ (decir) que perdemos mucho tiempo. Tiene prisa por llegar al Bosque de Chapultepec.
3. Mi padre tiene suerte, porque él siempre _____ (conseguir) lo que (*that which*) desea.
4. Cuando llegamos al parque, mis hermanos y yo _____ (seguir) conversando (*talking*) con nuestros padres.
5. Mis padres siempre _____ (repetir) la misma cosa: "Nosotros tomamos el sol aquí sin ustedes".
6. Yo siempre _____ (pedir) permiso para volver a casa un poco más tarde porque me gusta mucho el parque.

NOTA CULTURAL

A popular weekend destination for residents and tourists, **el Bosque de Chapultepec** is a beautiful park located in Mexico City. It occupies over 1.5 square miles and includes lakes, wooded areas, several museums, and a botanical garden. You may recognize this park from **Fotonovela, Lección 2**.

2 **Combinar** Combine words from the two columns to create sentences about yourself and people you know.

A	B
yo	(no) pedir muchos favores
mi madre	nunca (*never*) pedir perdón
mi mejor (*best*) amigo/a	nunca seguir las instrucciones
mi familia	siempre seguir las instrucciones
mis amigos/as	conseguir libros en Internet
mis amigos/as y yo	repetir el vocabulario
mis padres	poder hablar dos lenguas
mi hermano/a	dormir hasta el mediodía
mi profesor(a) de español	siempre perder sus libros

3 **¿Sí o no?** Indicate whether you do the following.

> *modelo*
>
> pedir consejos con frecuencia
> *Pido consejos con frecuencia./No pido consejos con frecuencia.*

1. conseguir libros en la librería
2. almorzar en casa
3. perder cosas con frecuencia
4. pedir favores
5. seguir las instrucciones de un manual
6. volver tarde a casa
7. dormir mucho
8. jugar al tenis

Comunicación

4 **Una entrevista** Read this interview with actress Andrea de la Palma. Then indicate whether the following conclusions are **lógico** or **ilógico**, based on what you read.

MANUEL Andrea, ¿qué tipo de persona eres?

ANDREA Creo que soy una persona introvertida. No les pido demasiados favores a mis amigos. En general, pienso que soy una buena amiga; siempre digo la verdad.

MANUEL ¿Qué pides en un restaurante?

ANDREA Siempre (*Always*) pido comida (*food*) vegetariana. Hay un restaurante español muy bueno. Siempre pido tortilla española (*potato omelet*) y ¡siempre repito!

MANUEL ¿Qué deportes sigues?

ANDREA Sigo el béisbol, pero no consigo entender bien los partidos.

MANUEL Sí, ¡pueden ser muy complicados! Andrea, muchas gracias por la entrevista y por ser tan buena actriz. Siempre veo tus películas.

ANDREA El gusto es mío. ¡Muchas gracias!

	Lógico	Ilógico
1. Andrea es honesta.	○	○
2. Andrea siempre come en casa.	○	○
3. Andrea pide pollo (*chicken*) en los restaurantes.	○	○
4. A Manuel le gustan las películas.	○	○
5. Manuel sigue la carrera de Andrea.	○	○

5 **Las películas** Answer your partner's questions.

1. ¿Prefieres las películas románticas, las películas de acción o las películas de terror? ¿Por qué?
2. ¿Dónde consigues información sobre (*about*) cine y televisión?
3. ¿Dónde consigues las entradas (*tickets*) para el cine?
4. Para decidir qué películas vas a ver, ¿sigues las recomendaciones de los críticos de cine? ¿Qué dicen los críticos en general?
5. ¿Qué cines de tu comunidad muestran las mejores (*best*) películas?
6. ¿Vas a ver una película esta semana? ¿A qué hora empieza la película?

6 **El cine** With a partner, discuss good and bad movies you have seen. Use stem-changing verbs in your conversation.

> **modelo**
> **Estudiante 1:** Pienso que *Gravedad* es una película muy buena. Los efectos especiales son excelentes.
> **Estudiante 2:** Sí. Digo que Sandra Bullock es la mejor actriz...

Síntesis

7 **Mi película favorita** Write a paragraph about your favorite movie. Use stem-changing verbs in your description.

4.4 Verbs with irregular **yo** forms

ANTE TODO In Spanish, several verbs have irregular **yo** forms in the present tense. You have already seen three verbs with the **-go** ending in the **yo** form: **decir → digo, tener → tengo,** and **venir → vengo**.

▶ Here are some common expressions with **decir**.

decir la verdad	**decir mentiras**
to tell the truth	*to tell lies*
decir que	**decir la respuesta**
to say that	*to say the answer*

▶ The verb **hacer** is often used to ask questions about what someone does. Note that when answering, **hacer** is frequently replaced with another, more specific action verb.

Verbs with irregular yo forms				
hacer *(to do; to make)*	**poner** *(to put; to place)*	**salir** *(to leave)*	**suponer** *(to suppose)*	**traer** *(to bring)*
hago	**pongo**	**salgo**	**supongo**	**traigo**
haces	pones	sales	supones	traes
hace	pone	sale	supone	trae
hacemos	ponemos	salimos	suponemos	traemos
hacéis	ponéis	salís	suponéis	traéis
hacen	ponen	salen	suponen	traen

SINGULAR FORMS applies to the first three rows; PLURAL FORMS applies to the last three rows.

Salgo mucho los fines de semana.

Yo no salgo, yo hago la tarea y veo películas en la televisión.

▶ **Poner** can also mean to *turn on* a household appliance.

Carlos **pone** la radio.	María **pone** la televisión.
Carlos turns on the radio.	*María turns on the television.*

▶ **Salir de** is used to indicate that someone is leaving a particular place.

Hoy **salgo del** hospital.	**Sale de** la clase a las cuatro.
Today I leave the hospital.	*He leaves class at four.*

▶ **Salir para** is used to indicate someone's destination.

> Mañana **salgo para** México.
> *Tomorrow I leave for Mexico.*

> Hoy **salen para** España.
> *Today they leave for Spain.*

▶ **Salir con** means *to leave with someone* or *something*, or *to date someone*.

> Alberto **sale con** su mochila.
> *Alberto is leaving with his backpack.*

> Margarita **sale con** Guillermo.
> *Margarita is going out with Guillermo.*

The verbs ver and oír

▶ The verb **ver** (*to see*) has an irregular **yo** form. The other forms of **ver** are regular.

The verb **ver** (*to see*)			
Singular forms		**Plural forms**	
yo	**veo**	nosotros/as	vemos
tú	ves	vosotros/as	veis
Ud./él/ella	ve	Uds./ellos/ellas	ven

▶ The verb **oír** (*to hear*) has an irregular **yo** form and the spelling change **i:y** in the **tú**, **usted/él/ella**, and **ustedes/ellos/ellas** forms. The **nosotros/as** and **vosotros/as** forms have an accent mark.

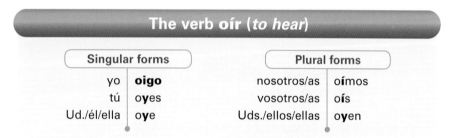

The verb **oír** (*to hear*)			
Singular forms		**Plural forms**	
yo	**oigo**	nosotros/as	oímos
tú	oyes	vosotros/as	oís
Ud./él/ella	oye	Uds./ellos/ellas	oyen

▶ While most commonly translated as *to hear*, **oír** is also used in contexts where the verb *to listen* would be used in English.

> **Oigo** a unas personas en la otra sala.
> *I hear some people in the other room.*

> ¿**Oyes** la radio por la mañana?
> *Do you listen to the radio in the morning?*

¡INTÉNTALO!   Provide the appropriate forms of these verbs.

1. salir   Isabel ___sale___.   Nosotros _____.   Yo _____.
2. ver   Yo _____.   Uds. _____.   Tú _____.
3. poner   Rita y yo _____.   Yo _____.   Los niños _____.
4. hacer   Yo _____.   Tú _____.   Ud. _____.
5. oír   Él _____.   Nosotros _____.   Yo _____.
6. traer   Ellas _____.   Yo _____.   Tú _____.
7. suponer   Yo _____.   Mi amigo _____.   Nosotras _____.

Práctica

1   **Completar** Complete this conversation with the appropriate forms of the verbs.

ERNESTO David, ¿qué (1)_____ (hacer) hoy?

DAVID Ahora estudio biología, pero esta noche (2)_____ (salir) con Luisa. Vamos al cine. Los críticos (3)_____ (decir) que la nueva (*new*) película de Almodóvar es buena.

ERNESTO ¿Y Diana? ¿Qué (4)_____ (hacer) ella?

DAVID (5)_____ (Salir) a comer con sus padres.

ERNESTO ¿Qué (6)_____ (hacer) Andrés y Javier?

DAVID Tienen que (7)_____ (hacer) las maletas. (8)_____ (Salir) para Monterrey mañana.

ERNESTO Pues, ¿qué (9)_____ (hacer) yo?

DAVID Yo (10)_____ (suponer) que puedes estudiar o (11)_____ (ver) la televisión.

ERNESTO No quiero estudiar. Mejor (12)_____ (poner) la televisión. Mi programa favorito empieza en unos minutos.

2   **Oraciones** Form sentences using the cues provided and verbs from **Estructura 4.4**.

> **modelo**
>
> tú / _____ / cosas / en / su lugar / antes de (*before*) / salir
> *Tú pones las cosas en su lugar antes de salir.*

1. mis amigos / _____ / conmigo / centro
2. tú / _____ / mentiras / pero / yo _____ / verdad
3. Alberto / _____ / música del café Pasatiempos
4. yo / no / _____ / muchas películas
5. domingo / nosotros / _____ / mucha / tarea
6. si / yo / _____ / que / yo / querer / ir / cine / mis amigos / ir / también

3   **Describir** Use the verbs from **Estructura 4.4** to describe what these people are doing.

1. Fernán

2. los aficionados

3. yo

4. nosotros

5. la señora Vargas

6. el estudiante

Comunicación

4

El día de Francisco Listen to Francisco's description of his day. Then indicate whether the following conclusions are **lógico** or **ilógico**, based on what you heard.

	Lógico	Ilógico
1. Francisco duerme hasta (*until*) el mediodía.	○	○
2. A Francisco no le gustan las matemáticas.	○	○
3. Francisco almuerza en casa.	○	○
4. A Francisco le gustan los deportes.	○	○
5. Francisco sale para la casa antes de las cinco.	○	○

5

Tu rutina Answer your partner's questions.

1. ¿Siempre (*Always*) pones tus cosas en su lugar?
2. ¿Qué prefieres hacer, oír la radio o ver la televisión?
3. ¿Oyes música cuando estudias?
4. ¿Ves películas en casa o prefieres ir al cine?
5. ¿Haces mucha tarea los fines de semana?
6. ¿Sales con tus amigos los fines de semana? ¿A qué hora? ¿Qué hacen?

6

Un día típico Write a short paragraph about what you do on a typical day. Use at least six of the verbs you have learned in this lesson.

> **modelo**
>
> Hola, me llamo Julia y vivo en Houston. Por la mañana, yo...

Síntesis

7

Situación Imagine that you are speaking with a member of your family. With a partner, prepare a conversation using these cues.

Estudiante 1	Estudiante 2
Ask your partner what he or she is doing.	→ Tell your partner that you are watching TV.
Say what you suppose he or she is watching.	→ Say that you like the show _____. Ask if he or she wants to watch.
Say no, because you are going out with friends, and tell where you are going.	→ Say you think it's a good idea, and ask what your partner and his or her friends are doing there.
Say what you are going to do, and ask your partner whether he or she wants to come along.	→ Say no and tell your partner what you prefer to do.

Recapitulación

SUBJECT
Javier
CONJUGATED FORM
empiezo
Main clause
Dudan

Review the grammar concepts you have learned in this lesson by completing these activities.

1 **Completar** Complete the chart with the correct verb forms. **30 pts.**

Infinitive	yo	nosotros/as	ellos/as
	vuelvo		
comenzar		comenzamos	
		hacemos	hacen
ir			
	juego		
repetir			repiten

2 **Un día típico** Complete the paragraph with the appropriate forms of the verbs in the word list. Not all verbs will be used. Some may be used more than once. **30 pts.**

almorzar	ir	salir
cerrar	jugar	seguir
empezar	mostrar	ver
hacer	querer	volver

¡Hola! Me llamo Cecilia y vivo en Puerto Vallarta, México. ¿Cómo es un día típico en mi vida (*life*)? Por la mañana bebo café con mis padres y juntos (*together*) (1) _____ las noticias (*news*) en la televisión. A las siete y media, (yo) (2) _____ de mi casa y tomo el autobús. Me gusta llegar temprano (*early*) a la escuela porque siempre (*always*) (3) _____ a mis amigos en la cafetería. Tomamos jugo y planeamos lo que (4) _____ hacer cada (*each*) día. A las ocho y cuarto, mi amiga Sandra y yo (5) _____ al laboratorio de lenguas. La clase de francés (6) _____ a las ocho y media. ¡Es mi clase favorita! A las doce y media (yo) (7) _____ en la cafetería con mis amigos. Después (*Afterwards*), yo (8) _____ con mis clases. Por las tardes, mis amigos (9) _____ a sus casas, pero yo (10) _____ al vóleibol con mi amigo Tomás.

RESUMEN GRAMATICAL

4.1 **Present tense of ir** *p. 36*

yo	voy	nos.	vamos
tú	vas	vos.	vais
él	va	ellas	van

► **ir a** + [*infinitive*] = *to be going* + [*infinitive*]
► **a** + **el** = **al**
► **vamos a** + [*infinitive*] = *let's* (*do something*)

4.2 **Stem-changing verbs e:ie, o:ue, u:ue**
pp. 39–40

	empezar	volver	jugar
yo	empiezo	vuelvo	juego
tú	empiezas	vuelves	juegas
él	empieza	vuelve	juega
nos.	empezamos	volvemos	jugamos
vos.	empezáis	volvéis	jugáis
ellas	empiezan	vuelven	juegan

► Other e:ie verbs: **cerrar, comenzar, entender, pensar, perder, preferir, querer**
► Other o:ue verbs: **almorzar, contar, dormir, encontrar, mostrar, poder, recordar**

4.3 **Stem-changing verbs e:i** *p. 43*

	pedir		
yo	pido	nos.	pedimos
tú	pides	vos.	pedís
él	pide	ellas	piden

► Other e:i verbs: **conseguir, decir, repetir, seguir**

4.4 **Verbs with irregular yo forms** *pp. 46–47*

hacer	poner	salir	suponer	traer
hago	pongo	salgo	supongo	traigo

► **ver**: veo, ves, ve, vemos, veis, ven
► **oír**: oigo, oyes, oye, oímos, oís, oyen

3 **Oraciones** Arrange the cues provided in the correct order to form complete sentences. Make all necessary changes. **36 pts.**

1. tarea / los / hacer / sábados / nosotros / la

    _____

2. en / pizza / Andrés / una / restaurante / el / pedir

    _____

3. a / ? / museo / ir / ¿ / el / (tú)

    _____

4. de / oír / amigos / bien / los / no / Elena

    _____

5. libros / traer / yo / clase / mis / a

    _____

6. película / ver / en / Jorge y Carlos / pensar / cine / una / el

    _____

7. unos / escribir / Mariana / electrónicos / querer / mensajes

    _____

8. centro / conseguir / en / nosotros / el / videojuegos

    _____

9. tú / favores / el / pedir / tiempo / todo

    _____

4 **Rima** Complete the rhyme with the appropriate forms of the correct verbs from the list. **4 pts.**

contar	poder
oír	suponer

❝ Si no _____ dormir
y el sueño deseas,
lo vas a conseguir
si _____ ovejas°. **❞**

ovejas *sheep*

Lectura

Antes de leer

Estrategia
Predicting content from visuals

When you are reading in Spanish, be sure to look for visual clues that will orient you as to the content and purpose of what you are reading. Photos and illustrations, for example, will often give you a good idea of the main points that the reading covers. You may also encounter very helpful visuals that are used to summarize large amounts of data in a way that is easy to comprehend; these include bar graphs, pie charts, flow charts, lists of percentages, and other sorts of diagrams.

Examinar el texto

Take a quick look at the visual elements of the magazine article in order to generate a list of ideas about its content.

Contestar

Read the list of ideas you wrote in **Examinar el texto**, and look again at the visual elements of the magazine article. Then answer these questions:

1. Who is the woman in the photo, and what is her role?
2. What is the article about?
3. What is the subject of the pie chart?
4. What is the subject of the bar graph?

por María Úrsula Echevarría

El fútbol es el deporte más popular en el mundo° hispano, según° una encuesta° reciente realizada entre estudiantes de secundaria. Mucha gente practica este deporte y tiene un equipo de fútbol favorito. Cada cuatro años se realiza la Copa Mundial°. Argentina y Uruguay han ganado° este campeonato° más de una vez°. Los aficionados siguen los partidos de fútbol en casa por tele y en muchos otros lugares como bares, restaurantes, estadios y clubes deportivos. Los jóvenes juegan al fútbol con sus amigos en parques y gimnasios.

Países hispanos en campeonatos mundiales de fútbol (1930–2014)

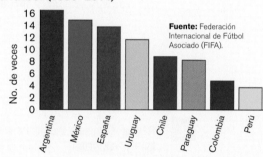

Fuente: Federación Internacional de Fútbol Asociado (FIFA).

Pero, por supuesto°, en los países de habla hispana también hay otros deportes populares. ¿Qué deporte sigue al fútbol en estos países? Bueno, ¡depende del país y de otros factores!

Después de leer

Evaluación y predicción

Which of the following sporting events would be most popular among the high school students surveyed? Rate them from one (most popular) to five (least popular). Which would be the most popular at your school?

_____ 1. la Copa Mundial de Fútbol

_____ 2. los Juegos Olímpicos

_____ 3. el Campeonato de Wimbledon

_____ 4. la Serie Mundial de Béisbol

_____ 5. el Tour de Francia

No sólo el fútbol

En Colombia, el béisbol también es muy popular después del fútbol, aunque° esto varía según la región del país. En la costa del norte de Colombia, el béisbol es una pasión. Y el ciclismo también es un deporte que los colombianos siguen con mucho interés.

Donde el béisbol es más popular
En los países del Caribe, el béisbol es el deporte predominante. Éste es el caso en Puerto Rico, Cuba y la República Dominicana. Los niños empiezan a jugar cuando son muy pequeños. En Puerto Rico y la República Dominicana, la gente también quiere participar en otros deportes, como el baloncesto, o ver los partidos en la tele. Y para los espectadores aficionados del Caribe, el boxeo es número dos.

Donde el fútbol es más popular
En México, el béisbol es el segundo° deporte más popular después° del fútbol. Pero en Argentina, después del fútbol, el rugby tiene mucha importancia. En Perú a la gente le gusta mucho ver partidos de vóleibol. ¿Y en España? Muchas personas prefieren el baloncesto, el tenis y el ciclismo.

Deportes más populares

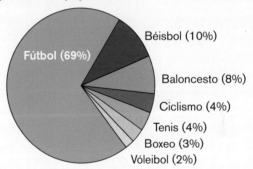

- Fútbol (69%)
- Béisbol (10%)
- Baloncesto (8%)
- Ciclismo (4%)
- Tenis (4%)
- Boxeo (3%)
- Vóleibol (2%)

mundo *world* según *according to* encuesta *survey* se realiza la Copa Mundial *the World Cup is held* han ganado *have won* campeonato *championship* más de una vez *more than once* por supuesto *of course* segundo *second* después *after* aunque *although*

¿Cierto o falso?
Indicate whether each sentence is **cierto** or **falso**, then correct the false statements.

	Cierto	Falso
1. El vóleibol es el segundo deporte más popular en México.	○	○
2. En España a la gente le gustan varios deportes como el baloncesto y el ciclismo.	○	○
3. En la costa del norte de Colombia, el tenis es una pasión.	○	○
4. En el Caribe, el deporte más popular es el béisbol.	○	○

Preguntas
Answer these questions in Spanish.

1. ¿Dónde ven el fútbol los aficionados? Y tú, ¿cómo ves tus deportes favoritos?
2. ¿Te gusta el fútbol? ¿Por qué?
3. ¿Miras la Copa Mundial en la televisión?
4. ¿Qué deportes miras en la televisión?
5. En tu opinión, ¿cuáles son los tres deportes más populares en tu escuela? ¿En tu comunidad? ¿En tu país?
6. ¿Practicas deportes en tus ratos libres?

Escritura

Estrategia
Using a dictionary

A common mistake made by beginning language learners is to embrace the dictionary as the ultimate resource for reading, writing, and speaking. While it is true that the dictionary is a useful tool that can provide valuable information about vocabulary, using the dictionary correctly requires that you understand the elements of each entry.

If you glance at a Spanish-English dictionary, you will notice that its format is similar to that of an English dictionary. The word is listed first, usually followed by its pronunciation. Then come the definitions, organized by parts of speech. Sometimes the most frequently used definitions are listed first.

To find the best word for your needs, you should refer to the abbreviations and the explanatory notes that appear next to the entries. For example, imagine that you are writing about your pastimes. You want to write, "I want to buy a new racket for my match tomorrow," but you don't know the Spanish word for "racket." In the dictionary, you may find an entry like this:

> **racket** *s* **1.** alboroto; **2.** raqueta (*dep.*)

The abbreviation key at the front of the dictionary says that *s* corresponds to **sustantivo** (*noun*). Then, the first word you see is **alboroto**. The definition of **alboroto** is *noise* or *racket*, so **alboroto** is probably not the word you're looking for. The second word is **raqueta**, followed by the abbreviation *dep.*, which stands for **deportes**. This indicates that the word **raqueta** is the best choice for your needs.

Tema
Escribir un folleto

Choose one topic to write a brochure.

1. You are the head of the Homecoming Committee at your school this year. Create a pamphlet that lists events for Friday night, Saturday, and Sunday. Include a brief description of each event and its time and location. Include activities for different age groups, since some alumni will bring their families.

2. You are on the Freshman Student Orientation Committee and are in charge of creating a pamphlet for new students that describes the sports offered at your school. Write the flyer and include activities for both men and women.

3. You volunteer at your community's recreation center. It is your job to market your community to potential residents. Write a brief pamphlet that describes the recreational opportunities your community provides, the areas where the activities take place, and the costs, if any. Be sure to include activities that will appeal to singles as well as couples and families; you should include activities for all age groups and for both men and women.

Escuchar

Estrategia
Listening for the gist

Listening for the general idea, or gist, can help you follow what someone is saying even if you can't hear or understand some of the words. When you listen for the gist, you simply try to capture the essence of what you hear without focusing on individual words.

🔊 To help you practice this strategy, you will listen to a paragraph made up of three sentences. Jot down a brief summary of what you hear.

Preparación

Based on the photo, what do you think Anabela is like? Do you and Anabela have similar interests?

Ahora escucha 🔊

You will hear first José talking, then Anabela. As you listen, check off each person's favorite activities.

Pasatiempos favoritos de José

1. _____ leer el correo electrónico
2. _____ jugar al béisbol
3. _____ ver películas de acción
4. _____ ir al café
5. _____ ir a partidos de béisbol
6. _____ ver películas románticas
7. _____ dormir la siesta
8. _____ escribir mensajes electrónicos

Pasatiempos favoritos de Anabela

9. _____ esquiar
10. _____ nadar
11. _____ practicar el ciclismo
12. _____ jugar al golf
13. _____ jugar al baloncesto
14. _____ ir a ver partidos de tenis
15. _____ escalar montañas
16. _____ ver televisión

Comprensión

Preguntas
Answer these questions about José's and Anabela's pastimes.

1. ¿Quién practica más deportes?
2. ¿Quién piensa que es importante descansar?
3. ¿A qué deporte es aficionado José?
4. ¿Por qué Anabela no practica el baloncesto?
5. ¿Qué películas le gustan a la novia de José?
6. ¿Cuál es el deporte favorito de Anabela?

Seleccionar
Which person do these statements best describe?

1. Le gusta practicar deportes.
2. Prefiere las películas de acción.
3. Le gustan las computadoras.
4. Le gusta nadar.
5. Siempre (*Always*) duerme una siesta por la tarde.
6. Quiere ir de vacaciones a las montañas.

Ejes

A mí me gusta la bici y
me quedo con la bici°.

Preparación

Answer these questions in English.

1. What role do sports play in your life? Which sports do you enjoy? Why?
2. Is there a sport you enjoy with other members of your family? With a group of friends? Is there a special season for that sport?

Más que un deporte

For many, extreme sports aren't just games but an art form and a lifestyle. BMX, skateboarding, surfing, and other sports are passions for many young men and women who, in search of speed and adrenaline, make their bikes and boards the center of their lives. Communities around the world are responding to the demand for extreme sports by constructing bike and skate parks, and Spanish-speaking countries are no exception. The UCI BMX World Championship was held in Medellín in 2016. Colombian Olympic Gold Medalist Mariana Pajón has won gold at the games three times (2011, 2014, 2016). Argentinian professional BMX cyclist Gabriela Díaz won the championship in 2001, 2002, and 2004.

Me quedo con la bici *I stay with the bike*

Vocabulario útil

andar	*go*
bici	*bike*
callejón	*alley*
campeonato	*championship*
conocer	*to be acquainted with*
molar	*be cool*
rampas	*ramps*

Comprensión

Indicate whether each statement is **cierto** or **falso.**

	Cierto	Falso
1. A Diego le gusta la bici.	○	○
2. Sarini cree que patinar es un arte.	○	○
3. Pequesaurio prefiere la patineta.	○	○
4. A Pequesaurio le gusta la rampa.	○	○

 Conversación

With a partner, discuss these questions in Spanish.

1. ¿Qué deportes se pueden practicar fácilmente en tu comunidad? ¿Qué deportes son fomentados (*encouraged*) en tu comunidad?
2. ¿Cuál es la diferencia entre un deporte y un juego? ¿Cuál es la diferencia entre un deporte y un deporte extremo?

 Aplicación

Participation in sports and other physical activities is important for one's well-being. With two classmates, prepare an oral presentation for your community. Your objective is to convince families and communities to encourage participation in sports among kids from an early age. Include illustrations in your presentation.

The rivalry between the teams **Real Madrid** and **FC Barcelona** is perhaps the fiercest in all of soccer—just imagine if they occupied the same city! Well, each team also has competing clubs within its respective city: Spain's capital has the **Club Atlético de Madrid**, and Barcelona is home to **Espanyol**. In fact, across the Spanish-speaking world, it is common for a city to have more than one professional team, often with strikingly dissimilar origins, identity, and fan base. For example, in Bogotá, the **Millonarios** were so named for the large sums spent on players, while the **Santa Fe** team is one of the most traditional in Colombian soccer. **River Plate** and **Boca Juniors**, who enjoy a famous rivalry, are just two of twenty-four clubs in Buenos Aires—the city with the most professional soccer teams in the world.

Vocabulario útil	
afición	fans
celebran	they celebrate
preferido/a	favorite
rivalidad	rivalry
se junta con	it's tied up with

Preparación

What is the most popular sport at your school? What teams are your rivals? How do students celebrate a win?

Escoger

Select the correct answer.

1. Un partido entre el Barça y el Real Madrid es un _____ (deporte/evento) importante en toda España.

2. Los aficionados _____ (miran/celebran) las victorias de sus equipos en las calles (*streets*).

3. La rivalidad entre el Real Madrid y el Barça está relacionada con la _____ (religión/política).

¡Fútbol en España!

(Hay mucha afición al fútbol en España.)

¿Y cuál es vuestro jugador favorito?

—**¿Y quién va a ganar?**
—**El Real Madrid.**

México

El país en cifras

▶ **Área:** 1.972.550 km² (761.603 millas²), *casi°* *tres veces°* el área de Texas

La situación geográfica de México, al sur° de los Estados Unidos, ha influido en° la economía y la sociedad de los dos países. Una de las consecuencias es la emigración de la población mexicana al país vecino°. Hoy día, más de 33 millones de personas de ascendencia mexicana viven en los Estados Unidos.

▶ **Población:** 118.818.000

▶ **Capital:** México, D.F. (y su área metropolitana)—19.319.000

▶ **Ciudades principales:** Guadalajara —4.338.000, Monterrey—3.838.000, Puebla—2.278.000, Ciudad Juárez—1.321.000

▶ **Moneda:** peso mexicano

▶ **Idiomas:** español (oficial), náhuatl, otras lenguas indígenas

Bandera de México

Mexicanos célebres

▶ **Benito Juárez,** héroe nacional (1806–1872)

▶ **Octavio Paz,** poeta (1914–1998)

▶ **Elena Poniatowska,** periodista y escritora (1932–)

▶ **Mario Molina,** Premio Nobel de Química, 1995; químico (1943–)

▶ **Paulina Rubio,** cantante (1971–)

casi *almost* veces *times* sur *south* ha influido en *has influenced* vecino *neighboring* se llenan de luz *get filled with light* flores *flowers* Muertos *Dead* se ríen *laugh* muerte *death* lo cual se refleja *which is reflected* calaveras de azúcar *sugar skulls* pan *bread* huesos *bones*

Cabo San Lucas

ESTADOS UNIDOS

Autorretrato con mono (*Self-portrait with monkey*), 1938, Frida Kahlo

Ciudad Juárez

Golfo de California

Baja California

Río Grande

Río Bravo del Norte

Sierra Madre Oriental

Sierra Madre Occidental

ESTADOS UNIDOS

MÉXICO

OCÉANO ATLÁNTICO

OCÉANO PACÍFICO

AMÉRICA DEL SUR

Océano Pacífico

Monterrey

Puerto Vallarta

Ciudad de México

Guadalajara

Puebla

Acapulco

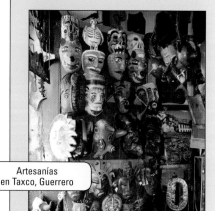
Artesanías en Taxco, Guerrero

Pirámide de Kukulcán en Chichén Itzá

¡Increíble pero cierto!

Cada dos de noviembre los cementerios de México se llenan de luz°, música y flores°. El Día de Muertos° no es un evento triste; es una fiesta en honor a las personas muertas. En ese día, los mexicanos se ríen° de la muerte°, lo cual se refleja° en detalles como las calaveras de azúcar° y el pan° de muerto —pan en forma de huesos°.

Ciudades • México, D.F.

La Ciudad de México, fundada° en 1525, también se llama el D.F. o Distrito Federal. Muchos turistas e inmigrantes vienen a la ciudad porque es el centro cultural y económico del país. El crecimiento° de la población es de los más altos° del mundo. El D.F. tiene una población mayor que las de Nueva York, Madrid o París.

Artes • Diego Rivera y Frida Kahlo

Frida Kahlo y Diego Rivera eran° artistas mexicanos muy famosos. Se casaron° en 1929. Los dos se interesaron° en las condiciones sociales de la gente indígena de su país. Puedes ver algunas° de sus obras° en el Museo de Arte Moderno de la Ciudad de México.

Historia • Los aztecas

Los aztecas dominaron° en México del siglo° XIV al siglo XVI. Sus canales, puentes° y pirámides con templos religiosos eran muy importantes. El fin del imperio azteca comenzó° con la llegada° de los españoles en 1519, pero la presencia azteca sigue hoy. La Ciudad de México está situada en la capital azteca de Tenochtitlán, y muchos turistas van a visitar sus ruinas.

Economía • La plata

México es el mayor productor de plata° del mundo°. Estados como Zacatecas y Durango tienen ciudades fundadas cerca de los más grandes yacimientos° de plata del país. Estas ciudades fueron° en la época colonial unas de las más ricas e importantes. Hoy en día, aún° conservan mucho de su encanto° y esplendor.

Golfo de México
Península de Yucatán
Bahía de Campeche
Mérida
Cancún
Veracruz
Istmo de Tehuantepec
BELICE
GUATEMALA

¿Qué aprendiste? Responde a cada pregunta con una oración completa.

1. ¿Qué lenguas hablan los mexicanos?
2. ¿Cómo es la población del D.F. en comparación con la de otras ciudades?
3. ¿En qué se interesaron Frida Kahlo y Diego Rivera?
4. Nombra algunas de las estructuras de la arquitectura azteca.
5. ¿Dónde está situada la capital de México?
6. ¿Qué estados de México tienen los mayores yacimientos de plata?

Conexión Internet Investiga estos temas en Internet.

1. Busca información sobre dos lugares de México. ¿Te gustaría (*Would you like*) vivir allí? ¿Por qué?
2. Busca información sobre dos artistas mexicanos. ¿Cómo se llaman sus obras más famosas?

fundada *founded* **crecimiento** *growth* **más altos** *highest* **eran** *were* **Se casaron** *They got married* **se interesaron** *were interested* **algunas** *some* **obras** *works* **dominaron** *dominated* **siglo** *century* **puentes** *bridges* **comenzó** *started* **llegada** *arrival* **plata** *silver* **mundo** *world* **yacimientos** *deposits* **fueron** *were* **aún** *still* **encanto** *charm*

Pasatiempos

andar en patineta	to skateboard
bucear	to scuba dive
escalar montañas (f., pl.)	to climb mountains
escribir una carta	to write a letter
escribir un mensaje electrónico	to write an e-mail
esquiar	to ski
ganar	to win
ir de excursión	to go on a hike
leer el correo electrónico	to read e-mail
leer un periódico	to read a newspaper
leer una revista	to read a magazine
nadar	to swim
pasear	to take a walk
pasear en bicicleta	to ride a bicycle
patinar (en línea)	to (inline) skate
practicar deportes (m., pl.)	to play sports
tomar el sol	to sunbathe
ver películas (f., pl.)	to watch movies
visitar monumentos (m., pl.)	to visit monuments
la diversión	fun activity; entertainment; recreation
el fin de semana	weekend
el pasatiempo	pastime; hobby
los ratos libres	spare (free) time
el videojuego	video game

Deportes

el baloncesto	basketball
el béisbol	baseball
el ciclismo	cycling
el equipo	team
el esquí (acuático)	(water) skiing
el fútbol	soccer
el fútbol americano	football
el golf	golf
el hockey	hockey
el/la jugador(a)	player
la natación	swimming
el partido	game; match
la pelota	ball
el tenis	tennis
el vóleibol	volleyball

Adjetivos

deportivo/a	sports-related
favorito/a	favorite

Lugares

el café	café
el centro	downtown
el cine	movie theater
el gimnasio	gymnasium
la iglesia	church
el lugar	place
el museo	museum
el parque	park
la piscina	swimming pool
la plaza	city or town square
el restaurante	restaurant

Verbos

almorzar (o:ue)	to have lunch
cerrar (e:ie)	to close
comenzar (e:ie)	to begin
conseguir (e:i)	to get; to obtain
contar (o:ue)	to count; to tell
decir (e:i)	to say; to tell
dormir (o:ue)	to sleep
empezar (e:ie)	to begin
encontrar (o:ue)	to find
entender (e:ie)	to understand
hacer	to do; to make
ir	to go
jugar (u:ue)	to play (a sport or a game)
mostrar (o:ue)	to show
oír	to hear
pedir (e:i)	to ask for; to request
pensar (e:ie)	to think
pensar (+ inf.)	to intend
pensar en	to think about
perder (e:ie)	to lose; to miss
poder (o:ue)	to be able to; can
poner	to put; to place
preferir (e:ie)	to prefer
querer (e:ie)	to want; to love
recordar (o:ue)	to remember
repetir (e:i)	to repeat
salir	to leave
seguir (e:i)	to follow; to continue
suponer	to suppose
traer	to bring
ver	to see
volver (o:ue)	to return

Decir expressions	See page 46.
Expresiones útiles	See page 31.

Las vacaciones

5

Communicative Goals

You will learn how to:

- Discuss and plan a vacation
- Describe a hotel
- Talk about how you feel
- Talk about the seasons and the weather

contextos

fotonovela

cultura

estructura

adelante

A PRIMERA VISTA
- ¿Están ellos en una montaña o en un museo?
- ¿Son viejos o jóvenes?
- ¿Pasean o ven una película? ¿Andan en patineta o van de excursión?
- ¿Es posible esquiar en este lugar?

Las vacaciones

Más vocabulario

la cama	bed
la habitación individual, doble	single, double room
el piso	floor (of a building)
la planta baja	ground floor
el campo	countryside
el paisaje	landscape
el equipaje	luggage
la estación de autobuses, del metro, de tren	bus, subway, train station
la llegada	arrival
el pasaje (de ida y vuelta)	(round-trip) ticket
la salida	departure; exit
la tabla de (wind)surf	surfboard/sailboard
acampar	to camp
estar de vacaciones	to be on vacation
hacer las maletas	to pack (one's suitcases)
hacer un viaje	to take a trip
hacer (wind)surf	to (wind)surf
ir de compras	to go shopping
ir de vacaciones	to go on vacation
ir en autobús (m.), auto(móvil) (m.), motocicleta (f.), taxi (m.)	to go by bus, car, motorcycle, taxi

Variación léxica

automóvil	⟷	coche (Esp.), carro (Amér. L.)
autobús	⟷	camión (Méx.), guagua (Caribe)
motocicleta	⟷	moto (coloquial)

la agente de viajes

el pasaporte

Confirma una reservación. (confirmar)

En la agencia de viajes

la habitación

el ascensor

el empleado

la llave

la huésped

el huésped

En el hotel

Saca/Toma fotos. (sacar, tomar)

BIENVENIDOS

el avión

el viajero

la inspectora de aduanas

En el aeropuerto

Pesca. (pescar)

Monta a caballo. (montar)

Va en barco. (ir)

el mar

Juegan a las cartas. (jugar)

la playa

En la playa

Práctica

1 Escuchar Indicate who would probably make each statement you hear. Each answer is used twice.

a. el agente de viajes
b. el inspector de aduanas
c. un empleado del hotel

1. _____   4. _____
2. _____   5. _____
3. _____   6. _____

2 ¿Cierto o falso? Mario and his wife, Natalia, are planning their next vacation with a travel agent. Indicate whether each statement is **cierto** or **falso** according to what you hear in the conversation.

	Cierto	Falso
1. Mario y Natalia están en Puerto Rico.	○	○
2. Ellos quieren hacer un viaje a Puerto Rico.	○	○
3. Natalia prefiere ir a la montaña.	○	○
4. Mario quiere pescar en Puerto Rico.	○	○
5. La agente de viajes va a confirmar la reservación.	○	○

3 Escoger Choose the best answer for each sentence.

1. Un huésped es una persona que _____.
   a. toma fotos   b. está en un hotel   c. pesca en el mar
2. Abrimos la puerta con _____.
   a. una llave   b. un caballo   c. una llegada
3. Enrique tiene _____ porque va a viajar a otro (*another*) país.
   a. un pasaporte   b. una foto   c. una llegada
4. Antes de (*Before*) ir de vacaciones, hay que _____.
   a. pescar   b. ir en tren   c. hacer las maletas
5. Nosotros vamos en _____ al aeropuerto.
   a. autobús   b. pasaje   c. viajero
6. Me gusta mucho ir al campo. El _____ es increíble.
   a. paisaje   b. pasaje   c. equipaje

4 Analogías Complete the analogies using the words below. Two words will not be used.

auto	huésped	mar	sacar
empleado	llegada	pasaporte	tren

1. acampar → campo ⊜ pescar →
2. agencia de viajes → agente ⊜ hotel →
3. llave → habitación ⊜ pasaje →
4. estudiante → libro ⊜ turista →
5. aeropuerto → viajero ⊜ hotel →
6. maleta → hacer ⊜ foto →

Las estaciones y los meses del año

el invierno: diciembre, enero, febrero

la primavera: marzo, abril, mayo

el verano: junio, julio, agosto

el otoño: septiembre, octubre, noviembre

—**¿Cuál es la fecha de hoy?**   *What is today's date?*
—**Es el primero de octubre.**   *It's the first of October.*
—**Es el dos de marzo.**   *It's March 2ⁿᵈ.*
—**Es el diez de noviembre.**   *It's November 10ᵗʰ.*

El tiempo

—**¿Qué tiempo hace?**   *How's the weather?*
—**Hace buen/mal tiempo.**   *The weather is good/bad.*

Hace (mucho) calor.
It's (very) hot.

Hace (mucho) frío.
It's (very) cold.

Llueve. (llover o:ue)
It's raining.

Está lloviendo.
It's raining.

Nieva. (nevar e:ie)
It's snowing.

Está nevando.
It's snowing.

Más vocabulario

Está (muy) nublado.	*It's (very) cloudy.*
Hace fresco.	*It's cool.*
Hace (mucho) sol.	*It's (very) sunny.*
Hace (mucho) viento.	*It's (very) windy.*

5 | **El Hotel Regis** Label the floors of the hotel.

Números ordinales	
primer *(before a masculine singular noun)*, **primero/a**	*first*
segundo/a	*second*
tercer *(before a masculine singular noun)*, **tercero/a**	*third*
cuarto/a	*fourth*
quinto/a	*fifth*
sexto/a	*sixth*
séptimo/a	*seventh*
octavo/a	*eighth*
noveno/a	*ninth*
décimo/a	*tenth*

a. _____ piso
b. _____ piso
c. _____ piso
d. _____ piso
e. _____ piso
f. _____ piso
g. _____ piso
h. _____ baja

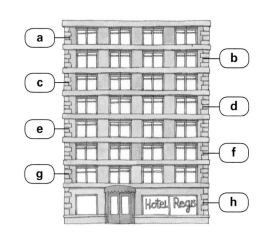

6 | **Contestar** Look at the illustrations of the months and seasons on the previous page. Then answer these questions.

> **modelo**
>
> **Estudiante 1:** *¿Cuál es el primer mes de la primavera?*
> **Estudiante 2:** *marzo*

1. ¿Cuál es el primer mes del invierno?
2. ¿Cuál es el segundo mes de la primavera?
3. ¿Cuál es el tercer mes del otoño?
4. ¿Cuál es el primer mes del año?
5. ¿Cuál es el quinto mes del año?
6. ¿Cuál es el octavo mes del año?
7. ¿Cuál es el décimo mes del año?
8. ¿Cuál es el segundo mes del verano?
9. ¿Cuál es el tercer mes del invierno?
10. ¿Cuál es el sexto mes del año?

7 | **Las estaciones** Name the season that applies to the description.

1. Las clases terminan.
2. Vamos a la playa.
3. Acampamos.
4. Nieva mucho.
5. Las clases empiezan.
6. Hace mucho calor.
7. Llueve mucho.
8. Esquiamos.
9. el entrenamiento (*training*) de béisbol
10. el Día de Acción de Gracias (*Thanksgiving*)

8 | **¿Cuál es la fecha?** Give the dates for these holidays.

> **modelo**
>
> el día de San Valentín   *14 de febrero*

1. el día de San Patricio
2. el día de Halloween
3. el primer día de verano
4. el Año Nuevo
5. mi cumpleaños (*birthday*)
6. mi día de fiesta favorito

9 **Seleccionar** Paco is talking about his family and friends. Choose the word or phrase that best completes each sentence.

1. A mis padres les gusta ir a Yucatán porque (hace sol, nieva).
2. Mi primo de Kansas dice que durante (*during*) un tornado, hace mucho (sol, viento).
3. Mis amigos van a esquiar si (nieva, está nublado).
4. Tomo el sol cuando (hace calor, llueve).
5. Nosotros vamos a ver una película si hace (buen, mal) tiempo.
6. Mi hermana prefiere correr cuando (hace mucho calor, hace fresco).
7. Mis tíos van de excursión si hace (buen, mal) tiempo.
8. Mi padre no quiere jugar al golf si (hace fresco, llueve).
9. Cuando hace mucho (sol, frío) no salgo de casa y tomo chocolate caliente (*hot*).
10. Hoy mi sobrino va al parque porque (está lloviendo, hace buen tiempo).

10 **El clima** With a partner, take turns asking and answering questions about the weather and temperatures in these cities. Use the model as a guide.

> **modelo**
>
> **Estudiante 1:** ¿Qué tiempo hace hoy en Nueva York?
> **Estudiante 2:** Hace frío y hace viento.
> **Estudiante 1:** ¿Cuál es la temperatura máxima?
> **Estudiante 2:** Treinta y un grados (*degrees*).
> **Estudiante 1:** ¿Y la temperatura mínima?
> **Estudiante 2:** Diez grados.

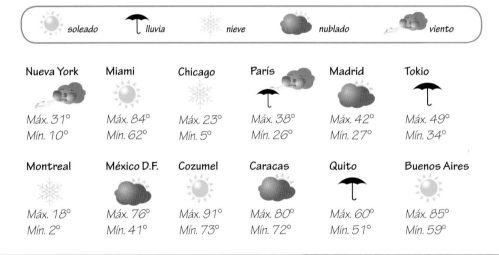

soleado · lluvia · nieve · nublado · viento

Nueva York	Miami	Chicago	París	Madrid	Tokio
Máx. 31°	Máx. 84°	Máx. 23°	Máx. 38°	Máx. 42°	Máx. 49°
Mín. 10°	Mín. 62°	Mín. 5°	Mín. 26°	Mín. 27°	Mín. 34°

Montreal	México D.F.	Cozumel	Caracas	Quito	Buenos Aires
Máx. 18°	Máx. 76°	Máx. 91°	Máx. 80°	Máx. 60°	Máx. 85°
Mín. 2°	Mín. 41°	Mín. 73°	Mín. 72°	Mín. 51°	Mín. 59°

NOTA CULTURAL

In most Spanish-speaking countries, temperatures are given in degrees Celsius. Use these formulas to convert between **grados centígrados** and **grados Fahrenheit**.
degrees C. × 9 ÷ 5 + 32 = degrees F.
degrees F. - 32 × 5 ÷ 9 = degrees C.

11 **Completar** Complete these sentences with your own ideas.

1. Cuando hace sol, yo…
2. Cuando llueve, mis amigos y yo…
3. Cuando hace calor, mi familia…
4. Cuando hace viento, la gente…
5. Cuando hace frío, yo…
6. Cuando hace mal tiempo, mis amigos…
7. Cuando nieva, muchas personas…
8. Cuando está nublado, mis amigos y yo…
9. Cuando hace fresco, mis padres…
10. Cuando hace buen tiempo, mis amigos…

CONSULTA

Calor and **frío** can apply to both weather and people. Use **hacer** to describe weather conditions or climate.
(**Hace frío en Santiago**. *It's cold in Santiago.*)
Use **tener** to refer to people.
(**El viajero tiene frío**. *The traveler is cold.*)
See **Senderos 1A, Estructura 3.4**, p. 125.

Comunicación

12

En la agencia de viajes Listen to the conversation between Mr. Vega and a travel agent. Then indicate whether the following conclusions are **lógico** or **ilógico**, based on what you heard.

	Lógico	Ilógico
1. El señor Vega quiere visitar la Antártida.	○	○
2. Hace calor en Puerto Rico.	○	○
3. El señor Vega va a ver el mar en Puerto Rico.	○	○
4. El señor Vega va a comprar un pasaje de ida y vuelta.	○	○
5. El señor Vega viaja con su familia.	○	○

13

Preguntas personales Answer your partner's questions.

1. ¿Cuál es la fecha de hoy? ¿Qué estación es?
2. ¿Te gusta esta estación? ¿Por qué?
3. ¿Qué estación prefieres? ¿Por qué?
4. ¿Prefieres el mar o las montañas? ¿La playa o el campo? ¿Por qué?
5. Cuando haces un viaje, ¿qué te gusta hacer y ver?
6. ¿Piensas ir de vacaciones este verano? ¿Adónde quieres ir? ¿Por qué?
7. ¿Qué deseas ver y qué lugares quieres visitar?
8. ¿Cómo te gusta viajar? ¿En avión? ¿En motocicleta...?

14

Itinerario Create a trip itinerary for a friend, a relative, or someone famous. First, choose a destination. Include information about transportation and accommodations, as well as a section for each day with activities.

- fechas
- lugar
- transporte
- hotel
- actividades

Síntesis

15

Un viaje With a partner, role-play a conversation between a travel agent and a client planning a trip. Discuss destinations, dates, transportation, hotel accommodations, and activities for the trip.

¡Vamos a la playa!

Los seis amigos hacen un viaje a la playa.

PERSONAJES   FELIPE   JUAN CARLOS

TÍA ANA MARÍA ¿Están listos para su viaje a la playa?

TODOS Sí.

TÍA ANA MARÍA Excelente... ¡A la estación de autobuses!

MARU ¿Dónde está Miguel?

FELIPE Yo lo traigo.

(*se escucha un grito de Miguel*)

FELIPE Ya está listo. Y tal vez enojado. Ahorita vamos.

EMPLEADO Bienvenidas. ¿En qué puedo servirles?

MARU Hola. Tenemos una reservación para seis personas para esta noche.

EMPLEADO ¿A nombre de quién?

JIMENA ¿Díaz? ¿López? No estoy segura.

EMPLEADO No encuentro su nombre. Ah, no, ahora sí lo veo, aquí está. Díaz. Dos habitaciones en el primer piso para seis huéspedes.

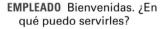

FELIPE No está nada mal el hotel, ¿verdad? Limpio, cómodo... ¡Oye, Miguel! ¿Todavía estás enojado conmigo? (*a Juan Carlos*) Miguel está de mal humor. No me habla.

JUAN CARLOS ¿Todavía?

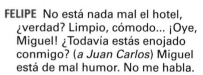

EMPLEADO Aquí están las llaves de sus habitaciones.

MARU Gracias. Una cosa más. Mi novio y yo queremos hacer windsurf, pero no tenemos tablas.

EMPLEADO El botones las puede conseguir para ustedes.

MARISSA
 JIMENA
 MARU
 MIGUEL
 MAITE FUENTES
 ANA MARÍA
EMPLEADO

JUAN CARLOS ¿Qué hace este libro aquí? ¿Estás estudiando en la playa?

JIMENA Sí, es que tengo un examen la próxima semana.

JUAN CARLOS Ay, Jimena. ¡No! ¿Vamos a nadar?

JIMENA Bueno, como estudiar es tan aburrido y el tiempo está tan bonito...

MARISSA Yo estoy un poco cansada. ¿Y tú? ¿Por qué no estás nadando?

FELIPE Es por causa de Miguel.

MARISSA Hmm, estoy confundida.

FELIPE Esta mañana. ¡Sigue enojado conmigo!

MARISSA No puede seguir enojado tanto tiempo.

Expresiones útiles

Talking with hotel personnel

¿En qué puedo servirles?
How can I help you?
Tenemos una reservación.
We have a reservation.
¿A nombre de quién?
In whose name?
¿Quizás López? ¿Tal vez Díaz?
Maybe López? Maybe Díaz?
Ahora lo veo, aquí está. Díaz.
Now I see it. Here it is. Díaz.
Dos habitaciones en el primer piso para seis huéspedes.
Two rooms on the first floor for six guests.
Aquí están las llaves.
Here are the keys.

Describing a hotel

No está nada mal el hotel.
The hotel isn't bad at all.
Todo está tan limpio y cómodo.
Everything is so clean and comfortable.
Es excelente/estupendo/fabuloso/ fenomenal/increíble/magnífico/ maravilloso/perfecto.
It's excellent/stupendous/fabulous/ phenomenal/incredible/magnificent/ marvelous/perfect.

Talking about how you feel

Yo estoy un poco cansado/a.
I am a little tired.
Estoy confundido/a. *I'm confused.*
Todavía estoy/Sigo enojado/a contigo.
I'm still angry with you.

Additional vocabulary

afuera *outside*
amable *nice; friendly*
el balde *bucket*
el/la botones *bellhop*
la crema de afeitar
shaving cream
el frente (frío) *(cold) front*
el grito *scream*
la temporada *period of time*
entonces *so, then*
es igual *it's the same*

¿Qué pasó?

1

Completar Complete these sentences with the correct term from the word bank.

aburrido	botones	la llave
el aeropuerto	la estación de autobuses	montar a caballo
amable	habitaciones	reservación

1. Los amigos van a _____ para ir a la playa.
2. La _____ del hotel está a nombre de los Díaz.
3. Los amigos tienen dos _____ para seis personas.
4. El _____ puede conseguir tablas de windsurf para Maru.
5. Jimena dice que estudiar en vacaciones es muy _____.

> **CONSULTA**
>
> The meaning of some adjectives, such as **aburrido**, changes depending on whether they are used with **ser** or **estar**. See **Estructura 5.3**, pp. 80–81.

2

Identificar Identify the person who would make each statement.

EMPLEADO   **MARU**   **TÍA ANA MARÍA**   **FELIPE**   **JUAN CARLOS**

1. No lo encuentro, ¿a nombre de quién está su reservación?
2. ¿Por qué estás estudiando en la playa? ¡Mejor vamos a nadar!
3. Nuestra reservación es para seis personas en dos habitaciones.
4. El hotel es limpio y cómodo, pero estoy triste porque Miguel no me habla.
5. Suban al autobús y ¡buen viaje a la playa!

3

Ordenar Place these events in the correct order.

_____ a. El empleado busca la reservación.
_____ b. Marissa dice que está confundida.
_____ c. Los amigos están listos para ir a la playa.
_____ d. El empleado da (*gives*) las llaves de las habitaciones a las chicas.
_____ e. Miguel grita (*screams*).

4

Conversar With a partner, use these cues to create a conversation between a hotel employee and a guest in Mexico.

Huésped	**Empleado/a**
Say hi to the employee and ask for your reservation.	→ Tell the guest that you can't find his/her reservation.
Tell the employee that the reservation is in your name.	→ Tell him/her that you found the reservation and that it's for a double room.
Tell the employee that the hotel is very clean and comfortable.	→ Say that you agree with the guest, welcome him/her, and give him/her the keys.
Ask the employee to call the bellhop to help you with your luggage.	→ Call the bellhop to help the guest with his/her luggage.

Pronunciación ◁))
Spanish b and v

bueno	**vóleibol**	**biblioteca**	**vivir**

There is no difference in pronunciation between the Spanish letters **b** and **v**. However, each letter can be pronounced two different ways, depending on which letters appear next to them.

bonito	**viajar**	**también**	**investigar**

B and **v** are pronounced like the English hard *b* when they appear either as the first letter of a word, at the beginning of a phrase, or after **m** or **n**.

deber	**novio**	**abril**	**favor**

In all other positions, **b** and **v** have a softer pronunciation, which has no equivalent in English. Unlike the hard **b**, which is produced by tightly closing the lips and stopping the flow of air, the soft **b** is produced by keeping the lips slightly open.

bola	**vela**	**Caribe**	**declive**

In both pronunciations, there is no difference in sound between **b** and **v**. The English *v* sound, produced by friction between the upper teeth and lower lip, does not exist in Spanish. Instead, the soft **b** comes from friction between the two lips.

Verónica y su esposo cantan boleros.

When **b** or **v** begins a word, its pronunciation depends on the previous word. At the beginning of a phrase or after a word that ends in **m** or **n**, it is pronounced as a hard **b**.

Benito es de Boquerón pero vive en Victoria.

Words that begin with **b** or **v** are pronounced with a soft **b** if they appear immediately after a word that ends in a vowel or any consonant other than **m** or **n**.

Práctica Read these words aloud to practice the **b** and the **v**.

1. hablamos	4. van	7. doble	10. nublado
2. trabajar	5. contabilidad	8. novia	11. llave
3. botones	6. bien	9. béisbol	12. invierno

No hay mal que por bien no venga.[1]

Hombre prevenido vale por dos.[2]

Oraciones Read these sentences aloud to practice the **b** and the **v**.

1. Vamos a Guaynabo en autobús.
2. Voy de vacaciones a la Isla Culebra.
3. Tengo una habitación individual en el octavo piso.
4. Víctor y Eva van en avión al Caribe.
5. La planta baja es bonita también.
6. ¿Qué vamos a ver en Bayamón?
7. Beatriz, la novia de Víctor, es de Arecibo, Puerto Rico.

Refranes Read these sayings aloud to practice the **b** and the **v**.

1 Every cloud has a silver lining.
2 An ounce of prevention equals a pound of cure.

Las cataratas
del Iguazú

Imagine the impressive and majestic Niagara Falls, the most powerful waterfall in North America. Now, if you can, imagine a waterfall four times as wide and almost twice as tall that caused Eleanor Roosevelt to exclaim "Poor Niagara!" upon seeing it for the first time. Welcome to **las cataratas del Iguazú!**

Garganta del Diablo
Isla San Martín

Iguazú is located in Iguazú National Park, an area of subtropical jungle where Argentina meets Brazil. Its name comes from the indigenous Guaraní word for "great water." A UNESCO World Heritage Site, **las cataratas del Iguazú** span three kilometers and comprise 275 cascades split into two main sections by San Martín Island. Most of the falls are about 82 meters (270 feet) high. The horseshoe-shaped cataract **Garganta del Diablo** (Devil's Throat) has the greatest water flow and is considered to be the most impressive; it also marks the border between Argentina and Brazil.

Each country offers different views and tourist options. Most visitors opt to use the numerous catwalks that are available on both sides; however, from the Argentinean side, tourists can get very close to the falls, whereas Brazil provides more panoramic views. If you don't mind getting wet, a jet boat tour is a good choice; those looking for wildlife—such as toucans, ocelots, butterflies, and jaguars—should head for San Martín Island. Brazil boasts less conventional ways to view the falls, such as helicopter rides and rappelling, while Argentina focuses on sustainability with its **Tren Ecológico de la Selva** (*Ecological Jungle Train*), an environmentally friendly way to reach the walkways.

No matter which way you choose to enjoy the falls, you are certain to be captivated.

Más cascadas° en Latinoamérica

Nombre	País	Altura°	Datos
Salto Ángel	Venezuela	979 metros	la más alta° del mundo°
Catarata del Gocta	Perú	771 metros	descubierta° en 2006
Piedra Volada	México	453 metros	la más alta de México

cascadas *waterfalls* Altura *Height* más alta *tallest* mundo *world* descubierta *discovered*

1 **¿Cierto o falso?** Indicate whether these statements are **cierto** or **falso**. Correct the false statements.

1. Iguazú Falls is located on the border of Argentina and Brazil.

2. Niagara Falls is four times as wide as Iguazú Falls.

3. Iguazú Falls has a few cascades, each about 82 meters.

4. Tourists visiting Iguazú can see exotic wildlife.

5. *Iguazú* is the Guaraní word for "blue water."

6. You can access the walkways by taking the **Garganta del Diablo**.

7. It is possible for tourists to visit Iguazú Falls by air.

8. **Salto Ángel** is the tallest waterfall in the world.

9. There are no waterfalls in Mexico.

10. For the best views of Iguazú Falls, tourists should visit the Brazilian side.

ASÍ SE DICE

Viajes y turismo

el asiento del medio, del pasillo, de la ventanilla	center, aisle, window seat
el itinerario	itinerary
media pensión	breakfast and one meal included
el ómnibus (Perú)	el autobús
pensión completa	all meals included
el puente	long weekend (lit., bridge)

EL MUNDO HISPANO

Destinos populares

- **Las playas del Parque Nacional Manuel Antonio** (Costa Rica) ofrecen° la oportunidad de nadar y luego caminar por el bosque tropical°.

- **Teotihuacán** (México) Desde antes de la época° de los aztecas, aquí se celebra el equinoccio de primavera en la Pirámide del Sol.

- **Puerto Chicama** (Perú), con sus olas° de cuatro kilómetros de largo°, es un destino para surfistas expertos.

- **Tikal** (Guatemala) Aquí puedes ver las maravillas de la selva° y ruinas de la civilización maya.

- **Las playas de Rincón** (Puerto Rico) Son ideales para descansar y observar ballenas°.

ofrecen *offer* bosque tropical *rainforest*
Desde antes de la época *Since before the time* olas *waves*
de largo *in length* selva *jungle* ballenas *whales*

PERFIL

Punta del Este

One of South America's largest and most fashionable beach resort towns is Uruguay's **Punta del Este**, a narrow strip of land containing twenty miles of pristine beaches. Its peninsular shape gives it two very different seascapes. **La Playa Mansa**, facing the bay and therefore the more protected side, has calm waters. Here, people practice water sports like swimming, water skiing, windsurfing, and diving. **La Playa Brava**, facing the east, receives the Atlantic Ocean's powerful, wave-producing winds, making it popular for surfing, body boarding, and kite surfing. Besides the beaches, posh shopping, and world-famous nightlife, **Punta** offers its 600,000 yearly visitors yacht and fishing clubs, golf courses, and excursions to observe sea lions at the **Isla de Lobos** nature reserve.

Conexión Internet

¿Cuáles son los sitios más populares para el turismo en Puerto Rico?

Use the Web to find more cultural information related to this **Cultura** section.

ACTIVIDADES

2 **Comprensión** Complete the sentences.

1. En las playas de Rincón puedes ver _____.
2. Cerca de 600.000 turistas visitan _____ cada año.
3. En el avión pides un _____ si te gusta ver el paisaje.
4. En Punta del Este, la gente prefiere nadar en la Playa _____.
5. El _____ es un medio de transporte en Perú.

3 **De vacaciones** Spring break is coming up, and you want to go on a short vacation with your family. Decide which of the locations featured on these pages best suits your likes and interests. Come to an agreement about how you will get there, where you prefer to stay and for how long, and what each of you will do during your free time.

5.1 Estar with conditions and emotions

ANTE TODO As you learned in **Lecciones 1** and **2**, the verb **estar** is used to talk about how you feel and to say where people, places, and things are located. **Estar** is also used with adjectives to talk about certain emotional and physical conditions.

CONSULTA

To review the present tense of **estar**, see **Senderos 1A, Estructura 2.3**, p. 83.

•••

To review the present tense of **ser**, see **Senderos 1A, Estructura 1.3**, p. 44.

▶ Use **estar** with adjectives to describe the physical condition of places and things.

La habitación **está** sucia.
The room is dirty.

La puerta **está** cerrada.
The door is closed.

▶ Use **estar** with adjectives to describe how people feel, both mentally and physically.

Yo estoy cansada.

¿Están listos para su viaje?

▶ **¡Atención!** Two important expressions with **estar** that you can use to talk about conditions and emotions are **estar de buen humor** (*to be in a good mood*) and **estar de mal humor** (*to be in a bad mood*).

Adjectives that describe emotions and conditions

abierto/a	open	**contento/a**	content	**listo/a**	ready
aburrido/a	bored	**desordenado/a**	disorderly	**nervioso/a**	nervous
alegre	happy	**enamorado/a (de)**	in love (with)	**ocupado/a**	busy
avergonzado/a	embarrassed			**ordenado/a**	orderly
cansado/a	tired	**enojado/a**	angry	**preocupado/a (por)**	worried (about)
cerrado/a	closed	**equivocado/a**	wrong		
cómodo/a	comfortable	**feliz**	happy	**seguro/a**	sure
confundido/a	confused	**limpio/a**	clean	**sucio/a**	dirty
				triste	sad

¡INTÉNTALO! Provide the present tense forms of **estar**, and choose which adjective best completes the sentence.

1. La biblioteca ___está___ (cerrada / nerviosa) los domingos por la noche. cerrada
2. Nosotros _____ muy (ocupados / equivocados) todos los lunes.
3. Ellas _____ (alegres / confundidas) porque tienen vacaciones.
4. Javier _____ (enamorado / ordenado) de Maribel.
5. Diana _____ (enojada / limpia) con su hermano.
6. Yo _____ (nerviosa / abierta) por el viaje.
7. La habitación siempre _____ (ordenada / segura) cuando vienen sus padres.
8. Ustedes no comprenden; _____ (equivocados / tristes).

Práctica y Comunicación

1 **¿Cómo están?** Complete Martín's statements about how he and other people are feeling. In the first blank, fill in the correct form of **estar**. In the second blank, fill in the adjective that best fits the context.

1. Yo _____ un poco _____ porque tengo un examen mañana.
2. Mi hermana Patricia _____ muy _____ porque mañana va a hacer una excursión al campo.
3. Mis hermanos Juan y José salen de la casa a las cinco de la mañana. Por la noche, siempre _____ muy _____ .
4. Mi amigo Ramiro _____ _____ ; su novia se llama Adela.
5. Mi papá y sus colegas _____ muy _____ hoy. ¡Hay mucho trabajo!
6. Patricia y yo _____ un poco _____ por ellos porque trabajan mucho.
7. Mi amiga Mónica _____ un poco _____ porque sus amigos no pueden salir esta noche.
8. Esta clase no es muy interesante. ¿Tú _____ _____ también?

2 **Describir** Describe these people and places.

1. Anabela

2. Juan y Luisa

3. la habitación de Teresa

4. la habitación de César

3 **Situaciones** With a partner, use **estar** to talk about how you feel in these situations.

1. Cuando hace sol...
2. Cuando tomas un examen...
3. Cuando viajas en avión...
4. Cuando llueve...
5. Cuando ves una película con tu actor/actriz favorito/a...

4 **Emociones** Write an e-mail to a friend explaining what you do when you feel a certain way. Use five adjectives of emotion.

> **modelo**
>
> Cuando estoy preocupado, hablo por teléfono con mi madre.
> Cuando estoy aburrido, miro la televisión...

5.2 The present progressive

ANTE TODO Both Spanish and English use the present progressive, which consists of the present tense of the verb *to be* and the present participle of another verb (the *-ing* form in English).

Las chicas están hablando con el empleado del hotel.

¿Estás estudiando en la playa?

▶ Form the present progressive with the present tense of **estar** and a present participle.

FORM OF **ESTAR** + PRESENT PARTICIPLE		FORM OF **ESTAR** + PRESENT PARTICIPLE	
Estoy	**pescando.**	**Estamos**	**comiendo.**
I am	*fishing.*	*We are*	*eating.*

▶ The present participle of regular **-ar**, **-er**, and **-ir** verbs is formed as follows:

INFINITIVE	STEM	ENDING	PRESENT PARTICIPLE
hablar	habl-	**-ando**	habl**ando**
comer	com-	**-iendo**	com**iendo**
escribir	escrib-	**-iendo**	escrib**iendo**

▶ **¡Atención!** When the stem of an **-er** or **-ir** verb ends in a vowel, the present participle ends in **-yendo**.

INFINITIVE	STEM	ENDING	PRESENT PARTICIPLE
leer	le-	**-yendo**	le**yendo**
oír	o-	**-yendo**	o**yendo**
traer	tra-	**-yendo**	tra**yendo**

▶ **Ir**, **poder**, and **venir** have irregular present participles (**yendo**, **pudiendo**, **viniendo**). Several other verbs have irregular present participles that you will need to learn.

▶ **-Ir** stem-changing verbs have a stem change in the present participle.

-ir stem-changing verbs

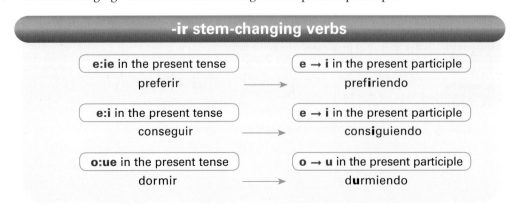

e:ie in the present tense	e → i in the present participle
preferir ⟶	prefir**i**endo

e:i in the present tense	e → i in the present participle
conseguir ⟶	consig**u**iendo

o:ue in the present tense	o → u in the present participle
dormir ⟶	d**u**rmiendo

The use of the present progressive is much more restricted in Spanish than in English. In Spanish, the present progressive is mainly used to emphasize that an action is in progress at the time of speaking.

Maru **está escuchando** música latina **ahora mismo**.
Maru is listening to Latin music right now.

Felipe y su amigo **todavía están jugando** al fútbol.
Felipe and his friend are still playing soccer.

In English, the present progressive is often used to talk about situations and actions that occur over an extended period of time or in the future. In Spanish, the simple present tense is often used instead.

Xavier **estudia** computación este semestre.
Xavier is studying computer science this semester.

Marissa **sale** mañana para los Estados Unidos.
Marissa is leaving tomorrow for the United States.

¿Está pensando en su futuro?
Nosotros, sí.

🏛 BANCO 🏛
CONGRESO

Preparándolo para el mañana

¡INTÉNTALO! Create complete sentences by putting the verbs in the present progressive.

1. mis amigos / descansar en la playa _Mis amigos están descansando en la playa._
2. nosotros / practicar deportes _____
3. Carmen / comer en casa _____
4. nuestro equipo / ganar el partido _____
5. yo / leer el periódico _____
6. él / pensar comprar una bicicleta _____
7. ustedes / jugar a las cartas _____
8. José y Francisco / dormir _____
9. Marisa / leer correo electrónico _____
10. yo / preparar sándwiches _____
11. Carlos / tomar fotos _____
12. ¿dormir / tú? _____

Práctica

1 Completar Alfredo's Spanish class is preparing to travel to Puerto Rico. Use the present progressive of the verb in parentheses to complete Alfredo's description of what everyone is doing.

1. Yo _____ (investigar) la situación política de la isla (*island*).
2. La esposa del profesor _____ (hacer) las maletas.
3. Marta y José Luis _____ (buscar) información sobre San Juan en Internet.
4. Enrique y yo _____ (leer) un correo electrónico de nuestro amigo puertorriqueño.
5. Javier _____ (aprender) mucho sobre la cultura puertorriqueña.
6. Y tú _____ (practicar) el español, ¿verdad?

2 ¿Qué están haciendo? María and her friends are vacationing at a resort in San Juan, Puerto Rico. Complete her description of what everyone is doing right now.

CONSULTA

For more information about Puerto Rico, see **Panorama**, pp. 96–97.

1. Yo   2. Javier   3. Alejandro y Rebeca

4. Celia y yo   5. Samuel   6. Lorenzo

3 Personajes famosos Say what these celebrities are doing right now, using the cues provided.

modelo

Shakira

Shakira está cantando una canción ahora mismo.

A		B	
Isabel Allende	Nelly Furtado	bailar	hacer
Rachael Ray	Dwight Howard	cantar	jugar
James Cameron	Las Rockettes de	correr	preparar
Venus y Serena	Nueva York	escribir	¿?
Williams	¿?	hablar	¿?
Joey Votto	¿?		

AYUDA

Isabel Allende: **novelas**
Rachael Ray: **televisión, negocios** (*business*)
James Cameron: **cine**
Venus y Serena Williams: **tenis**
Joey Votto: **béisbol**
Nelly Furtado: **canciones**
Dwight Howard: **baloncesto**
Las Rockettes de Nueva York: **baile**

Comunicación

4 **Las vacaciones** Read Elena's description of her family vacation. Then indicate whether these conclusions are **lógico** or **ilógico**, based on what you read.

> Está lloviendo. Mis tres hermanos están jugando a las cartas. Mi hermana está leyendo una revista. Mi madre está buscando la llave de la habitación. Mi padre está durmiendo. ¿Y yo? Estoy escribiendo este mensaje electrónico...

	Lógico	Ilógico
1. Hace mal tiempo.	○	○
2. La familia es pequeña.	○	○
3. La madre está contenta.	○	○
4. El padre está en la cama.	○	○
5. La familia está en un hotel.	○	○

5 **Preguntar** Answer your partner's questions about what you are doing at these times.

> **modelo**
> 8:00 a.m.
> **Estudiante 1:** Son las ocho de la mañana. ¿Qué estás haciendo?
> **Estudiante 2:** Estoy desayunando.

1. 5:00 a.m.	3. 11:00 a.m.	5. 2:00 p.m.	7. 9:00 p.m.
2. 9:30 a.m.	4. 12:00 p.m.	6. 5:00 p.m.	8. 11:30 p.m.

6 **Describir** Use the present progressive to write a description of what is happening in this Spanish beach scene.

Síntesis

7 **¿Qué están haciendo?** With a partner, take turns asking each other what people are doing right now. You could ask about other students, professors, or even celebrities.

bailar	comer	escribir	estudiar	leer
cantar	enseñar	escuchar	jugar	mirar

5.3 Ser and estar

ANTE TODO You have already learned that **ser** and **estar** both mean *to be* but are used for different purposes. These charts summarize the key differences in usage between **ser** and **estar**.

Uses of ser

1. **Nationality and place of origin** . . . .   Juan Carlos **es** argentino.
   Es de Buenos Aires.

2. **Profession or occupation** . . . .   Adela **es** agente de viajes.
   Francisco **es** médico.

3. **Characteristics of people and things** . . .   José y Clara **son** simpáticos.
   El clima de Puerto Rico **es** agradable.

4. **Generalizations** . . . .   ¡**Es** fabuloso viajar!
   Es difícil estudiar a la una de la mañana.

5. **Possession** . . . .   **Es** la pluma de Jimena.
   Son las llaves del señor Díaz.

6. **What something is made of** . . . .   La bicicleta **es** de metal.
   Los pasajes **son** de papel.

7. **Time and date** . . . .   Hoy **es** martes. **Son** las dos.
   Hoy **es** el primero de julio.

8. **Where or when an event takes place** . . .   El partido **es** en el estadio Santa Fe.
   La conferencia **es** a las siete.

Ellos son mis amigos.

Miguel está enojado conmigo.

Uses of estar

1. **Location or spatial relationships** . . . . .   El aeropuerto **está** lejos de la ciudad.
   Tu habitación **está** en el tercer piso.

2. **Health** . . . .   ¿Cómo **estás**?
   Estoy bien, gracias.

3. **Physical states and conditions** . . . .   El profesor **está** ocupado.
   Las ventanas **están** abiertas.

4. **Emotional states** . . . .   Marissa **está** feliz hoy.
   Estoy muy enojado con Maru.

5. **Certain weather expressions** . . . .   **Está** lloviendo.
   Está nublado.

6. **Ongoing actions (progressive tenses)** . .   **Estamos** estudiando para un examen.
   Ana **está** leyendo una novela.

Ser and estar with adjectives

▶ With many descriptive adjectives, **ser** and **estar** can both be used, but the meaning will change.

Juan **es** delgado.	Ana **es** nerviosa.
Juan is thin.	*Ana is a nervous person.*
Juan **está** más delgado hoy.	Ana **está** nerviosa por el examen.
Juan looks thinner today.	*Ana is nervous because of the exam.*

▶ In the examples above, the statements with **ser** are general observations about the inherent qualities of Juan and Ana. The statements with **estar** describe conditions that are variable.

▶ Here are some adjectives that change in meaning when used with **ser** and **estar**.

With ser	With estar
El chico **es listo**.	El chico **está listo**.
*The boy is **smart**.*	*The boy is **ready**.*
La profesora **es mala**.	La profesora **está mala**.
*The professor is **bad**.*	*The professor is **sick**.*
Jaime **es aburrido**.	Jaime **está aburrido**.
*Jaime is **boring**.*	*Jaime is **bored**.*
Las peras **son verdes**.	Las peras **están verdes**.
*Pears are **green**.*	*The pears are **not ripe**.*
El gato **es muy vivo**.	El gato **está vivo**.
*The cat is very **clever**.*	*The cat is **alive**.*
Iván **es un hombre seguro**.	Iván no **está seguro**.
*Iván is a **confident** man.*	*Iván is not **sure**.*

¡ATENCIÓN!

When referring to objects, **ser seguro/a** means *to be safe.*
El puente es seguro.
The bridge is safe.

¡INTÉNTALO! Form complete sentences by using the correct form of **ser** or **estar** and making any other necessary changes.

1. Alejandra / cansado
   Alejandra está cansada.

2. ellos / pelirrojo
   _____

3. Carmen / alto
   _____

4. yo / la clase de español
   _____

5. película / a las once
   _____

6. hoy / viernes
   _____

7. nosotras / enojado
   _____

8. Antonio / médico
   _____

9. Romeo y Julieta / enamorado
   _____

10. libros / de Ana
    _____

11. Marisa y Juan / estudiando
    _____

12. partido de baloncesto / gimnasio
    _____

Práctica

1 **¿Ser o estar?** Indicate whether each adjective takes **ser** or **estar**. **¡Ojo!**
Three of them can take both verbs.

	ser	estar			ser	estar
1. delgada	○	○		5. seguro	○	○
2. canadiense	○	○		6. enojada	○	○
3. enamorado	○	○		7. importante	○	○
4. lista	○	○		8. avergonzada	○	○

2 **Completar** Complete this conversation with the appropriate forms of **ser** and **estar**.

EDUARDO ¡Hola, Ceci! ¿Cómo (1)_____?

CECILIA Hola, Eduardo. Bien, gracias. ¡Qué guapo (2)_____ hoy!

EDUARDO Gracias. (3)_____ muy amable. Oye, ¿qué (4)_____ haciendo?
(5)¿_____ ocupada?

CECILIA No, sólo le (6)_____ escribiendo una carta a mi prima Pilar.

EDUARDO ¿De dónde (7)_____ ella?

CECILIA Pilar (8)_____ de Ecuador. Su papá (9)_____ médico en Quito. Pero
ahora Pilar y su familia (10)_____ de vacaciones en Ponce, Puerto Rico.

EDUARDO Y… ¿cómo (11)_____ Pilar?

CECILIA (12)_____ muy lista. Y también (13)_____ alta, rubia y muy bonita.

3 **En el parque** Describe the people in the drawing. Your descriptions should answer
the questions provided.

1. ¿Quiénes son?
2. ¿Dónde están?
3. ¿Cómo son?
4. ¿Cómo están?

5. ¿Qué están haciendo?
6. ¿Qué estación es?
7. ¿Qué tiempo hace?
8. ¿Quiénes están de vacaciones?

Comunicación

4   🔊

Ponce Listen to Carolina's description of her vacation. Then indicate whether the following conclusions are **lógico** or **ilógico**, based on what you heard.

	Lógico	Ilógico
1. Carolina es una turista.	○	○
2. Carolina prefiere acampar.	○	○
3. A Carolina no le gusta ir a la playa.	○	○
4. Carolina vive en Ponce.	○	○
5. A Carolina le gustan los museos.	○	○

5

Una persona famosa Describe a celebrity using these items as a guide.

- descripción física
- origen
- qué está haciendo ahora
- cómo está ahora
- dónde está ahora
- profesión u ocupación

6   👥

En el aeropuerto With a partner, take turns assuming the identity of a character from this drawing. Your partner will ask you questions using **ser** and **estar** to figure out who you are.

> **modelo**
>
> **Estudiante 2:** ¿Dónde estás?
> **Estudiante 1:** Estoy cerca de la puerta.
> **Estudiante 2:** ¿Qué estás haciendo?
> **Estudiante 1:** Estoy escuchando a otra persona.
> **Estudiante 2:** ¿Eres uno de los pasajeros?
> **Estudiante 1:** No, soy empleado del aeropuerto.
> **Estudiante 2:** ¿Eres Camilo?

Síntesis

7

Un hotel magnífico Write a radio ad for a vacation resort somewhere in the Spanish-speaking world. Use **ser** and **estar** in as many different ways as you can.

5.4   Direct object nouns and pronouns

SUBJECT	VERB	DIRECT OBJECT NOUN
Juan Carlos y Jimena	están tomando	fotos.
Juan Carlos and Jimena	*are taking*	*photos.*

▶ A direct object noun receives the action of the verb directly and generally follows the verb. In the example above, the direct object noun answers the question *What are Juan Carlos and Jimena taking?*

▶ When a direct object noun in Spanish is a person or a pet, it is preceded by the word **a**. This is called the personal **a**; there is no English equivalent for this construction.

Mariela mira **a** Carlos.   Mariela mira televisión.
Mariela is watching Carlos.   *Mariela is watching TV.*

▶ In the first sentence above, the personal **a** is required because the direct object is a person. In the second sentence, the personal **a** is not required because the direct object is a thing, not a person.

Miguel no me perdona.

No tenemos tablas de windsurf.

El botones las puede conseguir para ustedes.

▶ Direct object pronouns are words that replace direct object nouns. Like English, Spanish uses a direct object pronoun to avoid repeating a noun already mentioned.

	DIRECT OBJECT			DIRECT OBJECT PRONOUN	
Maribel hace	las maletas.	▶	Maribel	las	hace.
Felipe compra	el sombrero.		Felipe	lo	compra.
Vicky tiene	la llave.		Vicky	la	tiene.

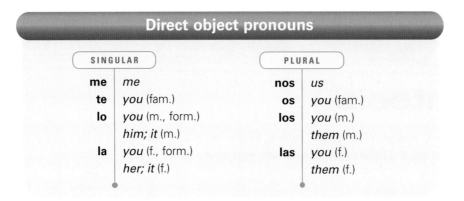

Direct object pronouns

SINGULAR		PLURAL	
me	*me*	**nos**	*us*
te	*you* (fam.)	**os**	*you* (fam.)
lo	*you* (m., form.)	**los**	*you* (m.)
	him; it (m.)		*them* (m.)
la	*you* (f., form.)	**las**	*you* (f.)
	her; it (f.)		*them* (f.)

▶ In affirmative sentences, direct object pronouns generally appear before the conjugated verb. In negative sentences, the pronoun is placed between the word **no** and the verb.

Adela practica **el tenis.**   Gabriela no tiene **las llaves.**
Adela **lo** practica.   Gabriela **no las** tiene.

Carmen compra **los pasajes.**   Diego no hace **las maletas.**
Carmen **los** compra.   Diego **no las** hace.

▶ When the verb is an infinitive construction, such as **ir a** + [*infinitive*], the direct object pronoun can be placed before the conjugated form or attached to the infinitive.

Ellos van a escribir **unas postales.**   Ellos **las** van a escribir.
                                            Ellos van a escribir**las.**

Lidia quiere ver **una película.**   Lidia **la** quiere ver.
                                            Lidia quiere ver**la.**

▶ When the verb is in the present progressive, the direct object pronoun can be placed before the conjugated form or attached to the present participle. **¡Atención!** When a direct object pronoun is attached to the present participle, an accent mark is added to maintain the proper stress.

Gerardo está leyendo **la lección.**   Gerardo **la** está leyendo.
                                            Gerardo está leyéndo**la.**

Toni está mirando **el partido.**   Toni **lo** está mirando.
                                            Toni está mirándo**lo.**

CONSULTA

To learn more about accents, see **Lección 4, Pronunciación,** p. 33.

¡INTÉNTALO!   Choose the correct direct object pronoun for each sentence.

1. Tienes el libro de español. *c*
   a. La tienes.   b. Los tienes.   c. Lo tienes.
2. Voy a ver el partido de baloncesto.
   a. Voy a verlo.   b. Voy a verte.   c. Voy a vernos.
3. El artista quiere dibujar a Luisa y a su mamá.
   a. Quiere dibujarme.   b. Quiere dibujarla.   c. Quiere dibujarlas.
4. Marcos busca la llave.
   a. Me busca.   b. La busca.   c. Las busca.
5. Rita me lleva al aeropuerto y también lleva a Tomás.
   a. Nos lleva.   b. Las lleva.   c. Te lleva.
6. Puedo oír a Gerardo y a Miguel.
   a. Puedo oírte.   b. Puedo oírlos.   c. Puedo oírlo.
7. Quieren estudiar la gramática.
   a. Quieren estudiarnos. b. Quieren estudiarlo. c. Quieren estudiarla.
8. ¿Practicas los verbos irregulares?
   a. ¿Los practicas?   b. ¿Las practicas?   c. ¿Lo practicas?
9. Ignacio ve la película.
   a. La ve.   b. Lo ve.   c. Las ve.
10. Sandra va a invitar a Mario a la excursión. También me va a invitar a mí.
    a. Los va a invitar. b. Lo va a invitar.   c. Nos va a invitar.

Práctica

1 **Simplificar** Professor Vega's class is planning a trip to Costa Rica. Describe their preparations by changing the direct object nouns into direct object pronouns.

> **modelo**
> La profesora Vega tiene su pasaporte.
> *La profesora Vega lo tiene.*

1. Gustavo y Héctor confirman las reservaciones.
2. Nosotros leemos los folletos (*brochures*).
3. Ana María estudia el mapa.
4. Yo aprendo los nombres de los monumentos de San José.
5. Alicia escucha a la profesora.
6. Miguel escribe las instrucciones para ir al hotel.
7. Esteban busca el pasaje.
8. Nosotros planeamos una excursión.

¡LENGUA VIVA!
There are many Spanish words that correspond to *ticket*. **Billete** and **pasaje** usually refer to a ticket for travel, such as an airplane ticket. **Entrada** refers to a ticket to an event, such as a concert or a movie. **Boleto** can be used in either case.

2 **Vacaciones** Ramón is going to San Juan, Puerto Rico, with his friends, Javier and Marcos. Express his thoughts more succinctly using direct object pronouns.

> **modelo**
> Quiero hacer una excursión.
> *Quiero hacerla./La quiero hacer.*

1. Voy a hacer mi maleta.
2. Necesitamos llevar los pasaportes.
3. Marcos está pidiendo el folleto turístico.
4. Javier debe llamar a sus padres.
5. Ellos desean visitar el Viejo San Juan.
6. Puedo llamar a Javier por la mañana.
7. Prefiero llevar mi cámara.
8. No queremos perder nuestras reservaciones de hotel.

NOTA CULTURAL
Puerto Rico is a U.S. territory, so people do not need travel documents when traveling to and from Puerto Rico from the U.S. mainland. However, everyone must meet all requirements for entering the U.S. when traveling directly to Puerto Rico from abroad.

3 **¿Quién?** The Garza family is preparing to go on a vacation to Puerto Rico. Based on the clues, answer the questions. Use direct object pronouns in your answers.

> **modelo**
> ¿Quién hace las reservaciones para el hotel? (el Sr. Garza)
> *El Sr. Garza las hace.*

1. ¿Quién compra los pasajes para el vuelo (*flight*)? (la Sra. Garza)
2. ¿Quién tiene que hacer las maletas de los niños? (María)
3. ¿Quiénes buscan los pasaportes? (Antonio y María)
4. ¿Quién va a confirmar las reservaciones de hotel? (la Sra. Garza)
5. ¿Quién busca la cámara? (María)
6. ¿Quién compra un mapa de Puerto Rico? (Antonio)

Comunicación

4 🔊 **Escuchar** Listen to Mercedes and Gabriel, two students in Chicago, talk about their winter break. Then indicate whether the following conclusions are **lógico** or **ilógico**, based on what you heard.

	Lógico	Ilógico
1. Gabriel va a la playa.	○	○
2. Gabriel está listo para salir.	○	○
3. Va a hacer frío en Chicago.	○	○
4. Gabriel viaja a España.	○	○
5. Mercedes va a viajar también.	○	○

5 👥 **Entrevista** Answer your partner's questions. Use direct object pronouns.

1. ¿Ves mucho la televisión?
2. ¿Cuándo vas a ver tu programa favorito?
3. ¿Quién prepara la comida (*food*) en tu casa?
4. ¿Te visita mucho tu familia?
5. ¿Visitas mucho a tus abuelos?
6. ¿Nos entienden nuestros padres a nosotros?
7. ¿Cuándo ves a tus amigos/as?
8. ¿Cuándo te llaman tus amigos/as?

6 👥 **De mal humor** The weather has ruined your plans to go to the beach. Using words from the list, your partner offers some suggestions to cheer you up. Use direct object pronouns in your responses.

> **modelo**
>
> **Estudiante 1:** ¿Quieres ver la película de Ryan Gosling?
> **Estudiante 2:** No la quiero ver.

computadora	fotos	libro
película	revista	videojuegos

Síntesis

7 **Adivinanzas** Write five riddles with descriptions of people, places, or things. Follow the model. Then see whether your teacher can solve your riddles.

> **modelo**
>
> Lo uso para (*I use it to*) escribir en mi cuaderno.
> No es muy grande y tiene borrador. ¿Qué es?

Javier
SUBJECT
CONJUGATED FORM
empiezo
Main clause
dudan

Recapitulación

Review the grammar concepts you have learned in this lesson by completing these activities.

1 **Completar** Complete the chart with the correct present participle of these verbs. **16 pts.**

Infinitive	Present participle	Infinitive	Present participle
hacer		estar	
acampar		ser	
tener		vivir	
venir		estudiar	

2 **Vacaciones en París** Complete this paragraph about Julia's trip to Paris with the correct form of **ser** or **estar**. **24 pts.**

Hoy (1) _____ (es/está) el 3 de julio y voy a París por tres semanas. (Yo) (2) _____ (Soy/Estoy) muy feliz porque voy a ver a mi mejor amiga. Ella (3) _____ (es/está) de Puerto Rico, pero ahora (4) _____ (es/está) viviendo en París. También (yo) (5) _____ (soy/estoy) un poco nerviosa porque (6) _____ (es/está) mi primer viaje a Francia. El vuelo (*flight*) (7) _____ (es/está) hoy por la tarde, pero ahora (8) _____ (es/está) lloviendo. Por eso (9) _____ (somos/estamos) preocupadas, porque probablemente el avión va a salir tarde. Mi equipaje ya (10) _____ (es/está) listo. (11) _____ (Es/Está) tarde y me tengo que ir. ¡Va a (12) _____ (ser/ estar) un viaje fenomenal!

3 **¿Qué hacen?** Respond to these questions by indicating what people do with the items mentioned. Use direct object pronouns. **20 pts.**

> **modelo**
> ¿Qué hacen ellos con la película? (ver)
> La ven.

1. ¿Qué haces tú con el libro de viajes? (leer) _____
2. ¿Qué hacen los turistas en la ciudad? (explorar) _____
3. ¿Qué hace el botones con el equipaje? (llevar) _____
4. ¿Qué hace la agente con las reservaciones? (confirmar) _____
5. ¿Qué hacen ustedes con los pasaportes? (mostrar) _____

RESUMEN GRAMATICAL

5.1 **Estar with conditions and emotions** *p. 74*

▶ Yo **estoy** aburrido/a, feliz, nervioso/a.
▶ El cuarto **está** desordenado, limpio, ordenado.
▶ Estos libros **están** abiertos, cerrados, sucios.

5.2 **The present progressive** *pp. 76–77*

▶ The present progressive is formed with the present tense of estar plus the present participle.

Forming the present participle

infinitive	stem	ending	present participle
hablar	habl-	-ando	hablando
comer	com-	-iendo	comiendo
escribir	escrib-	-iendo	escribiendo

-ir stem-changing verbs

	infinitive	present participle
e:ie	preferir	prefiriendo
e:i	conseguir	consiguiendo
o:ue	dormir	durmiendo

▶ Irregular present participles: **yendo (ir), pudiendo (poder), viniendo (venir)**

5.3 **Ser and estar** *pp. 80–81*

▶ Uses of **ser**: nationality, origin, profession or occupation, characteristics, generalizations, possession, what something is made of, time and date, time and place of events

▶ Uses of **estar**: location, health, physical states and conditions, emotional states, weather expressions, ongoing actions

▶ Many adjectives can be used with both **ser** and **estar**, but the meaning of the adjectives will change.

Juan **es** delgado.   Juan **está** más delgado hoy.
Juan is thin.   *Juan looks thinner today.*

4 **Opuestos** Complete these sentences with the appropriate form of the verb **estar** and an antonym for the underlined adjective. **20 pts.**

> **modelo**
>
> Mis respuestas están <u>bien</u>, pero las de Susana *están mal*.

1. Las tiendas están <u>abiertas</u>, pero la agencia de viajes _____ _____.
2. No me gustan las habitaciones <u>desordenadas</u>. Incluso (*Even*) mi habitación de hotel _____ _____.
3. Nosotras estamos <u>tristes</u> cuando trabajamos. Hoy comienzan las vacaciones y _____ _____.
4. En esta ciudad los autobuses están <u>sucios</u>, pero los taxis _____ _____.
5. —El avión sale a las 5:30, ¿verdad? —No, estás <u>confundida</u>. Yo _____ _____ de que el avión sale a las 5:00.

5.4 **Direct object nouns and pronouns** *pp. 84–85*

Direct object pronouns

Singular		Plural	
me	lo	nos	los
te	la	os	las

In affirmative sentences:
Adela practica el tenis. → Adela lo practica.

In negative sentences: Adela **no** lo practica.

With an infinitive:
Adela lo va a practicar./Adela va a practicarlo.

With the present progressive:
Adela lo está practicando./Adela está practicándolo.

5 **En la playa** Describe what these people are doing. Complete the sentences using the present progressive tense. **16 pts.**

1. El Sr. Camacho _____.
2. Felicia _____.
3. Leo _____.
4. Nosotros _____.

6 **Refrán** Complete this Spanish saying by filling in the missing present participles. Refer to the translation and the drawing. **4 pts.**

¡LA CIUDAD ESTÁ MUY SUCIA!

❝Se consigue más _____ que _____.**❞**

(You can accomplish more by doing than by saying.)

Lectura

Antes de leer

Estrategia

Scanning

Scanning involves glancing over a document in search of specific information. For example, you can scan a document to identify its format, to find cognates, to locate visual clues about the document's content, or to find specific facts. Scanning allows you to learn a great deal about a text without having to read it word for word.

Examinar el texto

Scan the reading selection for cognates and write down a few of them.

1. _____   4. _____
2. _____   5. _____
3. _____   6. _____

Based on the cognates you found, what do you think this document is about?

_____

Preguntas

Read these questions. Then scan the document again to look for answers.

1. What is the format of the reading selection?

   _____

2. Which place is the document about?

   _____

3. What are some of the visual cues this document provides? What do they tell you about the content of the document?

   _____

4. Who produced the document, and what do you think it is for?

   _____

Turismo ecológico en Puerto Rico

Hotel Vistahermosa

~ Lajas, Puerto Rico ~

- 40 habitaciones individuales
- 15 habitaciones dobles
- Teléfono/TV por cable/Internet
- Aire acondicionado
- Restaurante (Bar)
- Piscina
- Área de juegos
- Cajero automático°

El hotel está situado en Playa Grande, un pequeño pueblo de pescadores del mar Caribe. Es el lugar perfecto para el viajero que viene de vacaciones. Las playas son seguras y limpias, ideales para tomar el sol, descansar, tomar fotografías y nadar. Está abierto los 365 días del año. Hay una rebaja° especial para estudiantes universitarios.

DIRECCIÓN: Playa Grande 406, Lajas, PR 00667, cerca del Parque Nacional Foresta.

Cajero automático *ATM* rebaja *discount*

Atracciones cercanas

Playa Grande ¿Busca la playa perfecta? Playa Grande es la playa que está buscando. Usted puede pescar, sacar fotos, nadar y pasear en bicicleta. Playa Grande es un paraíso para el turista que quiere practicar deportes acuáticos. El lugar es bonito e interesante y usted va a tener muchas oportunidades para descansar y disfrutar en familia.

Valle Niebla Ir de excursión, tomar café, montar a caballo, caminar, hacer picnics. Más de cien lugares para acampar.

Bahía Fosforescente Sacar fotos, salidas de noche, excursión en barco. Una maravillosa experiencia llena de luz°.

Arrecifes de Coral Sacar fotos, bucear, explorar. Es un lugar único en el Caribe.

Playa Vieja Tomar el sol, pasear en bicicleta, jugar a las cartas, escuchar música. Ideal para la familia.

Parque Nacional Foresta Sacar fotos, visitar el Museo de Arte Nativo. Reserva Mundial de la Biosfera.

Santuario de las Aves Sacar fotos, observar aves°, seguir rutas de excursión.

llena de luz *full of light* **aves** *birds*

Después de leer

Listas
Which amenities of Hotel Vistahermosa would most interest these potential guests? Explain your choices.

1. dos padres con un hijo de seis años y una hija de ocho años

2. un hombre y una mujer en su luna de miel (*honeymoon*)

3. una persona en un viaje de negocios (*business trip*)

Conversaciones
Answer your partner's questions.

1. ¿Quieres visitar el Hotel Vistahermosa? ¿Por qué?
2. Tienes tiempo de visitar sólo tres de las atracciones turísticas que están cerca del hotel. ¿Cuáles vas a visitar? ¿Por qué?
3. ¿Qué prefieres hacer en Valle Niebla? ¿En Playa Vieja? ¿En el Parque Nacional Foresta?

Situaciones
You have just arrived at Hotel Vistahermosa. Your partner is the concierge. Use the phrases below to express your interests and ask for suggestions about where to go.

1. montar a caballo
2. bucear
3. pasear en bicicleta
4. pescar
5. observar aves

Contestar
Answer these questions.

1. ¿Quieres visitar Puerto Rico? Explica tu respuesta.

2. ¿Adónde quieres ir de vacaciones el verano que viene? Explica tu respuesta.

Escritura

Estrategia

Making an outline

When we write to share information, an outline can serve to separate topics and subtopics, providing a framework for the presentation of data. Consider the following excerpt from an outline of the tourist brochure on pages 90–91.

IV. Descripción del sitio (con foto)
   A. Playa Grande
      1. Playas seguras y limpias
      2. Ideal para tomar el sol, descansar, tomar fotografías, nadar
   B. El hotel
      1. Abierto los 365 días del año
      2. Rebaja para estudiantes universitarios

Mapa de ideas

Idea maps can be used to create outlines. The major sections of an idea map correspond to the Roman numerals in an outline. The minor idea map sections correspond to the outline's capital letters, and so on. Examine the idea map that led to the outline above.

Tema

Escribir un folleto

Write a tourist brochure for a hotel or resort you have visited. If you wish, you may write about an imaginary location. You may want to include some of this information in your brochure:

▶ the name of the hotel or resort
▶ phone and fax numbers that tourists can use to make contact
▶ the hotel website that tourists can consult
▶ an e-mail address that tourists can use to request information
▶ a description of the exterior of the hotel or resort
▶ a description of the interior of the hotel or resort, including facilities and amenities
▶ a description of the surrounding area, including its climate
▶ a listing of nearby scenic natural attractions
▶ a listing of nearby cultural attractions
▶ a listing of recreational activities that tourists can pursue in the vicinity of the hotel or resort

Escuchar

Estrategia
Listening for key words

By listening for key words or phrases, you can identify the subject and main ideas of what you hear, as well as some of the details.

🔊 To practice this strategy, you will now listen to a short paragraph. As you listen, jot down the key words that help you identify the subject of the paragraph and its main ideas.

Preparación

Based on the illustration, who do you think Hernán Jiménez is, and what is he doing? What key words might you listen for to help you understand what he is saying?

Ahora escucha 🔊

Now you are going to listen to a weather report by Hernán Jiménez. Note which phrases are correct according to the key words and phrases you hear.

Santo Domingo
1. hace sol
2. va a hacer frío
3. una mañana de mal tiempo
4. va a estar nublado
5. buena tarde para tomar el sol
6. buena mañana para la playa

San Francisco de Macorís
1. hace frío
2. hace sol
3. va a nevar
4. va a llover
5. hace calor
6. mal día para excursiones

Comprensión

¿Cierto o falso?
Indicate whether each statement is **cierto** or **falso**, based on the weather report. Correct the false statements.

1. Según el meteorólogo, la temperatura en Santo Domingo es de 26 grados.

2. La temperatura máxima en Santo Domingo hoy va a ser de 30 grados.

3. Está lloviendo ahora en Santo Domingo.

4. En San Francisco de Macorís la temperatura mínima de hoy va a ser de 20 grados.

5. Va a llover mucho hoy en San Francisco de Macorís.

Preguntas
Answer these questions about the weather report.

1. ¿Hace viento en Santo Domingo ahora?
2. ¿Está nublado en Santo Domingo ahora?
3. ¿Está nevando ahora en San Francisco de Macorís?
4. ¿Qué tiempo hace en San Francisco de Macorís?

Anuncio de Santander LANPASS

Con lo que realmente nos importa°.

Preparación

Answer these questions in Spanish.

1. ¿Te gusta viajar? ¿Por qué? ¿Adónde te gusta viajar?
2. ¿Qué te gusta hacer cuando estás de vacaciones?
3. ¿Qué modo de transporte prefieres usar? ¿Por qué?

El arte de viajar

Millions of people travel on airlines every year for business and pleasure. The number of airline passengers is expected to double between 2014 and 2034 worldwide. This is true for Latin America, too, as airlines are looking at how to attract all those customers to their planes. The airline of Chile, LAN, has partnered with the international bank Santander to create the loyalty program LANPASS to encourage frequent travel on LAN. What does an airline say to travelers that captures their attention and makes their business seem like your pleasure?

importa *matters*

Vocabulario útil

arena	*sand*
cambiar	*to change*
destino	*destination*
medir	*to measure*
mismo/a	*itself*
piel	*skin*
puestas de sol	*sunsets*
recuerdos	*memories*
sentirse	*to feel*
sino	*but*

Comprensión

Mark an X next to the phrases you hear in the ad.
Irse es volver a....

_ cambiar de piel   _ trabajar   _ la oficina
_ desconectarnos   _ castillos de arena   _ sentirse vivo
_ estudiar mucho   _ destinos exóticos   _ las siestas
_ un mundo sin Internet   _ la esencia de todo   _ tiempo en familia

Conversación

Answer these questions with a classmate.

1. Según el anuncio, ¿cuáles son algunas cosas positivas de viajar?
2. ¿Cuáles de estas cosas positivas son importantes para ti? ¿Por qué?
3. Para tener experiencias positivas, ¿a dónde viajas tú? ¿A dónde viaja tu familia? ¿Y tus amigos?

Aplicación

With a classmate, prepare an ad inviting other people to travel to a special place. Explain why it is a perfect or ideal place. What evocative words and images will you use? Present your ad to the class.

Between 1438 and 1533, when the vast and powerful Incan Empire was at its height, the Incas built an elaborate network of **caminos** (*trails*) that traversed the Andes Mountains and converged on the empire's capital, Cuzco. Today, hundreds of thousands of tourists come to Peru annually to walk the surviving trails and enjoy the spectacular scenery. The most popular trail, **el Camino Inca**, leads from Cuzco to **Intipunku** (*Sun Gate*), the entrance to the ancient mountain city of Machu Picchu.

¡Vacaciones en Perú!

Machu Picchu [...] se encuentra aislada sobre° esta montaña...

Vocabulario útil

ciudadela	*citadel*
de cultivo	*farming*
el/la guía	*guide*
maravilla	*wonder*
quechua	*Quechua (indigenous Peruvian)*
sector (urbano)	*(urban) sector*

... siempre he querido° venir [...] Me encantan° las civilizaciones antiguas°.

Preparación

Have you ever visited an archeological or historic site? Where? Why did you go there?

Completar

Complete these sentences. Make the necessary changes.

1. Las ruinas de Machu Picchu son una antigua _____ inca.

2. La ciudadela estaba (*was*) dividida en tres sectores: _____ , religioso y de cultivo.

3. Cada año los _____ reciben a cientos (*hundreds*) de turistas de diferentes países.

4. Hoy en día, la cultura _____ está presente en las comunidades andinas (*Andean*) de Perú.

Somos una familia francesa [...] Perú es un país muy, muy bonito de verdad.

se encuentra aislada sobre *it is isolated on* siempre he querido *I have always wanted* Me encantan *I love* antiguas *ancient*

Puerto Rico

El país en cifras

▶ **Área:** 8.959 km² (3.459 millas²)
  menor° que el área de Connecticut
▶ **Población:** 3.667.084
Puerto Rico es una de las islas más densamente pobladas° del mundo. Más de la mitad de la población vive en San Juan, la capital.
▶ **Capital:** San Juan—2.730.000
▶ **Ciudades principales:** Arecibo, Bayamón, Fajardo, Mayagüez, Ponce
▶ **Moneda:** dólar estadounidense
▶ **Idiomas:** español (oficial); inglés (oficial)
Aproximadamente la cuarta parte de la población puertorriqueña habla inglés, pero en las zonas turísticas este porcentaje es mucho más alto. El uso del inglés es obligatorio para documentos federales.

Bandera
de Puerto Rico

Puertorriqueños célebres
▶ **Raúl Juliá,** actor (1940–1994)
▶ **Roberto Clemente,** beisbolista (1934–1972)
▶ **Julia de Burgos,** escritora (1914–1953)
▶ **Benicio del Toro,** actor y productor (1967–)
▶ **Rosie Pérez,** actriz y bailarina (1964–)
▶ **José Rivera,** dramaturgo y guionista (1955–)

menor *less* pobladas *populated* río subterráneo *underground river* más largo *longest* cuevas *caves* bóveda *vault* fortaleza *fort* caber *fit*

Faro en Arecibo

Playa en San Juan

Océano Atlántico

Arecibo

San Juan ✪

Bayamón •

Río Grande de Añasco

Mayagüez

Cordillera Central

Sierra de Cayey

Ponce

Mar Caribe

Iglesia en Ponce

Pescadores en Mayagüez

OCÉANO ATLÁNTICO

PUERTO RICO

OCÉANO PACÍFICO

¡Increíble pero cierto!

El río Camuy es el tercer río subterráneo° más largo° del mundo y tiene el sistema de cuevas° más grande del hemisferio occidental.
La Cueva de los Tres Pueblos es una gigantesca bóveda°, tan grande que toda la fortaleza° del Morro puede caber° en su interior.

Lugares • El Morro

El Morro es una fortaleza que se construyó para proteger° la bahía° de San Juan desde principios del siglo° XVI hasta principios del siglo XX. Hoy día muchos turistas visitan este lugar, convertido en un museo. Es el sitio más fotografiado de Puerto Rico. La arquitectura de la fortaleza es impresionante. Tiene misteriosos túneles, oscuras mazmorras° y vistas fabulosas de la bahía.

Artes • Salsa

La salsa, un estilo musical de origen puertorriqueño y cubano, nació° en el barrio latino de la ciudad de Nueva York. Dos de los músicos de salsa más famosos son Tito Puente y Willie Colón, los dos de Nueva York. Las estrellas° de la salsa en Puerto Rico son Felipe Rodríguez y Héctor Lavoe. Hoy en día, Puerto Rico es el centro internacional de este estilo musical. El Gran Combo de Puerto Rico es una de las orquestas de salsa más famosas del mundo°.

Isla de Culebra

Fajardo

Isla de Vieques

Ciencias • El Observatorio de Arecibo

El Observatorio de Arecibo tiene uno de los radiotelescopios más grandes del mundo. Gracias a este telescopio, los científicos° pueden estudiar las propiedades de la Tierra°, la Luna° y otros cuerpos celestes. También pueden analizar fenómenos celestiales como los quasares y pulsares, y detectar emisiones de radio de otras galaxias, en busca de inteligencia extraterrestre.

Historia • Relación con los Estados Unidos

Puerto Rico pasó a ser° parte de los Estados Unidos después de° la guerra° de 1898 y se hizo° un estado libre asociado en 1952. Los puertorriqueños, ciudadanos° estadounidenses desde° 1917, tienen representación política en el Congreso, pero no votan en las elecciones presidenciales y no pagan impuestos° federales. Hay un debate entre los puertorriqueños: ¿debe la isla seguir como estado libre asociado, hacerse un estado como los otros° o volverse° independiente?

¿Qué aprendiste? Contesta las preguntas con una oración completa.

1. ¿Cuál es la moneda de Puerto Rico?
2. ¿Qué idiomas se hablan (*are spoken*) en Puerto Rico?
3. ¿Cuál es el sitio más fotografiado de Puerto Rico?
4. ¿Qué es el Gran Combo?
5. ¿Qué hacen los científicos en el Observatorio de Arecibo?

Conexión Internet Investiga estos temas en Internet.

1. Describe a dos puertorriqueños famosos. ¿Cómo son? ¿Qué hacen? ¿Dónde viven? ¿Por qué son célebres?
2. Busca información sobre lugares en los que se puede hacer ecoturismo en Puerto Rico.

proteger *protect* bahía *bay* siglo *century* mazmorras *dungeons* nació *was born* estrellas *stars* mundo *world* científicos *scientists* Tierra *Earth* Luna *Moon* pasó a ser *became* después de *after* guerra *war* se hizo *became* ciudadanos *citizens* desde *since* pagan impuestos *pay taxes* otros *others* volverse *to become*

Los viajes y las vacaciones

acampar	to camp
confirmar una reservación	to confirm a reservation
estar de vacaciones (*f. pl.*)	to be on vacation
hacer las maletas	to pack (one's suitcases)
hacer un viaje	to take a trip
hacer (wind)surf	to (wind)surf
ir de compras (*f. pl.*)	to go shopping
ir de vacaciones	to go on vacation
ir en autobús (*m.*), auto(móvil) (*m.*), avión (*m.*), barco (*m.*), moto(cicleta) (*f.*), taxi (*m.*)	to go by bus, car, plane, boat, motorcycle, taxi
jugar a las cartas	to play cards
montar a caballo (*m.*)	to ride a horse
pescar	to fish
sacar/tomar fotos (*f. pl.*)	to take photos
el/la agente de viajes	travel agent
el/la inspector(a) de aduanas	customs inspector
el/la viajero/a	traveler
el aeropuerto	airport
la agencia de viajes	travel agency
el campo	countryside
el equipaje	luggage
la estación de autobuses, del metro, de tren	bus, subway, train station
la llegada	arrival
el mar	sea
el paisaje	landscape
el pasaje (de ida y vuelta)	(round-trip) ticket
el pasaporte	passport
la playa	beach
la salida	departure; exit
la tabla de (wind)surf	surfboard/sailboard

El hotel

el ascensor	elevator
la cama	bed
el/la empleado/a	employee
la habitación individual, doble	single, double room
el hotel	hotel
el/la huésped	guest
la llave	key
el piso	floor (of a building)
la planta baja	ground floor

Adjetivos

abierto/a	open
aburrido/a	bored; boring
alegre	happy
amable	nice; friendly
avergonzado/a	embarrassed
cansado/a	tired
cerrado/a	closed
cómodo/a	comfortable
confundido/a	confused
contento/a	content
desordenado/a	disorderly
enamorado/a (de)	in love (with)
enojado/a	angry
equivocado/a	wrong
feliz	happy
limpio/a	clean
listo/a	ready; smart
nervioso/a	nervous
ocupado/a	busy
ordenado/a	orderly
preocupado/a (por)	worried (about)
seguro/a	sure; safe; confident
sucio/a	dirty
triste	sad

Los números ordinales

primer, primero/a	first
segundo/a	second
tercer, tercero/a	third
cuarto/a	fourth
quinto/a	fifth
sexto/a	sixth
séptimo/a	seventh
octavo/a	eighth
noveno/a	ninth
décimo/a	tenth

Palabras adicionales

ahora mismo	right now
el año	year
¿Cuál es la fecha (de hoy)?	What is the date (today)?
de buen/mal humor	in a good/bad mood
la estación	season
el mes	month
todavía	yet; still

Seasons, months, and dates	See page 64.
Weather expressions	See page 64.
Direct object pronouns	See page 84.
Expresiones útiles	See page 69.

¡De compras!

Communicative Goals

You will learn how to:

- Talk about and describe clothing
- Express preferences in a store
- Negotiate and pay for items you buy

contextos

fotonovela

cultura

estructura

adelante

A PRIMERA VISTA

- ¿Está comprando algo la chica?
- ¿Crees que busca una maleta o una blusa?
- ¿Está contenta o enojada?
- ¿Cómo es la chica?

¡De compras!

Más vocabulario

el abrigo	coat
los calcetines (el calcetín)	sock(s)
el cinturón	belt
las gafas (de sol)	(sun)glasses
los guantes	gloves
el impermeable	raincoat
la ropa	clothes
la ropa interior	underwear
las sandalias	sandals
el traje	suit
el vestido	dress
los zapatos de tenis	sneakers
el regalo	gift
el almacén	department store
el centro comercial	shopping mall
el mercado (al aire libre)	(open-air) market
el precio (fijo)	(fixed; set) price
la rebaja	sale
la tienda	store
costar (o:ue)	to cost
gastar	to spend (money)
pagar	to pay
regatear	to bargain
vender	to sell
hacer juego (con)	to match (with)
llevar	to wear; to take
usar	to wear; to use

Variación léxica

calcetines ←→ medias (Amér. L.)

cinturón ←→ correa (Col., Venez.)

gafas/lentes ←→ espejuelos (Cuba, P.R.),
anteojos (Arg., Chile)

zapatos de tenis ←→ zapatillas de deporte (Esp.),
zapatillas (Arg., Perú)

Damas

los pantalones cortos

el traje de baño

los pantalones

la camiseta

el dependiente/el vendedor

la camisa

la clienta

el dinero en efectivo

la blusa

hacer juego (con)

la bolsa

el suéter

la falda

las medias

Práctica

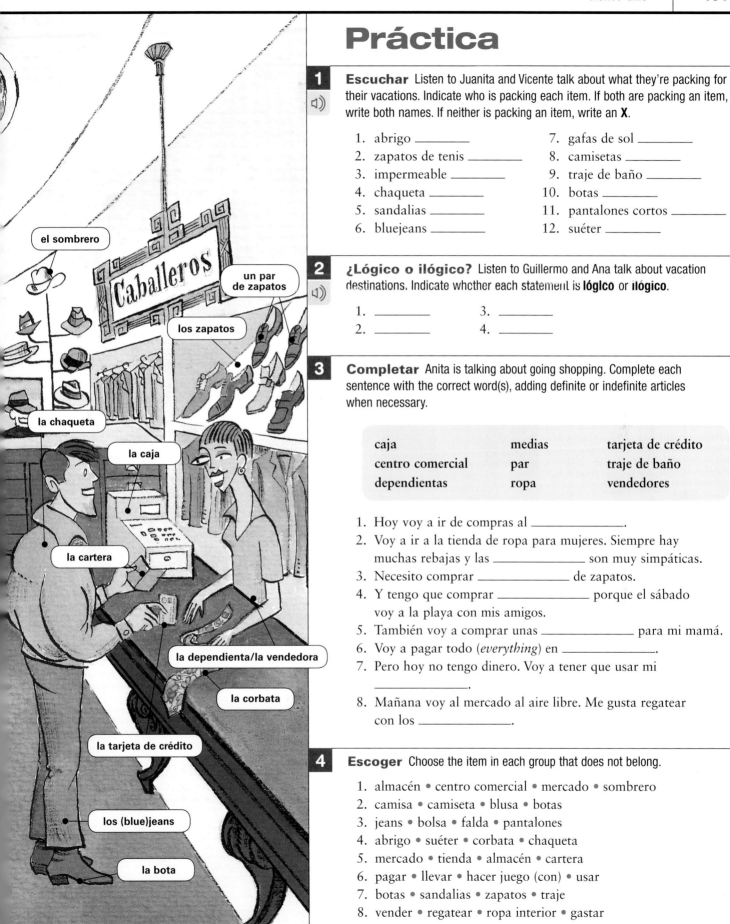

el sombrero

Caballeros

un par de zapatos

los zapatos

la chaqueta

la caja

la cartera

la dependienta/la vendedora

la corbata

la tarjeta de crédito

los (blue)jeans

la bota

1 Escuchar Listen to Juanita and Vicente talk about what they're packing for their vacations. Indicate who is packing each item. If both are packing an item, write both names. If neither is packing an item, write an **X**.

1. abrigo _____
2. zapatos de tenis _____
3. impermeable _____
4. chaqueta _____
5. sandalias _____
6. bluejeans _____
7. gafas de sol _____
8. camisetas _____
9. traje de baño _____
10. botas _____
11. pantalones cortos _____
12. suéter _____

2 ¿Lógico o ilógico? Listen to Guillermo and Ana talk about vacation destinations. Indicate whether each statement is **lógico** or **ilógico**.

1. _____   3. _____
2. _____   4. _____

3 Completar Anita is talking about going shopping. Complete each sentence with the correct word(s), adding definite or indefinite articles when necessary.

caja	medias	tarjeta de crédito
centro comercial	par	traje de baño
dependientas	ropa	vendedores

1. Hoy voy a ir de compras al _____.
2. Voy a ir a la tienda de ropa para mujeres. Siempre hay muchas rebajas y las _____ son muy simpáticas.
3. Necesito comprar _____ de zapatos.
4. Y tengo que comprar _____ porque el sábado voy a la playa con mis amigos.
5. También voy a comprar unas _____ para mi mamá.
6. Voy a pagar todo (*everything*) en _____.
7. Pero hoy no tengo dinero. Voy a tener que usar mi _____.
8. Mañana voy al mercado al aire libre. Me gusta regatear con los _____.

4 Escoger Choose the item in each group that does not belong.

1. almacén • centro comercial • mercado • sombrero
2. camisa • camiseta • blusa • botas
3. jeans • bolsa • falda • pantalones
4. abrigo • suéter • corbata • chaqueta
5. mercado • tienda • almacén • cartera
6. pagar • llevar • hacer juego (con) • usar
7. botas • sandalias • zapatos • traje
8. vender • regatear • ropa interior • gastar

Los colores

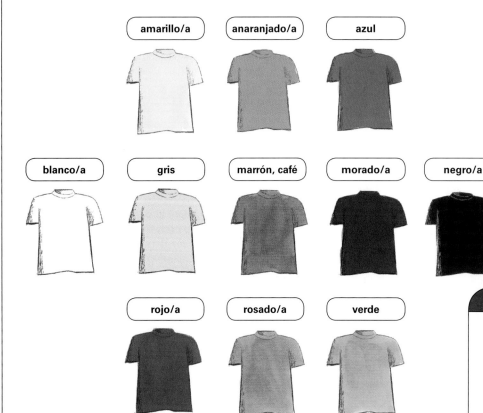

amarillo/a   anaranjado/a   azul

blanco/a   gris   marrón, café   morado/a   negro/a

rojo/a   rosado/a   verde

¡LENGUA VIVA!

The names of colors vary throughout the Spanish-speaking world. For example, in some countries, **anaranjado/a** may be referred to as **naranja**, **morado/a** as **púrpura**, and **rojo/a** as **colorado/a**.

Other terms that will prove helpful include **claro** (*light*) and **oscuro** (*dark*): **azul claro**, **azul oscuro**.

Adjetivos

barato/a	*cheap*
bueno/a	*good*
cada	*each*
caro/a	*expensive*
corto/a	*short (in length)*
elegante	*elegant*
hermoso/a	*beautiful*
largo/a	*long*
loco/a	*crazy*
nuevo/a	*new*
otro/a	*other; another*
pobre	*poor*
rico/a	*rich*

5 **Contrastes** Complete each phrase with the opposite of the underlined word.

1. una corbata <u>barata</u> • unas camisas…
2. unas vendedoras <u>malas</u> • unos dependientes…
3. un vestido <u>corto</u> • una falda…
4. un hombre muy <u>pobre</u> • una mujer muy…
5. una cartera <u>nueva</u> • un cinturón…
6. unos trajes <u>hermosos</u> • unos jeans…
7. un impermeable <u>caro</u> • unos suéteres…
8. unos calcetines <u>blancos</u> • unas medias…

CONSULTA

Like other adjectives you have seen, colors must agree in gender and number with the nouns they modify.

Ex: **las camisas verdes, el vestido amarillo.**

For a review of descriptive adjectives, see **Senderos 1A, Estructura 3.1,** pp. 112–113.

6 **Preguntas** Answer these questions.

1. ¿De qué color es la rosa de Texas?
2. ¿De qué color es la bandera (*flag*) de Canadá?
3. ¿De qué color es la casa donde vive el presidente de los EE.UU.?
4. ¿De qué color es el océano Atlántico?
5. ¿De qué color es la nieve?
6. ¿De qué color es el café?
7. ¿De qué color es el dólar de los EE.UU.?
8. ¿De qué color es la cebra (*zebra*)?

Comunicación

7

Los regalos Listen to the conversation between Victoria and her friend Juan Manuel. Then indicate whether the following conclusions are **lógico** or **ilógico**, based on what you heard.

	Lógico	Ilógico
1. Juan Manuel quiere ir de compras.	○	○
2. A la mamá de Victoria le gusta nadar.	○	○
3. El papá de Victoria usa camisas.	○	○
4. Victoria va a regatear.	○	○
5. Victoria le va a comprar a su hermano unas botas.	○	○

8

Preferencias Answer your partner's questions.

1. ¿Adónde vas a comprar ropa? ¿Por qué?
2. ¿Qué tipo de ropa prefieres? ¿Por qué?
3. ¿Cuáles son tus colores favoritos?
4. En tu opinión, ¿es importante comprar ropa nueva frecuentemente? ¿Por qué?
5. ¿Gastas mucho dinero en ropa cada mes? ¿Buscas rebajas?
6. ¿Regateas cuando compras ropa? ¿Usas tarjetas de crédito?

9

El viaje Write an e-mail to a relative about a trip you are taking with your family this summer. Include where you are going, what the weather is going to be like, what activities you are going to do, and what clothes you are taking.

10

Las maletas With a partner, take turns asking questions about the drawings. Include the topics from the list to talk about Carmela's vacation and Pepe's trip to Bariloche.

- ropa
- color
- lugar
- tiempo
- actividades

NOTA CULTURAL

Bariloche is a popular resort for skiing in South America. Located in Argentina's Patagonia region, the town is also known for its chocolate factories and its beautiful lakes, mountains, and forests.

CONSULTA

To review weather, see **Lección 5, Contextos**, p. 64.

En el mercado

Los chicos van de compras al mercado. ¿Quién hizo la mejor compra?

PERSONAJES   FELIPE   JUAN CARLOS

MARISSA Oigan, vamos al mercado.

JUAN CARLOS ¡Sí! Los chicos en un equipo y las chicas en otro.

FELIPE Tenemos dos horas para ir de compras.

MARU Y don Guillermo decide quién gana.

JIMENA Esta falda azul es muy elegante.

MARISSA ¡Sí! Además, este color está de moda.

MARU Éste rojo es de algodón.

(*Las chicas encuentran unas bolsas.*)

VENDEDOR Ésta de rayas cuesta 190 pesos, ésta 120 pesos y ésta 220 pesos.

MARISSA ¿Me das aquella blusa rosada? Me parece que hace juego con esta falda, ¿no? ¿No tienen otras tallas?

JIMENA Sí, aquí. ¿Qué talla usas?

MARISSA Uso talla 4.

JIMENA La encontré. ¡Qué ropa más bonita!

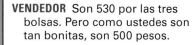

(*En otra parte del mercado*)

FELIPE Juan Carlos compró una camisa de muy buena calidad.

MIGUEL (*a la vendedora*) ¿Puedo ver ésos, por favor?

VENDEDORA Sí, señor. Le doy un muy buen precio.

VENDEDOR Son 530 por las tres bolsas. Pero como ustedes son tan bonitas, son 500 pesos.

MARU Señor, no somos turistas ricas. Somos estudiantes pobres.

VENDEDOR Bueno, son 480 pesos.

MARISSA **JIMENA** **MARU** **MIGUEL** **DON GUILLERMO** **VENDEDORA** **VENDEDOR**

7

JUAN CARLOS Miren, mi nueva camisa. Elegante, ¿verdad?

FELIPE A ver, Juan Carlos... te queda bien.

8

MARU ¿Qué compraste?

MIGUEL Sólo esto.

MARU ¡Qué bonitos aretes! Gracias, mi amor.

9

JUAN CARLOS Y ustedes, ¿qué compraron?

JIMENA Bolsas.

MARU Acabamos de comprar tres bolsas por sólo 480 pesos. ¡Una ganga!

10

FELIPE Don Guillermo, usted tiene que decidir quién gana. ¿Los chicos o las chicas?

DON GUILLERMO El ganador es... Miguel. ¡Porque no compró nada para él, sino para su novia!

Expresiones útiles

Talking about clothing

¡Qué ropa más bonita!
What nice clothing!
Esta falda azul es muy elegante.
This blue skirt is very elegant.
Está de moda.
It's in style.
Éste rojo es de algodón/lana.
This red one is cotton/wool.
Ésta de rayas/lunares/cuadros es de seda.
This striped / polka-dotted / plaid one is silk.
Es de muy buena calidad.
It's very good quality.
¿Qué talla usas/llevas?
What size do you wear?
Uso/Llevo talla 4.
I wear a size 4.
¿Qué número calza?
What size shoe do you wear?
Yo calzo siete.
I wear a size seven.

Negotiating a price

¿Cuánto cuesta?
How much does it cost?
Demasiado caro/a.
Too expensive.
Es una ganga.
It's a bargain.

Saying what you bought

¿Qué compraste?/¿Qué compró usted?
What did you buy?
Sólo compré esto.
I only bought this.
¡Qué bonitos aretes!
What beautiful earrings!
Y ustedes, ¿qué compraron?
And you guys, what did you buy?

Additional vocabulary

híjole *wow*

¿Qué pasó?

1 **¿Cierto o falso?** Indicate whether each sentence is **cierto** or **falso**. Correct the false statements.

	Cierto	Falso
1. Jimena dice que la falda azul no es elegante.	○	○
2. Juan Carlos compra una camisa.	○	○
3. Marissa dice que el azul es un color que está de moda.	○	○
4. Miguel compra unas sandalias para Maru.	○	○

2 **Identificar** Provide the first initial of the person who would make each statement.

____ 1. ¿Te gusta cómo se me ven mis nuevos aretes?
____ 2. Juan Carlos compró una camisa de muy buena calidad.
____ 3. No podemos pagar 500, señor, eso es muy caro.
____ 4. Aquí tienen ropa de muchas tallas.
____ 5. Esta falda me gusta mucho, el color azul es muy elegante.
____ 6. Hay que darnos prisa, sólo tenemos dos horas para ir de compras.

MARU

FELIPE

JIMENA

3 **Completar** Answer the questions using the information in the **Fotonovela**.

1. ¿Qué talla es Marissa?
2. ¿Cuánto les pide el vendedor por las tres bolsas?
3. ¿Cuál es el precio que pagan las tres amigas por las bolsas?
4. ¿Qué dice Juan Carlos sobre su nueva camisa?
5. ¿Quién ganó al hacer las compras? ¿Por qué?

4 **Conversar** With a partner, role-play a conversation between a customer and a salesperson in an open-air market. Use these expressions and also look at **Expresiones útiles** on the previous page.

¿Qué desea?	Estoy buscando...	Prefiero el/la rojo/a.
What would you like?	*I'm looking for...*	*I prefer the red one.*

Cliente/a

Say good afternoon.

Explain that you are looking for a particular item of clothing.

Discuss colors and sizes.

Ask for the price and begin bargaining.

Settle on a price and purchase the item.

Vendedor(a)

Greet the customer and ask what he/she would like.

Show him/her some items and ask what he/she prefers.

Discuss colors and sizes.

Tell him/her a price. Negotiate a price.

Accept a price and say thank you.

Pronunciación
The consonants d and t

¿Dónde?   **vender**   **nadar**   **verdad**

Like **b** and **v**, the Spanish **d** can have a hard sound or a soft sound, depending on which letters appear next to it.

Don   **dinero**   **tienda**   **falda**

At the beginning of a phrase and after **n** or **l**, the letter **d** is pronounced with a hard sound. This sound is similar to the English *d* in *dog*, but a little softer and duller. The tongue should touch the back of the upper teeth, not the roof of the mouth.

medias   **verde**   **vestido**   **huésped**

In all other positions, **d** has a soft sound. It is similar to the English *th* in *there*, but a little softer.

Don Diego no tiene el diccionario

When **d** begins a word, its pronunciation depends on the previous word. At the beginning of a phrase or after a word that ends in **n** or **l**, it is pronounced as a hard **d**.

Doña Dolores es de la capital

Words that begin with **d** are pronounced with a soft **d** if they appear immediately after a word that ends in a vowel or any consonant other than **n** or **l**.

traje   **pantalones**   **tarjeta**   **tienda**

When pronouncing the Spanish **t**, the tongue should touch the back of the upper teeth, not the roof of the mouth. Unlike the English *t*, no air is expelled from the mouth.

Práctica   Read these phrases aloud to practice the **d** and the **t**.

1. Hasta pronto.
2. De nada.
3. Mucho gusto.
4. Lo siento.
5. No hay de qué.
6. ¿De dónde es usted?
7. ¡Todos a bordo!
8. No puedo.
9. Es estupendo.
10. No tengo computadora.
11. ¿Cuándo vienen?
12. Son las tres y media.

Oraciones   Read these sentences aloud to practice the **d** and the **t**.

1. Don Teodoro tiene una tienda en un almacén en La Habana.
2. Don Teodoro vende muchos trajes, vestidos y zapatos todos los días.
3. Un día un turista, Federico Machado, entra en la tienda para comprar un par de botas.
4. Federico regatea con don Teodoro y compra las botas y también un par de sandalias.

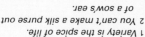

En la variedad está el gusto.[1]

Refranes   Read these sayings aloud to practice the **d** and the **t**.

Aunque la mona se vista de seda, mona se queda.[2]

[2] You can't make a silk purse out of a sow's ear.

[1] Variety is the spice of life.

Los mercados al aire libre

Mercados al aire libre are an integral part of commerce and culture in the Spanish-speaking world. Whether they take place daily or weekly, these markets are an important forum where tourists, locals, and vendors interact. People come to the marketplace to shop, socialize, taste local foods, and watch street performers. Wandering from one **puesto** (*stand*) to the next, one can browse for fresh fruits and vegetables, clothing, CDs and DVDs, and **artesanías** (*crafts*). Some markets offer a mix of products, while others specialize in food, fashion, or used merchandise, such as antiques and books.

When shoppers see an item they like, they can bargain with the vendor. Friendly bargaining is an expected ritual and may result in a significantly lower price. When selling food, vendors may give the customer a little extra of what they purchase; this free addition is known as **la ñapa**.

Many open-air markets are also tourist attractions. The market in Otavalo, Ecuador, is world-famous and has taken place every Saturday since pre-Incan times. This market is well-known for the colorful textiles woven by the **otavaleños**, the indigenous people of the area. One can also find leather goods and wood carvings from nearby towns.

Mercado de Otavalo

Another popular market is **El Rastro,** held every Sunday in Madrid, Spain. Sellers set up **puestos** along the streets to display their wares, which range from local artwork and antiques to inexpensive clothing and electronics.

mariscos *seafood* pescado *fish* verduras *vegetables* flores *flowers*

Otros mercados famosos

Mercado	Lugar	Productos
Feria Artesanal de Recoleta	Buenos Aires, Argentina	artesanías
Mercado Central	Santiago, Chile	mariscos°, pescado°, frutas, verduras°
Tianguis Cultural del Chopo	Ciudad de México, México	ropa, música, revistas, libros, arte, artesanías
El mercado de Chichicastenango	Chichicastenango, Guatemala	frutas y verduras, flores°, cerámica, textiles

1 **¿Cierto o falso?** Indicate whether these statements are cierto or falso. Correct the false statements.

1. Generally, open-air markets specialize in one type of goods.

2. Bargaining is commonplace at outdoor markets.

3. Only new goods can be found at open-air markets.

4. A Spaniard in search of antiques could search at **El Rastro.**

5. If you are in Guatemala and want to buy ceramics, you can go to Chichicastenango.

6. A **ñapa** is a tax on open-air market goods.

7. The **otavaleños** weave colorful textiles to sell on Saturdays.

8. Santiago's **Mercado Central** is known for books and music.

La ropa

la chamarra (Méx.)	la chaqueta
de manga corta/larga	*short/long-sleeved*
los mahones (P. Rico); el pantalón de mezclilla (Méx.); los tejanos (Esp.); los vaqueros (Arg., Cuba, Esp., Uru.)	los bluejeans
la marca	*brand*
la playera (Méx.); la remera (Arg.)	la camiseta

EL MUNDO HISPANO

Diseñadores de moda

- **Adolfo Domínguez** (España) Su ropa tiene un estilo minimalista y práctico. Usa telas° naturales y cómodas en sus diseños.

- **Silvia Tcherassi** (Colombia) Los colores vivos y las líneas asimétricas de sus vestidos y trajes muestran influencias tropicales.

- **Óscar de la Renta** (República Dominicana) Diseñó ropa opulenta para la mujer clásica.

- **Narciso Rodríguez** (EE.UU.) En sus diseños delicados y finos predominan los colores blanco y negro. Hizo° el vestido de boda° de Carolyn Bessette Kennedy. También diseñó varios vestidos para Michelle Obama.

telas *fabrics* Hizo *He made* de boda *wedding*

PERFIL

Carolina Herrera

In 1980, at the urging of some friends, **Carolina Herrera** created a fashion collection as a "test." The Venezuelan designer received such a favorable response that within one year she moved her family from Caracas to New York City and created her own label, Carolina Herrera, Ltd.

"I love elegance and intricacy, but whether it is in a piece of clothing or a fragrance, the intricacy must appear as simplicity," Herrera once stated. She quickly found that many sophisticated women agreed; from the start,

her sleek and glamorous designs have been in constant demand. Over the years, Herrera has grown her brand into a veritable fashion empire that encompasses her fashion and bridal collections, cosmetics, perfume, and accessories that are sold around the globe.

Conexión Internet

¿Qué marcas de ropa son populares en el mundo hispano?

Use the Web to find more cultural information related to this **Cultura** section.

ACTIVIDADES

2 **Comprensión** Complete these sentences.

1. Adolfo Domínguez usa telas _____ y _____ en su ropa.
2. Si hace fresco en el D.F., puedes llevar una _____.
3. La diseñadora _____ hace ropa, perfumes y más.
4. La ropa de _____ muestra influencias tropicales.
5. Los _____ son una ropa casual en Puerto Rico.

3 **Mi ropa favorita** Write a brief description of your favorite article of clothing. Mention what store it is from, the brand, colors, fabric, style, and any other information.

6.1 Saber and conocer

ANTE TODO Spanish has two verbs that mean *to know*: **saber** and **conocer**. They cannot be used interchangeably. Note the irregular **yo** forms.

The verbs saber and conocer

		saber *(to know)*	conocer *(to know)*
SINGULAR FORMS	yo	sé	conozco
	tú	sabes	conoces
	Ud./él/ella	sabe	conoce
PLURAL FORMS	nosotros/as	sabemos	conocemos
	vosotros/as	sabéis	conocéis
	Uds./ellos/ellas	saben	conocen

▶ **Saber** means *to know a fact or piece(s) of information* or *to know how to do something.*

No **sé** tu número de teléfono.
I don't know your telephone number.

Mi hermana **sabe** hablar francés.
My sister knows how to speak French.

▶ **Conocer** means *to know* or *be familiar/acquainted* with a person, place, or thing.

¿**Conoces** la ciudad de Nueva York?
Do you know New York City?

No **conozco** a tu amigo Esteban.
I don't know your friend Esteban.

▶ When the direct object of **conocer** is a person or pet, the personal **a** is used.

¿Conoces La Habana?   *but*   ¿Conoces **a** Celia Cruz?
Do you know Havana?   *Do you know Celia Cruz?*

▶ **¡Atención!** **Parecer** (*to seem*) and **ofrecer** (*to offer*) are conjugated like **conocer**.

▶ **¡Atención!** **Conducir** (*to drive*) and **traducir** (*to translate*) also have an irregular **yo** form, but since they are **-ir** verbs, they are conjugated differently from **conocer**.

conducir ▶ **conduzco, conduces, conduce, conducimos, conducís, conducen**
traducir ▶ **traduzco, traduces, traduce, traducimos, traducís, traducen**

NOTA CULTURAL

Cuban singer **Celia Cruz** (1925–2003), known as the "Queen of Salsa," recorded many albums over her long career. Adored by her fans, she was famous for her colorful and lively on-stage performances.

¡INTÉNTALO! Provide the appropriate forms of these verbs.

saber

1. José no ___*sabe*___ la hora.
2. Sara y yo _____ jugar al tenis.
3. ¿Por qué no _____ tú estos verbos?
4. Mis padres _____ hablar japonés.
5. Yo _____ a qué hora es la clase.
6. Usted no _____ dónde vivo.
7. Mi hermano no _____ nadar.
8. Nosotros _____ muchas cosas.

conocer

1. Usted y yo ___*conocemos*___ bien Miami.
2. ¿Tú _____ a mi amigo Manuel?
3. Sergio y Taydé _____ mi pueblo.
4. Emiliano _____ a mis padres.
5. Yo _____ muy bien el centro.
6. ¿Ustedes _____ la tienda Gigante?
7. Nosotras _____ una playa hermosa.
8. ¿Usted _____ a mi profesora?

Práctica y Comunicación

1 **Completar** Indicate the correct verb for each sentence.

1. Mis hermanos (conocen/saben) conducir, pero yo no (sé/conozco).
2. —¿(Conocen/Saben) ustedes dónde está el estadio? —No, no lo (conocemos/sabemos).
3. —¿(Conoces/Sabes) a Lady Gaga? —Bueno, (sé/conozco) quién es, pero no la (conozco/sé).
4. Mi profesora (sabe/conoce) Cuba y también (conoce/sabe) bailar salsa.

2 **Combinar** Combine elements from each column to create sentences.

A	B	C
Shakira	(no) conocer	Jimmy Fallon
los Yankees	(no) saber	cantar y bailar
el primer ministro		La Habana Vieja
de Canadá		muchas personas importantes
mis amigos y yo		hablar dos lenguas extranjeras
tú		jugar al béisbol

3 **Mi mejor amiga** Listen as Jennifer describes her best friend. Then indicate whether the following conclusions are **lógico** or **ilógico**, based on what you heard.

	Lógico	Ilógico
1. Jennifer y Laura son amigas.	○	○
2. Laura es antipática.	○	○
3. A Laura le gustan las lenguas extranjeras.	○	○
4. Laura prefiere comprar ropa cara.	○	○
5. Laura no tiene pasatiempos.	○	○
6. Laura conoce a muchas personas.	○	○

4 **Preguntas** Answer your partner's questions. Use complete sentences.

1. ¿Conoces a un(a) cantante famoso/a? ¿Te gusta cómo canta?
2. En tu familia, ¿quién sabe cantar bien? ¿Tu opinión es objetiva?
3. Y tú, ¿conduces bien o mal? ¿Y tus amigos?
4. Si un(a) amigo/a no conduce muy bien, ¿le ofreces crítica constructiva?
5. ¿Cómo parecen estar tus amigos hoy?

5 **Conocimientos** Tell about three things you know how to do, three places you are familiar with, and three people you know.

6 **Anuncio** Write an advertisement using two examples each of **saber** and **conocer**.

6.2 Indirect object pronouns

ANTE TODO   In **Lección 5**, you learned that a direct object receives the action of the verb directly. In contrast, an indirect object receives the action of the verb indirectly.

SUBJECT	I.O. PRONOUN	VERB	DIRECT OBJECT	INDIRECT OBJECT
Roberto	**le**	presta	cien pesos	**a Luisa**.
Roberto		*lends*	*100 pesos*	*to Luisa.*

An indirect object is a noun or pronoun that answers the question *to whom* or *for whom* an action is done. In the preceding example, the indirect object answers this question: **¿A quién le presta Roberto cien pesos?** *To whom does Roberto lend 100 pesos?*

Indirect object pronouns

Singular forms		Plural forms	
me	(to, for) *me*	**nos**	(to, for) *us*
te	(to, for) *you* (fam.)	**os**	(to, for) *you* (fam.)
le	(to, for) *you* (form.)	**les**	(to, for) *you*
	(to, for) *him; her*		(to, for) *them*

▶ **¡Atención!** The forms of indirect object pronouns for the first and second persons (**me**, **te**, **nos**, **os**) are the same as the direct object pronouns. Indirect object pronouns agree in number with the corresponding nouns, but not in gender.

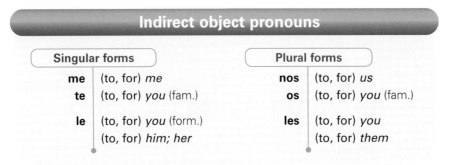

Using indirect object pronouns

▶ Spanish speakers commonly use both an indirect object pronoun and the noun to which it refers in the same sentence. This is done to emphasize and clarify to whom the pronoun refers.

I.O. PRONOUN	INDIRECT OBJECT	I.O. PRONOUN	INDIRECT OBJECT
Ella **le** vende la ropa **a Elena**.		**Les** prestamos el dinero **a Inés y a Álex**.	

▶ Indirect object pronouns are also used without the indirect object noun when the person for whom the action is being done is known.

Ana **le** presta la falda **a Elena**.   También **le** presta unos jeans.
Ana lends her skirt to Elena.   *She also lends her a pair of jeans.*

▶ Indirect object pronouns are usually placed before the conjugated form of the verb. In negative sentences the pronoun is placed between **no** and the conjugated verb.

CONSULTA

For more information on accents, see **Lección 4**, **Pronunciación**, p. 33.

Martín **me** compra un regalo.	Eva **no me** escribe cartas.
Martín is buying me a gift.	*Eva doesn't write me letters.*

▶ When a conjugated verb is followed by an infinitive or the present progressive, the indirect object pronoun may be placed before the conjugated verb or attached to the infinitive or present participle. **¡Atención!** When an indirect object pronoun is attached to a present participle, an accent mark is added to maintain the proper stress.

Él no quiere **pagarte**./	Él está **escribiéndole** una postal a ella./
Él no **te** quiere pagar.	Él **le** está escribiendo una postal a ella.
He does not want to pay you.	*He is writing a postcard to her.*

▶ Because the indirect object pronouns **le** and **les** have multiple meanings, Spanish speakers often clarify to whom the pronouns refer with the preposition **a** + [*pronoun*] or **a** + [*noun*].

UNCLARIFIED STATEMENTS	CLARIFIED STATEMENTS
Yo **le** compro un abrigo.	Yo **le** compro un abrigo **a usted/él/ella**.
Ella **le** describe un libro.	Ella **le** describe un libro **a Juan**.

UNCLARIFIED STATEMENTS	CLARIFIED STATEMENTS
Él **les** vende unos sombreros.	Él **les** vende unos sombreros **a ustedes/ellos/ellas**.
Ellos **les** hablan muy claro.	Ellos **les** hablan muy claro **a los clientes**.

▶ The irregular verbs **dar** (*to give*) and **decir** (*to say; to tell*) are often used with indirect object pronouns.

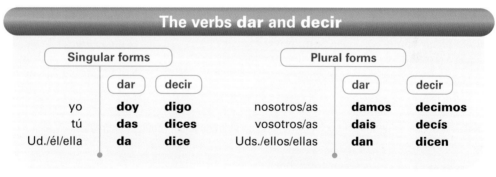

The verbs dar and decir

Singular forms	dar	decir	Plural forms	dar	decir
yo	**doy**	**digo**	nosotros/as	**damos**	**decimos**
tú	**das**	**dices**	vosotros/as	**dais**	**decís**
Ud./él/ella	**da**	**dice**	Uds./ellos/ellas	**dan**	**dicen**

Me dan una fiesta cada año.	**Te digo** la verdad.
They give (throw) me a party every year.	*I'm telling you the truth.*
Voy a **darle** consejos.	No **les digo** mentiras a mis padres.
I'm going to give her advice.	*I don't tell lies to my parents.*

¡INTÉNTALO!   Use the cues in parentheses to provide the correct indirect object pronoun for each sentence.

1. Juan _____le_____ quiere dar un regalo. (*to Elena*)
2. María _____ prepara un café. (*for us*)
3. Beatriz y Felipe _____ escriben desde (*from*) Cuba. (*to me*)
4. Marta y yo _____ compramos unos guantes. (*for them*)
5. Los vendedores _____ venden ropa. (*to you, fam. sing.*)
6. La dependienta _____ muestra los guantes. (*to us*)

Práctica

1 **Completar** Fill in the blanks with the correct pronouns to complete Mónica's description of her family's holiday shopping.

1. Juan y yo _____ damos una blusa a nuestra hermana Gisela.
2. Mi tía _____ da a nosotros una mesa para la casa.
3. Gisela _____ da dos corbatas a su papá.
4. A mi mamá yo _____ doy un par de guantes negros.
5. A mi profesora _____ doy dos libros de José Martí.
6. Juan _____ da un regalo a mis padres.
7. Mis padres _____ dan un traje nuevo a mí.
8. Y a ti, yo _____ doy un regalo también. ¿Quieres verlo?

◀

2 **En La Habana** Describe what happens on Pascual's trip to Cuba based on the cues provided.

1. ellos / cantar / canción / (mí)

2. él / comprar / libros / (sus hijos) / Plaza de Armas

3. yo / preparar el almuerzo (*lunch*) / (ti)

4. él / explicar cómo llegar / (conductor)

5. mi novia / sacar / foto / (nosotros)

6. el guía (*guide*) / mostrar / catedral de San Cristóbal / (ustedes)

◀

3 **Combinar** Use an item from each column and an indirect object pronoun to create logical sentences.

> **modelo**
> Mis padres les dan regalos a mis primos.

A	B	C	D
yo	comprar	mensajes electrónicos	mí
el dependiente	dar	corbata	ustedes
el profesor Arce	decir	dinero en efectivo	clienta
la vendedora	escribir	tarea	novia
mis padres	explicar	problemas	primos
tú	pagar	regalos	ti
nosotros/as	prestar	ropa	nosotros
¿?	vender	¿?	¿?

Comunicación

4 **Días locos** Gabriela is e-mailing her friend Sandra about her semester. Indicate whether the following conclusions are **lógico** or **ilógico**, based on what you read.

De:	Gabriela
Para:	Sandra
Asunto:	Días locos

Los profesores nos dan mucha tarea. ¡Vivo en la biblioteca! Mi mamá me escribe mensajes electrónicos cada dos horas. Obviamente, yo no tengo tiempo de contestarle, pero ¡ella no me entiende! Rodrigo, el hermano menor de Ana, viene a visitarme todo el tiempo y me da regalos. ¡También me canta! Le tengo que decir la verdad: ¡No quiero su atención!

	Lógico	Ilógico
1. Gabriela tiene muchos ratos libres.	○	○
2. La mamá de Gabriela está enojada con ella.	○	○
3. Rodrigo está enamorado de Gabriela.	○	○
4. Gabriela está enamorada de Rodrigo.	○	○
5. Rodrigo le debe dar más regalos a Gabriela.	○	○

5 **Entrevista** Answer your partner's questions.

1. ¿Qué tiendas, almacenes o centros comerciales prefieres?
2. ¿A quién le compras regalos cuando hay rebajas?
3. ¿A quién le prestas dinero cuando lo necesita?
4. ¿Me explicas cómo regatear?
5. ¿Te dan tus padres su tarjeta de crédito cuando vas de compras?

6 **¡Somos ricos!** You and another student chipped in on a lottery ticket and you won! Now you want to spend money on your loved ones. Write a paragraph telling what you plan to buy for your family and your friends.

> **modelo**
> Quiero comprarle un vestido de Carolina Herrera a mi madre...

Síntesis

7 **Minidrama** With a partner, role-play a conversation between a customer and a clerk in a clothing store. The customer should talk about the clothes he/she is looking for and for whom he/she is buying the clothes. The clerk should recommend different items based on the customer's descriptions. Use these expressions and also look at **Expresiones útiles** on page 105.

Me queda grande/pequeño. *It's big/small on me.*	**¿Está en rebaja?** *Is it on sale?*
¿Tiene otro color? *Do you have another color?*	**También estoy buscando...** *I'm also looking for...*

[6.3] Preterite tense of regular verbs

In order to talk about events in the past, Spanish uses two simple tenses: the preterite and the imperfect. In this lesson, you will learn how to form the preterite tense, which is used to express actions or states completed in the past.

Preterite of regular -ar, -er, and -ir verbs			
		-ar verbs	-er verbs	-ir verbs
		comprar	**vender**	**escribir**
SINGULAR FORMS	yo	compr**é** *I bought*	vend**í** *I sold*	escrib**í** *I wrote*
	tú	compr**aste**	vend**iste**	escrib**iste**
	Ud./él/ella	compr**ó**	vend**ió**	escrib**ió**
PLURAL FORMS	nosotros/as	compr**amos**	vend**imos**	escrib**imos**
	vosotros/as	compr**asteis**	vend**isteis**	escrib**isteis**
	Uds./ellos/ellas	compr**aron**	vend**ieron**	escrib**ieron**

▶ **¡Atención!** The **yo** and **Ud./él/ella** forms of all three conjugations have written accents on the last syllable to show that it is stressed.

▶ As the chart shows, the endings for regular **-er** and **-ir** verbs are identical in the preterite.

¿Qué compraste?

Compré estos aretes.

▶ Note that the **nosotros/as** forms of regular **-ar** and **-ir** verbs in the preterite are identical to the present tense forms. Context will help you determine which tense is being used.

En invierno **compramos** ropa.   Anoche **compramos** unos zapatos.
In the winter, we buy clothes.   *Last night we bought some shoes.*

▶ **-Ar** and **-er** verbs that have a stem change in the present tense are regular in the preterite. They do *not* have a stem change.

		PRESENT	PRETERITE
cerrar	(e:ie)	La tienda **cierra** a las seis.	La tienda **cerró** a las seis.
volver	(o:ue)	Carlitos **vuelve** tarde.	Carlitos **volvió** tarde.
jugar	(u:ue)	Él **juega** al fútbol.	Él **jugó** al fútbol.

▶ **¡Atención!** **-Ir** verbs that have a stem change in the present tense also have a stem change in the preterite.

▶ Verbs that end in **-car**, **-gar**, and **-zar** have a spelling change in the first person singular (**yo** form) in the preterite.

bus**car** ▶	bus**c**- ▶	**qu**- ▶	yo bus**qué**
lle**gar**	lle**g**-	**gu**-	yo lle**gué**
empe**zar**	empe**z**-	**c**-	yo empe**cé**

▶ Except for the **yo** form, all other forms of **-car**, **-gar**, and **-zar** verbs are regular in the preterite.

▶ Three other verbs—**creer**, **leer**, and **oír**—have spelling changes in the preterite. The **i** of the verb endings of **creer**, **leer**, and **oír** carries an accent in the **yo**, **tú**, **nosotros/as**, and **vosotros/as** forms, and changes to **y** in the **Ud./él/ella** and **Uds./ellos/ellas forms**.

creer ▶	cre- ▶	cre**í**, cre**í**ste, cre**y**ó, cre**í**mos, cre**í**steis, cre**y**eron
leer	le-	le**í**, le**í**ste, le**y**ó, le**í**mos, le**í**steis, le**y**eron
oír	o-	o**í**, o**í**ste, o**y**ó, o**í**mos, o**í**steis, o**y**eron

▶ **Ver** is regular in the preterite, but none of its forms has an accent.

ver ⟶ vi, viste, vio, vimos, visteis, vieron

Words commonly used with the preterite

anoche	*last night*	**pasado/a (adj.)**	*last; past*
anteayer	*the day before yesterday*	**el año pasado**	*last year*
		la semana pasada	*last week*
ayer	*yesterday*	**una vez**	*once*
de repente	*suddenly*	**dos veces**	*twice*
desde... hasta...	*from... until...*	**ya**	*already*

Ayer llegué a Santiago de Cuba.   **Anoche** oí un ruido extraño.
Yesterday I arrived in Santiago de Cuba.   *Last night I heard a strange noise.*

▶ **Acabar de** + [*infinitive*] is used to say that something has just occurred. Note that **acabar** is in the present tense in this construction.

Acabo de comprar una falda.   **Acabas de ir** de compras.
I just bought a skirt.   *You just went shopping.*

¡INTÉNTALO!   Provide the appropriate preterite forms of the verbs.

	comer	salir	comenzar	leer
1. ellas	comieron	salieron	comenzaron	leyeron
2. tú	_____	_____	_____	_____
3. usted	_____	_____	_____	_____
4. nosotros	_____	_____	_____	_____
5. yo	_____	_____	_____	_____

Práctica

1 **Completar** Andrea is talking about what happened last weekend. Complete each sentence by choosing the correct verb and putting it in the preterite.

1. El viernes a las cuatro de la tarde, la profesora Mora _____ (asistir, costar, usar) a una reunión (*meeting*) de profesores.
2. A la una, yo _____ (llegar, bucear, llevar) a la tienda con mis amigos.
3. Mis amigos y yo _____ (comprar, regatear, gastar) dos o tres cosas.
4. Yo _____ (costar, comprar, escribir) unos pantalones negros y mi amigo Mateo _____ (gastar, pasear, comprar) una camisa azul.
5. Después, nosotros _____ (llevar, vivir, comer) cerca de un mercado.
6. A las tres, Pepe _____ (hablar, pasear, nadar) con su amiga por teléfono.
7. El sábado por la tarde, mi mamá _____ (escribir, beber, vivir) una carta.
8. El domingo mi tía _____ (decidir, salir, escribir) comprarme un traje.
9. A las cuatro de la tarde, mi tía _____ (beber, salir, encontrar) el traje y después nosotras _____ (acabar, ver, salir) una película.

2 **Preguntas** Imagine that you have a pesky friend who keeps asking you questions. Respond that you already did or have just done what he/she asks. Make sure you and your partner take turns playing the role of the pesky friend and responding to his/her questions.

> **modelo**
>
> leer la lección
> **Estudiante 1:** ¿Leíste la lección?
> **Estudiante 2:** Sí, ya la leí./Sí, acabo de leerla.

1. escribir el mensaje electrónico
2. lavar (*to wash*) la ropa
3. oír las noticias (*news*)
4. comprar pantalones cortos
5. practicar los verbos
6. pagar la cuenta (*bill*)
7. empezar la composición
8. ver la película *Diarios de motocicleta*

3 **¿Cuándo?** Use the time expressions from the word bank to talk about when you and others did the activities listed.

anoche	anteayer	el mes pasado	una vez
ayer	la semana pasada	el año pasado	dos veces

1. mi maestro/a: llegar tarde a clase
2. mi mejor (*best*) amigo/a: salir con un(a) chico/a guapo/a
3. mis padres: ver una película
4. yo: llevar un traje/vestido
5. el presidente/primer ministro de mi país: asistir a una conferencia internacional
6. mis amigos y yo: comer en un restaurante
7. ¿?: comprar algo (*something*) bueno, bonito y barato

Comunicación

4

🔊

¿Estás listo? Listen to the conversation between Matilde and Hernán. Then indicate whether the following conclusions are **lógico** or **ilógico**, based on what you heard.

	Lógico	Ilógico
1. Hernán compró un pasaje de ida y vuelta.	○	○
2. Matilde va a viajar con Hernán.	○	○
3. Hernán buscó su pasaporte.	○	○
4. Los documentos personales de Hernán están en su mochila.	○	○
5. Hernán tiene mucho equipaje.	○	○

5

👥

Ayer Tell your partner at what time you did these activities yesterday.

1. desayunar
2. salir de la casa
3. almorzar
4. ver a un(a) amigo/a
5. volver a la casa
6. cenar

6

Las vacaciones Imagine that you took these photos on a vacation with friends. Use the pictures to describe the trip.

7

Mi última compra Write a short paragraph describing the last time you went shopping. Use at least four verbs in the preterite tense.

Síntesis

8

👥

Conversación With a partner, talk about what you did last week. Don't forget to include school activities, shopping, and pastimes.

6.4 Demonstrative adjectives and pronouns

Demonstrative adjectives

ANTE TODO   In Spanish, as in English, demonstrative adjectives are words that "demonstrate" or "point out" nouns. Demonstrative adjectives precede the nouns they modify and, like other Spanish adjectives you have studied, agree with them in gender and number. Observe these examples and then study the chart below.

esta camisa	**ese** vendedor	**aquellos** zapatos
this shirt	*that salesman*	*those shoes (over there)*

Demonstrative adjectives

Singular		Plural		
MASCULINE	FEMININE	MASCULINE	FEMININE	
este	**esta**	**estos**	**estas**	*this; these*
ese	**esa**	**esos**	**esas**	*that; those*
aquel	**aquella**	**aquellos**	**aquellas**	*that; those (over there)*

▶ There are three sets of demonstrative adjectives. To determine which one to use, you must establish the relationship between the speaker and the noun(s) being pointed out.

▶ The demonstrative adjectives **este**, **esta**, **estos**, and **estas** are used to point out things that are close to the speaker and the listener.

Me gustan estos zapatos.

▶ The demonstrative adjectives **ese**, **esa**, **esos**, and **esas** are used to point out things that are not close in space and time to the speaker. They may, however, be close to the listener.

Prefiero esos zapatos.

▶ The demonstrative adjectives **aquel**, **aquella**, **aquellos**, and **aquellas** are used to point out things that are far away from the speaker and the listener.

Aquel auto es de mi hermana.

Demonstrative pronouns

▶ Demonstrative pronouns are identical to their corresponding demonstrative adjectives, with the exception that they traditionally carry an accent mark on the stressed vowel. The **Real Academia** no longer requires this accent, but it is still commonly used.

Demonstrative pronouns			
Singular		**Plural**	
MASCULINE	FEMININE	MASCULINE	FEMININE
éste	**ésta**	**éstos**	**éstas**
ése	**ésa**	**ésos**	**ésas**
aquél	**aquélla**	**aquéllos**	**aquéllas**

—¿Quieres comprar **este suéter**?
Do you want to buy this sweater?

—No, no quiero **éste**. Quiero **ése**.
No, I don't want this one. I want that one.

—¿Vas a leer **estas revistas**?
Are you going to read these magazines?

—Sí, voy a leer **éstas**. También voy a leer **aquéllas**.
Yes, I'm going to read these. I'll also read those (over there).

▶ **¡Atención!** Like demonstrative adjectives, demonstrative pronouns agree in gender and number with the corresponding noun.

Este libro es de Pablito.   **Éstos** son de Juana.

▶ There are three neuter demonstrative pronouns: **esto**, **eso**, and **aquello**. These forms refer to unidentified or unspecified things, situations, ideas, and concepts. They do not change in gender or number and never carry an accent mark.

—¿Qué es **esto**?
What's this?

—**Eso** es interesante.
That's interesting.

—**Aquello** es bonito.
That's pretty.

¡INTÉNTALO!   Provide the correct form of the demonstrative adjective for these nouns.

1. la falda / este _____ *esta falda* _____
2. los estudiantes / este _____
3. los países / aquel _____
4. la ventana / ese _____

5. los periodistas / ese _____
6. el chico / aquel _____
7. las sandalias / este _____
8. las chicas / aquel _____

Práctica

1 **Cambiar** Make the singular sentences plural and the plural sentences singular.

> **modelo**
>
> Estas camisas son blancas.
> Esta camisa es blanca.

1. Aquellos sombreros son muy elegantes.
2. Ese abrigo es muy caro.
3. Estos cinturones son hermosos.
4. Esos precios son muy buenos.
5. Estas faldas son muy cortas.
6. ¿Quieres ir a aquel almacén?
7. Esas blusas son baratas.
8. Esta corbata hace juego con mi traje.

2 **Completar** Here are some things people might say while shopping. Complete the sentences with the correct demonstrative pronouns.

1. No me gustan esos zapatos. Voy a comprar _____. (*these*)
2. ¿Vas a comprar ese traje o _____? (*this one*)
3. Esta guayabera es bonita, pero prefiero _____. (*that one*)
4. Estas corbatas rojas son muy bonitas, pero _____ son fabulosas. (*those*)
5. Estos cinturones cuestan demasiado. Prefiero _____. (*those over there*)
6. ¿Te gustan esas botas o _____? (*these*)
7. Esa bolsa roja es bonita, pero prefiero _____. (*that one over there*)
8. No voy a comprar estas botas; voy a comprar _____. (*those over there*)
9. ¿Prefieres estos pantalones o _____? (*those*)
10. Me gusta este vestido, pero voy a comprar _____. (*that one*)
11. Me gusta ese almacén, pero _____ es mejor (*better*). (*that one over there*)
12. Esa blusa es bonita, pero cuesta demasiado. Voy a comprar _____. (*this one*)

3 **Describir** Look for two items that are one of these colors: **amarillo**, **azul**, **blanco**, **marrón**, **negro**, **verde**, **rojo**. Point them out, first using demonstrative adjectives, and then demonstrative pronouns.

> **modelo**
>
> azul
> Esta silla es azul. Aquella mochila es azul.
> Ésta es azul. Aquélla es azul.

Comunicación

4
🔊

De compras Listen to the conversation between Alejandra and a clerk. Then indicate whether the following conclusions are **lógico** or **ilógico**, based on what you heard.

	Lógico	Ilógico
1. A Alejandra no le gusta llevar faldas.	○	○
2. Alejandra va a comprar la blusa blanca.	○	○
3. La dependienta trabaja en un almacén.	○	○
4. A Alejandra le gustan los colores azul y gris.	○	○
5. El cinturón negro es muy caro.	○	○
6. Alejandra va a comprar una cartera también.	○	○

5
👥

En una tienda Imagine that you and a partner are in Madrid shopping at Zara. Study the floor plan, then have a conversation about your surroundings. Use demonstrative adjectives and pronouns.

modelo

Estudiante 1: Me gusta este suéter azul.
Estudiante 2: Yo prefiero aquella chaqueta.

Zara is an international clothing company based in Spain. Its innovative processes take a product from the design room to the manufacturing shelves in less than a month. This means that the merchandise is constantly changing to keep up with the most current trends.

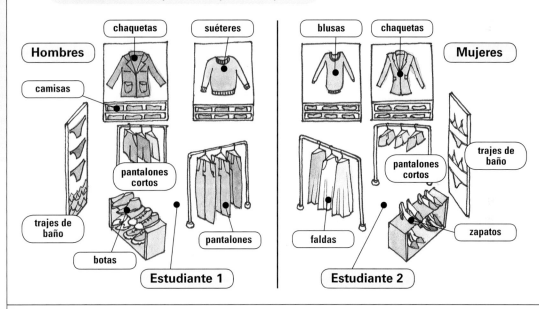

Síntesis

6

En el café Write a conversation between two people sitting at a busy sidewalk café. Use as many demonstrative adjectives and pronouns as possible to describe the people and things around them.

modelo

Carmen: Esa corbata es fea, ¿no?
Susana: Sí. No me gustan las corbatas rosadas y verdes. Y ese traje...

Recapitulación

RESUMEN GRAMATICAL

Review the grammar concepts you have learned in this lesson by completing these activities.

1   **Completar** Complete the chart with the correct preterite or infinitive form of the verbs. `30 pts.`

Infinitive	yo	ella	ellos
			tomaron
		abrió	
comprender			
	leí		
pagar			

2   **En la tienda** Look at the drawing and complete the conversation with demonstrative adjectives and pronouns. `14 pts.`

CLIENTE Buenos días, señorita. Deseo comprar (1) _____ corbata.

VENDEDORA Muy bien, señor. ¿No le interesa mirar (2) _____ trajes que están allá? Hay unos que hacen juego con la corbata.

CLIENTE (3) _____ de allá son de lana, ¿no? Prefiero ver (4) _____ traje marrón que está detrás de usted.

VENDEDORA Estupendo. Como puede ver, es de seda. Cuesta seiscientos cincuenta dólares.

CLIENTE Ah… eh… no, creo que sólo voy a comprar la corbata, gracias.

VENDEDORA Bueno… si busca algo más económico, hay rebaja en (5) _____ sombreros. Cuestan sólo treinta dólares.

CLIENTE ¡Magnífico! Me gusta (6) _____, el blanco que está hasta arriba (*at the top*). Y quiero pagar todo con (7) _____ tarjeta.

VENDEDORA Sí, señor. Ahora mismo le traigo el sombrero.

6.1   **Saber and conocer**   *p. 110*

saber	conocer
sé	conozco
sabes	conoces
sabe	conoce
sabemos	conocemos
sabéis	conocéis
saben	conocen

▶ **saber** = to know facts/how to do something

▶ **conocer** = to know a person, place, or thing

6.2   **Indirect object pronouns**   *pp. 112–113*

Indirect object pronouns

Singular	Plural
me	nos
te	os
le	les

▶ **dar** = doy, das, da, damos, dais, dan

▶ **decir (e:i)** = digo, dices, dice, decimos, decís, dicen

6.3   **Preterite tense of regular verbs**   *pp. 116–117*

comprar	vender	escribir
compré	vendí	escribí
compraste	vendiste	escribiste
compró	vendió	escribió
compramos	vendimos	escribimos
comprasteis	vendisteis	escribisteis
compraron	vendieron	escribieron

Verbs with spelling changes in the preterite

▶ **-car:** buscar → yo busqué

▶ **-gar:** llegar → yo llegué

▶ **-zar:** empezar → yo empecé

▶ **creer:** creí, creíste, creyó, creímos, creísteis, creyeron

▶ **leer:** leí, leíste, leyó, leímos, leísteis, leyeron

▶ **oír:** oí, oíste, oyó, oímos, oísteis, oyeron

▶ **ver:** vi, viste, vio, vimos, visteis, vieron

3 ¿Saber o conocer? Complete each dialogue with the correct form of **saber** or **conocer**. `20 pts.`

1. —¿Qué _____ hacer tú?
   —(Yo) _____ jugar al fútbol.
2. —¿_____ tú esta tienda de ropa?
   —No, (yo) no la _____. ¿Es buena?
3. —¿Tus amigos no _____ a tu hermana?
   —No, ¡ellos no _____ que tengo una hermana!
4. —Mi maestra todavía no me _____ bien.
   —Y tú, ¿la quieres _____ a ella?
5. —¿_____ ustedes dónde está el mercado?
   —No, nosotros no _____ bien esta ciudad.

6.4 Demonstrative adjectives and pronouns *pp. 120–121*

Demonstrative adjectives

Singular		Plural	
Masc.	Fem.	Masc.	Fem.
este	esta	estos	estas
ese	esa	esos	esas
aquel	aquella	aquellos	aquellas

Demonstrative pronouns

Singular		Plural	
Masc.	Fem.	Masc.	Fem.
éste	ésta	éstos	éstas
ése	ésa	ésos	ésas
aquél	aquélla	aquéllos	aquéllas

4 Oraciones Form complete sentences using the information provided. Use indirect object pronouns and the present tense of the verbs. `32 pts.`

1. Javier / prestar / el abrigo / a Maripili
   _____
2. nosotros / vender / ropa / a los clientes
   _____
3. el vendedor / traer / las camisetas / a mis amigos y a mí
   _____
4. yo / querer dar / consejos / a ti
   _____
5. ¿tú / ir a comprar / un regalo / a mí?
   _____
6. el dependiente / mostrar / las corbatas / a Santiago
   _____
7. los hijos / pedir / dinero / a sus padres
   _____
8. la profesora / escribir / mensajes electrónicos / a nosotros
   _____

5 Poema Write the missing words to complete the excerpt from the poem *Romance sonámbulo* by Federico García Lorca. `4 pts.`

" Verde que _____ quiero verde.
Verde viento. Verdes ramas°.
El barco sobre la mar
y el caballo en la montaña, [...]
Verde que te quiero _____ (*green*). "

ramas *branches*

Lectura

Antes de leer

Estrategia
Skimming

Skimming involves quickly reading through a document to absorb its general meaning. This allows you to understand the main ideas without having to read word for word. When you skim a text, you might want to look at its title and subtitles. You might also want to read the first sentence of each paragraph.

Examinar el texto

Look at the format of the reading selection. How is it organized? What does the organization of the document tell you about its content?

Buscar cognados

Scan the reading selection to locate at least five cognates. Based on the cognates, what do you think the reading selection is about?

1. _____   4. _____

2. _____   5. _____

3. _____

The reading selection is about _____.

Impresiones generales

Now skim the reading selection to understand its general meaning. Jot down your impressions. What new information did you learn about the document by skimming it? Based on all the information you now have, answer these questions in Spanish.

1. Who created this document?

2. What is its purpose?

3. Who is its intended audience?

Corona

http://corona.cl

Corona
¡Corona tiene las ofertas más locas del verano!

La tienda más elegante de la ciudad con precios increíbles

niños | **mujeres** | casa | baño | equipaje

Faldas largas
ROPA BONITA
Algodón. De distintos colores
Talla mediana
Precio especial: 8.000 pesos

Blusas de seda
BAMBÚ
De cuadros y de lunares
Ahora: 21.000 pesos
40% de rebaja

Vestido de algodón
PANAMÁ
Colores blanco, azul y verde
Ahora: 18.000 pesos
30% de rebaja

Accesorios
BELLEZA
Cinturones, gafas de sol, sombreros, medias
Diversos estilos
Todos con un 40% de rebaja

Carteras
ELEGANCIA
Colores anaranjado, blanco, rosado y amarillo
Ahora: 15.000 pesos
50% de rebaja

Sandalias de playa
GINO
Números del 35 al 38
A sólo 12.000 pesos
50% de descuento

Lunes a sábado de 9 a 21 horas.
Domingo de 10 a 14 horas.

Real° Liquidación ¡Grandes rebajas!
¡La rebaja está de moda en Corona!

y con la tarjeta de crédito más conveniente del mercado.

bebé | **hombres** | jardín | joyas | electrónica

Chaquetas CASINO
Microfibra. Colores negro, café y gris
Tallas: P, M, G, XG
Ahora: 22.500 pesos

Traje inglés GALES
Modelos originales
Ahora: 105.000 pesos
30% de rebaja

Pantalones OCÉANO
Colores negro, gris y café
Ahora: 11.500 pesos
30% de rebaja

Accesorios GUAPO
Gafas de sol, corbatas, cinturones, calcetines
Diversos estilos
Todos con un 40% de rebaja

Zapatos COLOR
Italianos y franceses
Números del 40 al 45
A sólo 20.000 pesos

Ropa interior ATLÁNTICO
Tallas: P, M, G
Colores blanco, negro y gris
40% de rebaja

Real *Royal* **Liquidación** *Clearance sale*

Por la compra de 40.000 pesos, puede llevar un regalo gratis.
- Un hermoso cinturón de mujer
- Un par de calcetines
- Una corbata de seda
- Una bolsa para la playa
- Una mochila
- Unas medias

Después de leer

Completar
Complete this paragraph about the reading selection with the correct forms of the words from the word bank.

almacén	hacer juego	tarjeta de crédito
caro	increíble	tienda
dinero	pantalones	verano
falda	rebaja	zapato

En este anuncio, el _____ Corona anuncia la liquidación de _____ con grandes _____. Con muy poco _____ usted puede conseguir ropa fina y elegante. Si no tiene dinero en efectivo, puede utilizar su _____ y pagar luego. Para el caballero con gustos refinados, hay _____ importados de París y Roma. La señora elegante puede encontrar blusas de seda que _____ con todo tipo de _____ o _____. Los precios de esta liquidación son realmente _____.

¿Cierto o falso?
Indicate whether each statement is **cierto** or **falso**. Correct the false statements.
1. Hay sandalias de playa.
2. Las corbatas tienen una rebaja del 30%.
3. El almacén Corona tiene un departamento de zapatos.
4. Normalmente las sandalias cuestan 22.000 pesos.
5. Cuando gastas 30.000 pesos en la tienda, llevas un regalo gratis.
6. Tienen carteras amarillas.

Preguntas
Answer these questions.
1. Imagina que vas a ir a la tienda Corona. ¿Qué departamentos vas a visitar? ¿El departamento de ropa para señoras, el departamento de ropa para caballeros…?
2. ¿Qué vas a buscar en Corona?
3. ¿Hay tiendas similares a la tienda Corona en tu pueblo o ciudad? ¿Cómo se llaman? ¿Tienen muchas gangas?

Escritura

Estrategia

How to report an interview

There are several ways to prepare a written report about an interview. For example, you can transcribe the interview verbatim, you can simply summarize it, or you can summarize it but quote the speakers occasionally. In any event, the report should begin with an interesting title and a brief introduction, which may include the five Ws (*what, where, when, who, why*) and the H (*how*) of the interview. The report should end with an interesting conclusion. Note that when you transcribe dialogue in Spanish, you should pay careful attention to format and punctuation.

Writing dialogue in Spanish

- If you need to transcribe an interview verbatim, you can use speakers' names to indicate a change of speaker.

CARMELA	¿Qué compraste? ¿Encontraste muchas gangas?
ROBERTO	Sí, muchas. Compré un suéter, una camisa y dos corbatas. Y tú, ¿qué compraste?
CARMELA	Una blusa y una falda muy bonitas. ¿Cuánto costó tu camisa?
ROBERTO	Sólo diez dólares. ¿Cuánto costó tu blusa?
CARMELA	Veinte dólares.

- You can also use a dash (*raya*) to mark the beginning of each speaker's words.

—¿Qué compraste?

—Un suéter y una camisa muy bonitos. Y tú, ¿encontraste muchas gangas?

—Sí... compré dos blusas, tres camisetas y un par de zapatos.

—¡A ver!

Tema

Escribe un informe

Write a report for the school newspaper about an interview you conducted with a student about his or her shopping habits and clothing preferences. First, brainstorm a list of interview questions. Then conduct the interview using the questions below as a guide, but feel free to ask other questions as they occur to you.

Examples of questions:

▶ ¿Cuándo vas de compras?

▶ ¿Adónde vas de compras?

▶ ¿Con quién vas de compras?

▶ ¿Qué tiendas, almacenes o centros comerciales prefieres?

▶ ¿Compras ropa de catálogos o por Internet?

▶ ¿Prefieres comprar ropa cara o barata? ¿Por qué? ¿Te gusta buscar gangas?

▶ ¿Qué ropa llevas cuando vas a clase?

▶ ¿Qué ropa llevas cuando sales a bailar?

▶ ¿Qué ropa llevas cuando practicas un deporte?

▶ ¿Cuáles son tus colores favoritos? ¿Compras mucha ropa de esos colores?

▶ ¿Les das ropa a tu familia o a tus amigos/as?

Escuchar

Estrategia
Listening for linguistic cues

You can enhance your listening comprehension by listening for specific linguistic cues. For example, if you listen for the endings of conjugated verbs, or for familiar constructions, such as **acabar de** + [*infinitive*] or **ir a** + [*infinitive*], you can find out whether an event already took place, is taking place now, or will take place in the future. Verb endings also give clues about who is participating in the action.

🔊 To practice listening for linguistic cues, you will now listen to four sentences. As you listen, note whether each sentence refers to a past, present, or future action. Also jot down the subject of each sentence.

Preparación

Based on the photograph, what do you think Marisol has recently done? What do you think Marisol and Alicia are talking about? What else can you guess about their conversation from the visual clues in the photograph?

Ahora escucha 🔊

Now you are going to hear Marisol and Alicia's conversation. Make a list of the clothing items that each person mentions. Then put a check mark after the item if the person actually purchased it.

Marisol	Alicia
1. _____	1. _____
2. _____	2. _____
3. _____	3. _____
4. _____	4. _____

Comprensión

¿Cierto o falso?
Indicate whether each statement is **cierto** or **falso.** Then correct the false statements.

1. Marisol y Alicia acaban de ir de compras juntas (*together*).
2. Marisol va a comprar unos pantalones y una blusa mañana.
3. Marisol compró una blusa de cuadros.
4. Alicia compró unos zapatos nuevos hoy.
5. Alicia y Marisol van a ir al café.
6. Marisol gastó todo el dinero de la semana en ropa nueva.

Preguntas
Answer the following questions. Be sure to explain your answers.

1. ¿Crees que Alicia y Marisol son buenas amigas? ¿Por qué?
2. ¿Cuál de las dos estudiantes es más ahorradora (*frugal*)? ¿Por qué?
3. ¿Crees que a Alicia le gusta la ropa que Marisol compró?
4. ¿Crees que la moda es importante para Alicia? ¿Para Marisol? ¿Por qué?
5. ¿Es importante para ti estar a la moda? ¿Por qué?

en pantalla

Preparación

Answer these questions in Spanish.

1. ¿Cómo eres? Escribe tres adjetivos que te describan.
2. ¿Qué actividades ilustran (*illustrates*) tu personalidad?

El Pais de Siempre Jugar

Juguettos, first established in Villena (Comunidad de Valencia), Spain, in the 1980s, now has chain stores all over the country. Juguettos offers both brand-name toys you would recognize (and maybe own) and those that specifically cater to a child's life and cultural experiences in Spain. When children dreaming of the perfect toy look in a Juguettos catalog, they may be looking for Legos® but also for Nenittos® or Hazlo tú®. But children's toys, like their imaginations, are very similar throughout the world. Indeed, the company declares it has founded its own "country," el País de Siempre Jugar.

Anuncio de jueguetería Juguettos

generosa

Me lo pido.

Vocabulario útil

copionas	*copycats*
despistado/a	*distracted*
sean	*they may be*
pidan	*they may ask for*

Comprensión

Match the personality trait with its visual representation in the ad.

_____ 1. valiente
_____ 2. galáctico/a
_____ 3. artista
_____ 4. generoso/a
_____ 5. intrépido/a

a. Tienen una batalla (*battle*) imaginaria.
b. Le compra juguetes a su mascota (*pet*).
c. Está en un cartón con forma de nave espacial (*spaceship*).
d. Hacen música con parte de una basurera (*trashcan*).
e. Imagina que puede volar (*fly*).

Conversación

Answer these questions with a classmate.

1. ¿Qué quieres hacer ahora en tu vida que no haces? ¿Por qué lo quieres hacer?
2. ¿Por qué es importante la imaginación en la vida de los niños?
3. ¿Qué importancia tiene la imaginación en la vida de los adultos?

Aplicación

The Spanish poet Gustavo Adolfo Bécquer wrote, **"Él que tiene imaginación, con qué facilidad saca de la nada un mundo."** Working with a partner, discuss your understanding of the quote. Then prepare and present a skit in Spanish that illustrates its point.

Comprar en los mercados

In the Spanish-speaking world, most city dwellers shop at large supermarkets and little stores that specialize in just one item, such as a butcher shop (**carnicería**), vegetable market (**verdulería**), perfume shop (**perfumería**), or hat shop (**sombrerería**). In small towns where supermarkets are less common, many people rely exclusively on specialty shops. This requires shopping more frequently—often every day or every other day for perishable items—but also means that the foods they consume are fresher and the goods are usually locally produced. Each neighborhood generally has its own shops, so people don't have to walk far to find fresh bread (at a **panadería**) for the midday meal.

Vocabulario útil	
colones (pl.)	*currency from Costa Rica*
¿Cuánto vale?	*¿Cuánto cuesta?*
descuento	*discount*
disculpe	*excuse me*
¿Dónde queda...?	*Where is... located?*
los helados	*ice cream*
el regateo	*bargaining*

Trescientos colones.

Preparación

Have you ever been to an open-air market? What did you buy? Have you ever negotiated a price? What did you say?

Comprensión

Select the option that best summarizes this episode.

a. Randy Cruz va al mercado al aire libre para comprar papayas. Luego va al Mercado Central. Él les pregunta a varios clientes qué compran, prueba (*tastes*) platos típicos y busca la heladería.

b. Randy Cruz va al mercado al aire libre para comprar papayas y pedir un descuento. Luego va al Mercado Central para preguntarles a los clientes qué compran en los mercados.

... pero me hace un buen descuento.

¿Qué compran en el Mercado Central?

Cuba

El país en cifras

▸ **Área**: 110.860 km² (42.803 millas²),
aproximadamente el área de Pensilvania
▸ **Población**: 11.061.886
▸ **Capital**: La Habana—2.116.000

La Habana Vieja fue declarada° Patrimonio° Cultural de la Humanidad por la UNESCO en 1982. Este distrito es uno de los lugares más fascinantes de Cuba. En La Plaza de Armas, se puede visitar el majestuoso Palacio de Capitanes Generales, que ahora es un museo. En la calle° Obispo, frecuentada por el autor Ernest Hemingway, hay hermosos cafés, clubes nocturnos y tiendas elegantes.

▸ **Ciudades principales**: Santiago de Cuba; Camagüey; Holguín; Guantánamo
▸ **Moneda**: peso cubano
▸ **Idiomas**: español (oficial)

Bandera de Cuba

Cubanos célebres

▸ **Carlos Finlay,** doctor y científico (1833–1915)
▸ **José Martí,** político y poeta (1853–1895)
▸ **Fidel Castro,** ex primer ministro, ex comandante en jefe° de las fuerzas armadas (1926–)
▸ **Zoé Valdés,** escritora (1959–)
▸ **Ibrahim Ferrer,** músico (1927–2005)
▸ **Carlos Acosta,** bailarín (1973–)

fue declarada *was declared* Patrimonio *Heritage* calle *street*
comandante en jefe *commander in chief* liviano *light*
colibrí abeja *bee hummingbird* ave *bird* mundo *world*
miden *measure* pesan *weigh*

Golfo de México

ESTADOS UNIDOS

Gran Teatro de La Habana

Los coco taxis son un medio de transporte cubano muy popular.

Océano Atlántico

Plaza del Capitolio

La Habana

Cordillera de los Órganos

ESTADOS UNIDOS

CUBA

OCÉANO PACÍFICO

OCÉANO ATLÁNTICO

AMÉRICA DEL SUR

Isla de la Juventud

Mar Caribe

Camagüey

La música es parte esencial de la vida en Cuba.

¡Increíble pero cierto!

Pequeño y liviano°, el colibrí abeja° de Cuba es una de las más de 320 especies de colibrí y es también el ave° más pequeña del mundo°. Menores que muchos insectos, estas aves minúsculas miden° 5 centímetros y pesan° sólo 1,95 gramos.

Baile • Ballet Nacional de Cuba

La bailarina Alicia Alonso fundó el Ballet Nacional de Cuba en 1948, después de° convertirse en una estrella° internacional en el Ballet de Nueva York y en Broadway. El Ballet Nacional de Cuba es famoso en todo el mundo por su creatividad y perfección técnica.

Economía • La caña de azúcar y el tabaco

La caña de azúcar° es el producto agrícola° que más se cultiva en la isla y su exportación es muy importante para la economía del país. El tabaco, que se usa para fabricar los famosos puros° cubanos, es otro cultivo° de mucha importancia.

Gente • Población

La población cubana tiene raíces° muy heterogéneas. La inmigración a la isla fue determinante° desde la colonia hasta mediados° del siglo° XX. Los cubanos de hoy son descendientes de africanos, europeos, chinos y antillanos, entre otros.

Música • Buena Vista Social Club

En 1997 nace° el fenómeno musical conocido como *Buena Vista Social Club*. Este proyecto reúne° a un grupo de importantes músicos de Cuba, la mayoría ya mayores, con una larga trayectoria interpretando canciones clásicas del son° cubano. Ese mismo año ganaron un *Grammy*. Hoy en día estos músicos son conocidos en todo el mundo, y personas de todas las edades bailan al ritmo° de su música.

Holguín

Santiago de Cuba
Guantánamo

Sierra Maestra

¿Qué aprendiste? Responde a las preguntas con una oración completa.
1. ¿Qué autor está asociado con la Habana Vieja?
2. ¿Por qué es famoso el Ballet Nacional de Cuba?
3. ¿Cuáles son los dos cultivos más importantes para la economía cubana?
4. ¿Qué fabrican los cubanos con la planta del tabaco?
5. ¿De dónde son muchos de los inmigrantes que llegaron a Cuba?
6. ¿En qué año ganó un *Grammy* el disco *Buena Vista Social Club*?

Conexión Internet Investiga estos temas en Internet.
1. Busca información sobre un(a) cubano/a célebre. ¿Por qué es célebre? ¿Qué hace? ¿Todavía vive en Cuba?
2. Busca información sobre una de las ciudades principales de Cuba. ¿Qué atracciones hay en esta ciudad?

después de *after* estrella *star* caña de azúcar *sugar cane* agrícola *farming* puros *cigars* cultivo *crop* raíces *roots* determinante *deciding* mediados *halfway through* siglo *century* nace *is born* reúne *gets together* son *Cuban musical genre* ritmo *rhythm*

La ropa

el abrigo	coat
los (blue)jeans	jeans
la blusa	blouse
la bolsa	purse; bag
la bota	boot
los calcetines (el calcetín)	sock(s)
la camisa	shirt
la camiseta	t-shirt
la cartera	wallet
la chaqueta	jacket
el cinturón	belt
la corbata	tie
la falda	skirt
las gafas (de sol)	(sun)glasses
los guantes	gloves
el impermeable	raincoat
las medias	pantyhose; stockings
los pantalones	pants
los pantalones cortos	shorts
la ropa	clothes
la ropa interior	underwear
las sandalias	sandals
el sombrero	hat
el suéter	sweater
el traje	suit
el traje de baño	bathing suit
el vestido	dress
los zapatos de tenis	sneakers

Verbos

conducir	to drive
conocer	to know; to be acquainted with
dar	to give
ofrecer	to offer
parecer	to seem
saber	to know; to know how
traducir	to translate

Ir de compras

el almacén	department store
la caja	cash register
el centro comercial	shopping mall
el/la cliente/a	customer
el/la dependiente/a	clerk
el dinero	money
(en) efectivo	cash
el mercado (al aire libre)	(open-air) market
un par (de zapatos)	a pair (of shoes)
el precio (fijo)	(fixed; set) price
la rebaja	sale
el regalo	gift
la tarjeta de crédito	credit card
la tienda	store
el/la vendedor(a)	salesperson
costar (o:ue)	to cost
gastar	to spend (money)
hacer juego (con)	to match (with)
llevar	to wear; to take
pagar	to pay
regatear	to bargain
usar	to wear; to use
vender	to sell

Adjetivos

barato/a	cheap
bueno/a	good
cada	each
caro/a	expensive
corto/a	short (in length)
elegante	elegant
hermoso/a	beautiful
largo/a	long
loco/a	crazy
nuevo/a	new
otro/a	other; another
pobre	poor
rico/a	rich

Los colores

el color	color
amarillo/a	yellow
anaranjado/a	orange
azul	blue
blanco/a	white
gris	gray
marrón, café	brown
morado/a	purple
negro/a	black
rojo/a	red
rosado/a	pink
verde	green

Palabras adicionales

acabar de (+ inf.)	to have just done something
anoche	last night
anteayer	the day before yesterday
ayer	yesterday
de repente	suddenly
desde	from
dos veces	twice
hasta	until
pasado/a (adj.)	last; past
el año pasado	last year
la semana pasada	last week
prestar	to lend; to loan
una vez	once
ya	already

Indirect object pronouns	See page 112.
Demonstrative adjectives and pronouns	See page 120.
Expresiones útiles	See page 105.

Vocabulario

Guide to Vocabulary

Note on alphabetization

For purposes of alphabetization, **ch** and **ll** are not treated as separate letters, but **ñ** follows **n**. Therefore, in this glossary you will find that **año**, for example, appears after **anuncio**.

Abbreviations used in this glossary

adj.	adjective	*form.*	formal	*pl.*	plural
adv.	adverb	*indef.*	indefinite	*poss.*	possessive
art.	article	*interj.*	interjection	*prep.*	preposition
conj.	conjunction	*i.o.*	indirect object	*pron.*	pronoun
def.	definite	*m.*	masculine	*ref.*	reflexive
d.o.	direct object	*n.*	noun	*sing.*	singular
f.	feminine	*obj.*	object	*sub.*	subject
fam.	familiar	*p.p.*	past participle	*v.*	verb

Spanish–English

A

a *prep.* at; to 1.1
  ¿A qué hora...? At what time...? 1.1
  a bordo aboard
  a dieta on a diet 3.3
  a la derecha de to the right of 1.2
  a la izquierda de to the left of 1.2
  a la plancha grilled 2.2
  a la(s) + *time* at + *time* 1.1
  a menos que *conj.* unless 3.1
  a menudo *adv.* often 2.4
  a nombre de in the name of 1.5
  a plazos in installments 3.2
  A sus órdenes. At your service.
  a tiempo *adv.* on time 2.4
  a veces *adv.* sometimes 2.4
  a ver let's see
abeja *f.* bee
abierto/a *adj.* open 1.5, 3.2
abogado/a *m., f.* lawyer 3.4
abrazar(se) *v.* to hug; to embrace (each other) 2.5
abrazo *m.* hug
abrigo *m.* coat 1.6
abril *m.* April 1.5
abrir *v.* to open 1.3
abuelo/a *m., f.* grandfather/grandmother 1.3
abuelos *pl.* grandparents 1.3
aburrido/a *adj.* bored; boring 1.5
aburrir *v.* to bore 2.1
aburrirse *v.* to get bored 3.5
acabar de (+ *inf.*) *v.* to have just done something 1.6
acampar *v.* to camp 1.5
accidente *m.* accident 2.4
acción *f.* action 3.5
  de acción action (genre) 3.5

aceite *m.* oil 2.2
aceptar: ¡Acepto casarme contigo! I'll marry you! 3.5
acompañar *v.* to accompany 3.2
aconsejar *v.* to advise 2.6
acontecimiento *m.* event 3.6
acordarse (de) (o:ue) *v.* to remember 2.1
acostarse (o:ue) *v.* to go to bed 2.1
activo/a *adj.* active 3.3
actor *m.* actor 3.4
actriz *f.* actress 3.4
actualidades *f., pl.* news; current events 3.6
adelgazar *v.* to lose weight; to slim down 3.3
además (de) *adv.* furthermore; besides 2.4
adicional *adj.* additional
adiós *m.* goodbye 1.1
adjetivo *m.* adjective
administración de empresas *f.* business administration 1.2
adolescencia *f.* adolescence 2.3
¿adónde? *adv.* where (to)? (destination) 1.2
aduana *f.* customs
aeróbico/a *adj.* aerobic 3.3
aeropuerto *m.* airport 1.5
afectado/a *adj.* affected 3.1
afeitarse *v.* to shave 2.1
aficionado/a *m., f.* fan 1.4
afirmativo/a *adj.* affirmative
afuera *adv.* outside 1.5
afueras *f., pl.* suburbs; outskirts 2.6
agencia de viajes *f.* travel agency 1.5
agente de viajes *m., f.* travel agent 1.5
agosto *m.* August 1.5
agradable *adj.* pleasant
agua *f.* water 2.2
  agua mineral mineral water 2.2

aguantar *v.* to endure, to hold up 3.2
ahora *adv.* now 1.2
  ahora mismo right now 1.5
ahorrar *v.* to save (money) 3.2
ahorros *m., pl.* savings 3.2
aire *m.* air 3.1
ajo *m.* garlic 2.2
al (*contraction of* **a** + **el**) 1.4
  al aire libre open-air 1.6
  al contado in cash 3.2
  (al) este (to the) east 3.2
  al lado de next to; beside 1.2
  (al) norte (to the) north 3.2
  (al) oeste (to the) west 3.2
  (al) sur (to the) south 3.2
alcoba *f.* bedroom
alegrarse (de) *v.* to be happy 3.1
alegre *adj.* happy; joyful 1.5
alegría *f.* happiness 2.3
alemán, alemana *adj.* German 1.3
alérgico/a *adj.* allergic 2.4
alfombra *f.* carpet; rug 2.6
algo *pron.* something; anything 2.1
algodón *m.* cotton 1.6
alguien *pron.* someone; somebody; anyone 2.1
algún, alguno/a(s) *adj.* any; some 2.1
alimento *m.* food
  alimentación *f.* diet
aliviar *v.* to reduce 3.3
  aliviar el estrés/la tensión to reduce stress/tension 3.3
allá *adv.* over there 1.2
allí *adv.* there 1.2
alma *f.* soul 2.3
almacén *m.* department store 1.6
almohada *f.* pillow 2.6
almorzar (o:ue) *v.* to have lunch 1.4
almuerzo *m.* lunch 1.4, 2.2

aló *interj.* hello (*on the telephone*) 2.5
alquilar *v.* to rent 2.6
alquiler *m.* rent (payment) 2.6
altar *m.* altar 2.3
altillo *m.* attic 2.6
alto/a *adj.* tall 1.3
aluminio *m.* aluminum 3.1
ama de casa *m., f.* housekeeper; caretaker 2.6
amable *adj.* nice; friendly 1.5
amarillo/a *adj.* yellow 1.6
amigo/a *m., f.* friend 1.3
amistad *f.* friendship 2.3
amor *m.* love 2.3
  amor a primera vista love at first sight 2.3
anaranjado/a *adj.* orange 1.6
ándale *interj.* come on 3.2
andar *v.* **en patineta** to skateboard 1.4
ángel *m.* angel 2.3
anillo *m.* ring 3.5
animal *m.* animal 3.1
aniversario (de bodas) *m.* (wedding) anniversary 2.3
anoche *adv.* last night 1.6
anteayer *adv.* the day before yesterday 1.6
antes *adv.* before 2.1
  antes (de) que *conj.* before 3.1
  antes de *prep.* before 2.1
antibiótico *m.* antibiotic 2.4
antipático/a *adj.* unpleasant 1.3
anunciar *v.* to announce; to advertise 3.6
anuncio *m.* advertisement 3.4
año *m.* year 1.5
  año pasado last year 1.6
apagar *v.* to turn off 2.5
aparato *m.* appliance
apartamento *m.* apartment 2.6
apellido *m.* last name 1.3
apenas *adv.* hardly; scarcely 2.4
aplaudir *v.* to applaud 3.5
aplicación *f.* app 2.5
apreciar *v.* to appreciate 3.5
aprender (a + *inf.*) *v.* to learn 1.3
apurarse *v.* to hurry; to rush 3.3
aquel, aquella *adj.* that (over there) 1.6
aquél, aquélla *pron.* that (over there) 1.6
aquello *neuter, pron.* that; that thing; that fact 1.6
aquellos/as *pl. adj.* those (over there) 1.6
aquéllos/as *pl. pron.* those (ones) (over there) 1.6
aquí *adv.* here 1.1
  Aquí está(n)... Here is/are... 1.5
árbol *m.* tree 3.1
archivo *m.* file 2.5
arete *m.* earring 1.6
argentino/a *adj.* Argentine 1.3
armario *m.* closet 2.6
arqueología *f.* archeology 1.2

arqueólogo/a *m., f.* archeologist 3.4
arquitecto/a *m., f.* architect 3.4
arrancar *v.* to start (*a car*) 2.5
arreglar *v.* to fix; to arrange 2.5; to neaten; to straighten up 2.6
arreglarse *v.* to get ready 2.1; to fix oneself (*clothes, hair, etc. to go out*) 2.1
arroba *f.* @ symbol 2.5
arroz *m.* rice 2.2
arte *m.* art 1.2
artes *f., pl.* arts 3.5
artesanía *f.* craftsmanship; crafts 3.5
artículo *m.* article 3.6
artista *m., f.* artist 1.3
artístico/a *adj.* artistic 3.5
arveja *f.* pea 2.2
asado/a *adj.* roast 2.2
ascenso *m.* promotion 3.4
ascensor *m.* elevator 1.5
así *adv.* like this; so (*in such a way*) 2.4
asistir (a) *v.* to attend 1.3
aspiradora *f.* vacuum cleaner 2.6
aspirante *m., f.* candidate; applicant 3.4
aspirina *f.* aspirin 2.4
atún *m.* tuna 2.2
aumentar *v.* to grow; to get bigger 3.1
aumentar *v.* **de peso** to gain weight 3.3
aumento *m.* increase
  aumento de sueldo pay raise 3.4
aunque although
autobús *m.* bus 1.1
automático/a *adj.* automatic
auto(móvil) *m.* auto(mobile) 1.5
autopista *f.* highway 2.5
ave *f.* bird 3.1
avenida *f.* avenue
aventura *f.* adventure 3.5
  de aventuras adventure (genre) 3.5
avergonzado/a *adj.* embarrassed 1.5
avión *m.* airplane 1.5
¡Ay! *interj.* Oh!
  ¡Ay, qué dolor! Oh, what pain!
ayer *adv.* yesterday 1.6
ayudar(se) *v.* to help (each other) 2.5
azúcar *m.* sugar 2.2
azul *adj. m., f.* blue 1.6

B

bailar *v.* to dance 1.2
bailarín/bailarina *m., f.* dancer 3.5
baile *m.* dance 3.5
bajar(se) de *v.* to get off of/out of (a vehicle) 2.5
bajo/a *adj.* short (*in height*) 1.3

balcón *m.* balcony 2.6
balde *m.* bucket 1.5
ballena *f.* whale 3.1
baloncesto *m.* basketball 1.4
banana *f.* banana 2.2
banco *m.* bank 3.2
banda *f.* band 3.5
bandera *f.* flag
bañarse *v.* to bathe; to take a bath 2.1
baño *m.* bathroom 2.1
barato/a *adj.* cheap 1.6
barco *m.* boat 1.5
barrer *v.* to sweep 2.6
  barrer el suelo *v.* to sweep the floor 2.6
barrio *m.* neighborhood 2.6
bastante *adv.* enough; rather 2.4
basura *f.* trash 2.6
baúl *m.* trunk 2.5
beber *v.* to drink 1.3
bebida *f.* drink 2.2
béisbol *m.* baseball 1.4
bellas artes *f., pl.* fine arts 3.5
belleza *f.* beauty 3.2
beneficio *m.* benefit 3.4
besar(se) *v.* to kiss (each other) 2.5
beso *m.* kiss 2.3
biblioteca *f.* library 1.2
bicicleta *f.* bicycle 1.4
bien *adv.* well 1.1
bienestar *m.* well-being 3.3
bienvenido(s)/a(s) *adj.* welcome 1.1
billete *m.* paper money; ticket
billón *m.* trillion
biología *f.* biology 1.2
bisabuelo/a *m., f.* great-grand-father/great-grandmother 1.3
bistec *m.* steak 2.2
blanco/a *adj.* white 1.6
blog *m.* blog 2.5
(blue)jeans *m., pl.* jeans 1.6
blusa *f.* blouse 1.6
boca *f.* mouth 2.4
boda *f.* wedding 2.3
boleto *m.* ticket 1.2, 3.5
bolsa *f.* purse, bag 1.6
bombero/a *m., f.* firefighter 3.4
bonito/a *adj.* pretty 1.3
borrador *m.* eraser 1.2
borrar *v.* to erase 2.5
bosque *m.* forest 3.1
  bosque tropical tropical forest; rain forest 3.1
bota *f.* boot 1.6
botella *f.* bottle 2.3
botones *m., f. sing.* bellhop 1.5
brazo *m.* arm 2.4
brindar *v.* to toast (*drink*) 2.3
bucear *v.* to scuba dive 1.4
buen, bueno/a *adj.* good 1.3, 1.6
  buena forma good shape (*physical*) 3.3

Buenas noches. Good evening; Good night. 1.1
Buenas tardes. Good afternoon. 1.1
Bueno. Hello. (*on telephone*) 2.5
Buenos días. Good morning. 1.1
bulevar *m.* boulevard
buscador *m.* browser 2.5
buscar *v.* to look for 1.2
buzón *m.* mailbox 3.2

C

caballero *m.* gentleman, sir 2.2
caballo *m.* horse 1.5
cabe: no cabe duda de there's no doubt 3.1
cabeza *f.* head 2.4
cada *adj. m., f.* each 1.6
caerse *v.* to fall (down) 2.4
café *m.* café 1.4; *adj. m., f.* brown 1.6; *m.* coffee 2.2
cafeína *f.* caffeine 3.3
cafetera *f.* coffee maker 2.6
cafetería *f.* cafeteria 1.2
caído/a *p.p.* fallen 3.2
caja *f.* cash register 1.6
cajero/a *m., f.* cashier
  cajero automático *m.* ATM 3.2
calavera de azúcar *f.* skull made out of sugar 2.3
calcetín (calcetines) *m.* sock(s) 1.6
calculadora *f.* calculator 1.2
calentamiento global *m.* global warming 3.1
calentarse (e:ie) *v.* to warm up 3.3
calidad *f.* quality 1.6
calle *f.* street 2.5
calor *m.* heat
caloría *f.* calorie 3.3
calzar *v.* to take size... shoes 1.6
cama *f.* bed 1.5
cámara de video *f.* video camera 2.5
cámara digital *f.* digital camera 2.5
camarero/a *m., f.* waiter/ waitress 2.2
camarón *m.* shrimp 2.2
cambiar (de) *v.* to change 2.3
cambio: de cambio in change 1.2
cambio *m.* **climático** climate change 3.1
cambio *m.* **de moneda** currency exchange
caminar *v.* to walk 1.2
camino *m.* road
camión *m.* truck; bus
camisa *f.* shirt 1.6
camiseta *f.* t-shirt 1.6
campo *m.* countryside 1.5
canadiense *adj.* Canadian 1.3

canal *m.* (TV) channel 2.5; 3.5
canción *f.* song 3.5
candidato/a *m., f.* candidate 3.6
canela *f.* cinnamon 2.4
cansado/a *adj.* tired 1.5
cantante *m., f.* singer 3.5
cantar *v.* to sing 1.2
capital *f.* capital city
capó *m.* hood 2.5
cara *f.* face 2.1
caramelo *m.* caramel 2.3
cargador *m.* charger 2.5
carne *f.* meat 2.2
  carne de res *f.* beef 2.2
carnicería *f.* butcher shop 3.2
caro/a *adj.* expensive 1.6
carpintero/a *m., f.* carpenter 3.4
carrera *f.* career 3.4
carretera *f.* highway; (main) road 2.5
carro *m.* car; automobile 2.5
carta *f.* letter 1.4; *(playing)* card 1.5
cartel *m.* poster 2.6
cartera *f.* wallet 1.4, 1.6
cartero *m.* mail carrier 3.2
casa *f.* house; home 1.2
casado/a *adj.* married 2.3
casarse (con) *v.* to get married (to) 2.3
casi *adv.* almost 2.4
catorce fourteen 1.1
cazar *v.* to hunt 3.1
cebolla *f.* onion 2.2
cederrón *m.* CD-ROM
celebrar *v.* to celebrate 2.3
cementerio *m.* cemetery 2.3
cena *f.* dinner 2.2
cenar *v.* to have dinner 1.2
centro *m.* downtown 1.4
  centro comercial shopping mall 1.6
cepillarse los dientes/el pelo *v.* to brush one's teeth/one's hair 2.1
cerámica *f.* pottery 3.5
cerca de *prep.* near 1.2
cerdo *m.* pork 2.2
cereales *m., pl.* cereal; grains 2.2
cero *m.* zero 1.1
cerrado/a *adj.* closed 1.5
cerrar (e:ie) *v.* to close 1.4
césped *m.* grass
ceviche *m.* marinated fish dish 2.2
  ceviche de camarón *m.* lemon-marinated shrimp 2.2
chaleco *m.* vest
champiñón *m.* mushroom 2.2
champú *m.* shampoo 2.1
chaqueta *f.* jacket 1.6
chatear *v.* to chat 2.5
chau *fam. interj.* bye 1.1
cheque *m.* (bank) check 3.2
  cheque (de viajero) *m.* (traveler's) check 3.2
chévere *adj., fam.* terrific

chico/a *m., f.* boy/girl 1.1
chino/a *adj.* Chinese 1.3
chocar (con) *v.* to run into
chocolate *m.* chocolate 2.3
choque *m.* collision 3.6
chuleta *f.* chop *(food)* 2.2
  chuleta de cerdo *f.* pork chop 2.2
cibercafé *m.* cybercafé 2.5
ciclismo *m.* cycling 1.4
cielo *m.* sky 3.1
cien(to) one hundred 1.2
ciencias *f., pl.* sciences 1.2
  ciencias ambientales environmental science 1.2
  de ciencia ficción *f.* science fiction (genre) 3.5
científico/a *m., f.* scientist 3.4
cierto/a *adj.* certain 3.1
  es cierto it's certain 3.1
  no es cierto it's not certain 3.1
cima *f.* top, peak 3.3
cinco five 1.1
cincuenta fifty 1.2
cine *m.* movie theater 1.4
cinta *f.* (audio)tape
cinta caminadora *f.* treadmill 3.3
cinturón *m.* belt 1.6
circulación *f.* traffic 2.5
cita *f.* date; appointment 2.3
ciudad *f.* city
ciudadano/a *m., f.* citizen 3.6
Claro (que sí). *fam.* Of course.
clase *f.* class 1.2
  clase de ejercicios aeróbicos *f.* aerobics class 3.3
clásico/a *adj.* classical 3.5
cliente/a *m., f.* customer 1.6
clínica *f.* clinic 2.4
cobrar *v.* to cash (a check) 3.2
coche *m.* car; automobile 2.5
cocina *f.* kitchen; stove 2.3, 2.6
cocinar *v.* to cook 2.6
cocinero/a *m., f.* cook, chef 3.4
cofre *m.* hood 3.2
cola *f.* line 3.2
colesterol *m.* cholesterol 3.3
color *m.* color 1.6
comedia *f.* comedy; play 3.5
comedor *m.* dining room 2.6
comenzar (e:ie) *v.* to begin 1.4
comer *v.* to eat 1.3
comercial *adj.* commercial; business-related 3.4
comida *f.* food; meal 1.4, 2.2
como like; as 2.2
¿cómo? what?; how? 1.1, 1.2
  ¿Cómo es...? What's... like?
  ¿Cómo está usted? *form.* How are you? 1.1
  ¿Cómo estás? *fam.* How are you? 1.1
  ¿Cómo se llama usted? *(form.)* What's your name? 1.1
  ¿Cómo te llamas? *fam.* What's your name? 1.1

cómoda *f.* chest of drawers **2.6**
cómodo/a *adj.* comfortable **1.5**
compañero/a de clase *m., f.* classmate **1.2**
compañero/a de cuarto *m., f.* roommate **1.2**
compañía *f.* company; firm **3.4**
compartir *v.* to share **1.3**
compositor(a) *m., f.* composer **3.5**
comprar *v.* to buy **1.2**
compras *f., pl.* purchases
  ir de compras to go shopping **1.5**
comprender *v.* to understand **1.3**
comprobar *v.* to check
comprometerse (con) *v.* to get engaged (to) **2.3**
computación *f.* computer science **1.2**
computadora *f.* computer **1.1**
computadora portátil *f.* portable computer; laptop **2.5**
comunicación *f.* communication **3.6**
comunicarse (con) *v.* to communicate (with) **3.6**
comunidad *f.* community **1.1**
con *prep.* with **1.2**
  Con él/ella habla. Speaking. (*on telephone*) **2.5**
  con frecuencia *adv.* frequently **2.4**
  Con permiso. Pardon me; Excuse me. **1.1**
  con tal (de) que *conj.* provided (that) **3.1**
concierto *m.* concert **3.5**
concordar *v.* to agree
concurso *m.* game show; contest **3.5**
conducir *v.* to drive **1.6, 2.5**
conductor(a) *m., f.* driver **1.1**
conexión *f.* **inalámbrica** wireless connection **2.5**
confirmar *v.* to confirm **1.5**
confirmar *v.* **una reservación** *f.* to confirm a reservation **1.5**
confundido/a *adj.* confused **1.5**
congelador *m.* freezer **2.6**
congestionado/a *adj.* congested; stuffed-up **2.4**
conmigo *pron.* with me **1.4, 2.3**
conocer *v.* to know; to be acquainted with **1.6**
conocido/a *adj.; p.p.* known
conseguir (e:i) *v.* to get; to obtain **1.4**
consejero/a *m., f.* counselor; advisor **3.4**
consejo *m.* advice
conservación *f.* conservation **3.1**
conservar *v.* to conserve **3.1**
construir *v.* to build
consultorio *m.* doctor's office **2.4**
consumir *v.* to consume **3.3**
contabilidad *f.* accounting **1.2**
contador(a) *m., f.* accountant **3.4**

contaminación *f.* pollution **3.1**
  contaminación del aire/del agua air/water pollution **3.1**
contaminado/a *adj.* polluted **3.1**
contaminar *v.* to pollute **3.1**
contar (o:ue) *v.* to count; to tell **1.4**
contento/a *adj.* content **1.5**
contestadora *f.* answering machine
contestar *v.* to answer **1.2**
contigo *fam. pron.* with you **1.5, 2.3**
contratar *v.* to hire **3.4**
control *m.* **remoto** remote control **2.5**
controlar *v.* to control **3.1**
conversación *f.* conversation **1.1**
conversar *v.* to converse, to chat **1.2**
corazón *m.* heart **2.4**
corbata *f.* tie **1.6**
corredor(a) *m., f.* **de bolsa** stockbroker **3.4**
correo *m.* mail; post office **3.2**
  correo de voz *m.* voice mail **2.5**
  correo electrónico *m.* e-mail **1.4**
correr *v.* to run **1.3**
cortesía *f.* courtesy
cortinas *f., pl.* curtains **2.6**
corto/a *adj.* short (*in length*) **1.6**
cosa *f.* thing **1.1**
costar (o:ue) *v.* to cost **1.6**
costarricense *adj.* Costa Rican **1.3**
cráter *m.* crater **3.1**
creer *v.* to believe **1.3, 3.1**
  creer (en) *v.* to believe (in) **1.3**
  no creer *v.* not to believe **3.1**
creído/a *adj., p.p.* believed **3.2**
crema de afeitar *f.* shaving cream **1.5, 2.1**
crimen *m.* crime; murder **3.6**
cruzar *v.* to cross **3.2**
cuaderno *m.* notebook **1.1**
cuadra *f.* (city) block **3.2**
¿cuál(es)? which?; which one(s)? **1.2**
  ¿Cuál es la fecha de hoy? What is today's date? **1.5**
cuadro *m.* picture **2.6**
cuando *conj.* when **2.1; 3.1**
¿cuándo? when? **1.2**
¿cuánto(s)/a(s)? how much/how many? **1.1, 1.2**
  ¿Cuánto cuesta...? How much does... cost? **1.6**
  ¿Cuántos años tienes? How old are you?
cuarenta forty **1.2**
cuarto de baño *m.* bathroom **2.1**
cuarto *m.* room **1.2; 2.1**
cuarto/a *adj.* fourth **1.5**
  menos cuarto quarter to (time) **1.1**
  y cuarto quarter after (time) **1.1**
cuatro four **1.1**
cuatrocientos/as four hundred **1.2**
cubano/a *adj.* Cuban **1.3**

cubiertos *m., pl.* silverware
cubierto/a *p.p.* covered
cubrir *v.* to cover
cuchara *f.* (table or large) spoon **2.6**
cuchillo *m.* knife **2.6**
cuello *m.* neck **2.4**
cuenta *f.* bill **2.2**; account **3.2**
  cuenta corriente *f.* checking account **3.2**
  cuenta de ahorros *f.* savings account **3.2**
cuento *m.* short story **3.5**
cuerpo *m.* body **2.4**
cuidado *m.* care
cuidar *v.* to take care of **3.1**
cultura *f.* culture **1.2, 3.5**
cumpleaños *m., sing.* birthday **2.3**
cumplir años *v.* to have a birthday
cuñado/a *m., f.* brother-in-law/ sister-in-law **1.3**
currículum *m.* résumé **3.4**
curso *m.* course **1.2**

D

danza *f.* dance **3.5**
dañar *v.* to damage; to break down **2.4**
dar *v.* to give **1.6**
  dar un consejo *v.* to give advice
  darse con *v.* to bump into; to run into (something) **2.4**
  darse prisa *v.* to hurry; to rush **3.3**
de *prep.* of; from **1.1**
  ¿De dónde eres? *fam.* Where are you from? **1.1**
  ¿De dónde es usted? *form.* Where are you from? **1.1**
  ¿De parte de quién? Who is speaking/calling? (*on telephone*) **2.5**
  ¿de quién...? whose...? (*sing.*) **1.1**
  ¿de quiénes...? whose...? (*pl.*) **1.1**
  de algodón (made) of cotton **1.6**
  de aluminio (made) of aluminum **3.1**
  de buen humor in a good mood **1.5**
  de compras shopping **1.5**
  de cuadros plaid **1.6**
  de excursión hiking **1.4**
  de hecho in fact
  de ida y vuelta roundtrip **1.5**
  de la mañana in the morning; A.M. **1.1**
  de la noche in the evening; at night; P.M. **1.1**
  de la tarde in the afternoon; in the early evening; P.M. **1.1**
  de lana (made) of wool **1.6**
  de lunares polka-dotted **1.6**
  de mal humor in a bad mood **1.5**
  de moda in fashion **1.6**

De nada. You're welcome. 1.1
de niño/a as a child 2.4
de parte de on behalf of 2.5
de plástico (made) of plastic 3.1
de rayas striped 1.6
de repente suddenly 1.6
de seda (made) of silk 1.6
de vaqueros western (genre) 3.5
de vez en cuando from time to time 2.4
de vidrio (made) of glass 3.1
debajo de *prep.* below; under 1.2
deber (+ inf.) *v.* should; must; ought to 1.3
deber *m.* responsibility; obligation 3.6
debido a due to (the fact that)
débil *adj.* weak 3.3
decidir (+ inf.) *v.* to decide 1.3
décimo/a *adj.* tenth 1.5
decir (e:i) *v.* **(que)** to say (that); to tell (that) 1.4
  decir la respuesta to say the answer 1.4
  decir la verdad to tell the truth 1.4
  decir mentiras to tell lies 1.4
declarar *v.* to declare; to say 3.6
dedo *m.* finger 2.4
dedo del pie *m.* toe 2.4
deforestación *f.* deforestation 3.1
dejar *v.* to let; to quit; to leave behind 3.4
  dejar de (+ inf.) *v.* to stop (*doing something*) 3.1
  dejar una propina *v.* to leave a tip
del (*contraction of* **de + el**) of the; from the 1.1
delante de *prep.* in front of 1.2
delgado/a *adj.* thin; slender 1.3
delicioso/a *adj.* delicious 2.2
demás *adj.* the rest
demasiado *adv.* too much 1.6
dentista *m., f.* dentist 2.4
dentro de (diez años) within (ten years) 3.4; inside
dependiente/a *m., f.* clerk 1.6
deporte *m.* sport 1.4
deportista *m.* sports person
deportivo/a *adj.* sports-related 1.4
depositar *v.* to deposit 3.2
derecha *f.* right 1.2
  a la derecha de to the right of 1.2
derecho *adv.* straight (ahead) 3.2
derechos *m., pl.* rights 3.6
desarrollar *v.* to develop 3.1
desastre (natural) *m.* (natural) disaster 3.6
desayunar *v.* to have breakfast 1.2
desayuno *m.* breakfast 2.2
descafeinado/a *adj.* decaffeinated 3.3
descansar *v.* to rest 1.2

descargar *v.* to download 2.5
descompuesto/a *adj.* not working; out of order 2.5
describir *v.* to describe 1.3
descrito/a *p.p.* described 3.2
descubierto/a *p.p.* discovered 3.2
descubrir *v.* to discover 3.1
desde *prep.* from 1.6
desear *v.* to wish; to desire 1.2
desempleo *m.* unemployment 3.6
desierto *m.* desert 3.1
desigualdad *f.* inequality 3.6
desordenado/a *adj.* disorderly 1.5
despacio *adv.* slowly 2.4
despedida *f.* farewell; goodbye
despedir (e:i) *v.* to fire 3.4
despedirse (de) (e:i) *v.* to say goodbye (to) 3.6
despejado/a *adj.* clear (*weather*)
despertador *m.* alarm clock 2.1
despertarse (e:ie) *v.* to wake up 2.1
después *adv.* afterwards; then 2.1
  después de after 2.1
  después de que *conj.* after 3.1
destruir *v.* to destroy 3.1
detrás de *prep.* behind 1.2
día *m.* day 1.1
  día de fiesta holiday 2.3
diario *m.* diary 1.1; newspaper 3.6
diario/a *adj.* daily 2.1
dibujar *v.* to draw 1.2
dibujo *m.* drawing
  dibujos animados *m., pl.* cartoons 3.5
diccionario *m.* dictionary 1.1
dicho/a *p.p.* said 3.2
diciembre *m.* December 1.5
dictadura *f.* dictatorship 3.6
diecinueve nineteen 1.1
dieciocho eighteen 1.1
dieciséis sixteen 1.1
diecisiete seventeen 1.1
diente *m.* tooth 2.1
dieta *f.* diet 3.3
  comer una dieta equilibrada to eat a balanced diet 3.3
diez ten 1.1
difícil *adj.* difficult; hard 1.3
Diga. Hello. (*on telephone*) 2.5
diligencia *f.* errand 3.2
dinero *m.* money 1.6
dirección *f.* address 3.2
  dirección electrónica *f.* e-mail address 2.5
director(a) *m., f.* director; (*musical*) conductor 3.5
dirigir *v.* to direct 3.5
disco compacto compact disc (CD) 2.5
discriminación *f.* discrimination 3.6
discurso *m.* speech 3.6
diseñador(a) *m., f.* designer 3.4
diseño *m.* design

disfraz *m.* costume 2.3
disfrutar (de) *v.* to enjoy; to reap the benefits (of) 3.3
disminuir *v.* to reduce 3.4
diversión *f.* fun activity; entertainment; recreation 1.4
divertido/a *adj.* fun
divertirse (e:ie) *v.* to have fun 2.3
divorciado/a *adj.* divorced 2.3
divorciarse (de) *v.* to get divorced (from) 2.3
divorcio *m.* divorce 2.3
doblar *v.* to turn 3.2
doble *adj.* double 1.5
doce twelve 1.1
doctor(a) *m., f.* doctor 1.3; 2.4
documental *m.* documentary 3.5
documentos de viaje *m., pl.* travel documents
doler (o:ue) *v.* to hurt 2.4
dolor *m.* ache; pain 2.4
  dolor de cabeza *m.* headache 2.4
doméstico/a *adj.* domestic 2.6
domingo *m.* Sunday 1.2
don *m.* Mr.; sir 1.1
doña *f.* Mrs.; ma'am 1.1
donde *adv.* where
  ¿Dónde está...? Where is...? 1.2
  ¿dónde? where? 1.1, 1.2
dormir (o:ue) *v.* to sleep 1.4
dormirse (o:ue) *v.* to go to sleep; to fall asleep 2.1
dormitorio *m.* bedroom 2.6
dos two 1.1
  dos veces *f.* twice; two times 1.6
doscientos/as two hundred 1.2
drama *m.* drama; play 3.5
dramático/a *adj.* dramatic 3.5
dramaturgo/a *m., f.* playwright 3.5
ducha *f.* shower 2.1
ducharse *v.* to shower; to take a shower 2.1
duda *f.* doubt 3.1
dudar *v.* to doubt 3.1
  no dudar *v.* not to doubt 3.1
dueño/a *m., f.* owner 2.2
dulces *m., pl.* sweets; candy 2.3
durante *prep.* during 2.1
durar *v.* to last 3.6

E

e *conj.* (*used instead of* **y** *before words beginning with* **i** *and* **hi**) and
echar *v.* to throw
  echar (una carta) al buzón *v.* to put (a letter) in the mailbox; to mail 3.2
ecología *f.* ecology 3.1
ecológico/a *adj.* ecological 3.1
ecologista *m., f.* ecologist 3.1
economía *f.* economics 1.2
ecoturismo *m.* ecotourism 3.1

ecuatoriano/a *adj.*
Ecuadorian 1.3
edad *f.* age 2.3
edificio *m.* building 2.6
edificio de apartamentos
apartment building 2.6
(en) efectivo *m.* cash 1.6
ejercer *v.* to practice/exercise
(a degree/profession) 3.4
ejercicio *m.* exercise 3.3
ejercicios aeróbicos
aerobic exercises 3.3
ejercicios de estiramiento
stretching exercises 3.3
ejército *m.* army 3.6
el *m., sing., def. art.* the 1.1
él *sub. pron.* he 1.1; *obj. pron.* him
elecciones *f., pl.* election 3.6
electricista *m., f.* electrician 3.4
electrodoméstico *m.* electric
appliance 2.6
elegante *adj. m., f.* elegant 1.6
elegir (e:i) *v.* to elect 3.6
ella *sub. pron.* she 1.1; *obj.
pron.* her
ellos/as *sub. pron.* they 1.1;
obj. pron. them
embarazada *adj.* pregnant 2.4
emergencia *f.* emergency 2.4
emitir *v.* to broadcast 3.6
emocionante *adj. m., f.* exciting
empezar (e:ie) *v.* to begin 1.4
empleado/a *m., f.* employee 1.5
empleo *m.* job; employment 3.4
empresa *f.* company; firm 3.4
en *prep.* in; on 1.2
en casa at home
en caso (de) que *conj.* in case
(that) 3.1
en cuanto *conj.* as soon as 3.1
en efectivo in cash 3.2
en exceso in excess; too
much 3.3
en línea in-line 1.4
en punto on the dot; exactly;
sharp (*time*) 1.1
en qué in what; how
¿En qué puedo servirles?
How can I help you? 1.5
en vivo live 2.1
enamorado/a (de) *adj.* in love
(with) 1.5
enamorarse (de) *v.* to fall in love
(with) 2.3
encantado/a *adj.* delighted;
pleased to meet you 1.1
encantar *v.* to like very much; to
love (*inanimate objects*) 2.1
encima de *prep.* on top of 1.2
encontrar (o:ue) *v.* to find 1.4
encontrar(se) (o:ue) *v.* to meet
(each other); to run into (each
other) 2.5
encontrarse con to meet up
with 2.1
encuesta *f.* poll; survey 3.6
energía *f.* energy 3.1

energía nuclear nuclear
energy 3.1
energía solar solar energy 3.1
enero *m.* January 1.5
enfermarse *v.* to get sick 2.4
enfermedad *f.* illness 2.4
enfermero/a *m., f.* nurse 2.4
enfermo/a *adj.* sick 2.4
enfrente de *adv.* opposite;
facing 3.2
engordar *v.* to gain weight 3.3
enojado/a *adj.* angry 1.5
enojarse (con) *v.* to get angry
(with) 2.1
ensalada *f.* salad 2.2
ensayo *m.* essay 1.3
enseguida *adv.* right away
enseñar *v.* to teach 1.2
ensuciar *v.* to get (something)
dirty 2.6
entender (e:ie) *v.* to understand 1.4
enterarse *v.* to find out 3.4
entonces *adv.* so, then 1.5, 2.1
entrada *f.* entrance 2.6; ticket
entre *prep.* between; among 1.2
entregar *v.* to hand in 2.5
entremeses *m., pl.* hors
d'oeuvres; appetizers 2.2
entrenador(a) *m., f.* trainer 3.3
entrenarse *v.* to practice;
to train 3.3
entrevista *f.* interview 3.4
entrevistador(a) *m., f.*
interviewer 3.4
entrevistar *v.* to interview 3.4
envase *m.* container 3.1
enviar *v.* to send; to mail 3.2
equilibrado/a *adj.* balanced 3.3
equipaje *m.* luggage 1.5
equipo *m.* team 1.4
equivocado/a *adj.* wrong 1.5
eres *fam.* you are 1.1
es he/she/it is 1.1
Es bueno que... It's good
that... 2.6
es cierto it's certain 3.1
es extraño it's strange 3.1
es igual it's the same 1.5
Es importante que... It's
important that... 2.6
es imposible it's
impossible 3.1
es improbable it's
improbable 3.1
Es malo que... It's bad
that... 2.6
Es mejor que... It's better
that... 2.6
Es necesario que... It's
necessary that... 2.6
es obvio it's obvious 3.1
es posible it's possible 3.1
es probable it's probable 3.1
es ridículo it's ridiculous 3.1
es seguro it's certain 3.1
es terrible it's terrible 3.1
es triste it's sad 3.1

Es urgente que... It's urgent
that... 2.6
Es la una. It's one o'clock. 1.1
es una lástima it's a shame 3.1
es verdad it's true 3.1
esa(s) *f., adj.* that; those 1.6
ésa(s) *f., pron.* that (one);
those (ones) 1.6
escalar *v.* to climb 1.4
escalar montañas to climb
mountains 1.4
escalera *f.* stairs; stairway 2.6
escalón *m.* step 3.3
escanear *v.* to scan 2.5
escoger *v.* to choose 2.2
escribir *v.* to write 1.3
**escribir un mensaje
electrónico** to write an
e-mail 1.4
escribir una carta to write a
letter 1.4
escrito/a *p.p.* written 3.2
escritor(a) *m., f.* writer 3.5
escritorio *m.* desk 1.2
escuchar *v.* to listen (to) 1.2
escuchar la radio to listen to
the radio 1.2
escuchar música to listen to
music 1.2
escuela *f.* school 1.1
esculpir *v.* to sculpt 3.5
escultor(a) *m., f.* sculptor 3.5
escultura *f.* sculpture 3.5
ese *m., sing., adj.* that 1.6
ése *m., sing., pron.* that one 1.6
eso *neuter, pron.* that;
that thing 1.6
esos *m., pl., adj.* those 1.6
ésos *m., pl., pron.* those (ones) 1.6
España *f.* Spain
español *m.* Spanish (*language*) 1.2
español(a) *adj. m., f.* Spanish 1.3
espárragos *m., pl.* asparagus 2.2
**especialidad: las especialidades
del día** today's specials 2.2
especialización *f.* major 1.2
espectacular *adj.* spectacular
espectáculo *m.* show 3.5
espejo *m.* mirror 2.1
esperar *v.* to hope; to wish 3.1
esperar (+ inf.) *v.* to wait
(for); to hope 1.2
esposo/a *m., f.* husband/wife;
spouse 1.3
esquí (acuático) *m.* (water)
skiing 1.4
esquiar *v.* to ski 1.4
esquina *f.* corner 3.2
está he/she/it is, you are
Está bien. That's fine.
Está (muy) despejado. It's
(very) clear. (*weather*)
Está lloviendo. It's raining. 1.5
Está nevando. It's snowing. 1.5
Está (muy) nublado. It's
(very) cloudy. (*weather*) 1.5
esta(s) *f., adj.* this; these 1.6

esta noche tonight
ésta(s) *f., pron.* this (one); these (ones) **1.6**
establecer *v.* to establish **3.4**
estación *f.* station; season **1.5**
  estación de autobuses bus station **1.5**
  estación del metro subway station **1.5**
  estación de tren train station **1.5**
estacionamiento *m.* parking lot **3.2**
estacionar *v.* to park **2.5**
estadio *m.* stadium **1.2**
estado civil *m.* marital status **2.3**
Estados Unidos *m., pl.* (EE.UU.; E.U.) United States
estadounidense *adj. m., f.* from the United States **1.3**
estampilla *f.* stamp **3.2**
estante *m.* bookcase; bookshelves **2.6**
estar *v.* to be **1.2**
  estar a dieta to be on a diet **3.3**
  estar aburrido/a to be bored **1.5**
  estar afectado/a (por) to be affected (by) **3.1**
  estar cansado/a to be tired **1.5**
  estar contaminado/a to be polluted **3.1**
  estar de acuerdo to agree **3.5**
    Estoy de acuerdo. I agree. **3.5**
    No estoy de acuerdo. I don't agree. **3.5**
  estar de moda to be in fashion **1.6**
  estar de vacaciones *f., pl.* to be on vacation **1.5**
  estar en buena forma to be in good shape **3.3**
  estar enfermo/a to be sick **2.4**
  estar harto/a de... to be sick of... **3.6**
  estar listo/a to be ready **1.5**
  estar perdido/a to be lost **3.2**
  estar roto/a to be broken
  estar seguro/a to be sure **1.5**
  estar torcido/a to be twisted; to be sprained **2.4**
  No está nada mal. It's not bad at all. **1.5**
estatua *f.* statue **3.5**
este *m.* east **3.2**
este *m., sing., adj.* this **1.6**
éste *m., sing., pron.* this (one) **1.6**
estéreo *m.* stereo **2.5**
estilo *m.* style
estiramiento *m.* stretching **3.3**
esto *neuter pron.* this; this thing **1.6**
estómago *m.* stomach **2.4**
estornudar *v.* to sneeze **2.4**
estos *m., pl., adj.* these **1.6**

éstos *m., pl., pron.* these (ones) **1.6**
estrella *f.* star **3.1**
  estrella de cine *m., f.* movie star **3.5**
estrés *m.* stress **3.3**
estudiante *m., f.* student **1.1, 1.2**
estudiantil *adj. m., f.* student **1.2**
estudiar *v.* to study **1.2**
estufa *f.* stove **2.6**
estupendo/a *adj.* stupendous **1.5**
etapa *f.* stage **2.3**
evitar *v.* to avoid **3.1**
examen *m.* test; exam **1.2**
  examen médico physical exam **2.4**
excelente *adj. m., f.* excellent **1.5**
exceso *m.* excess **3.3**
excursión *f.* hike; tour; excursion **1.4**
excursionista *m., f.* hiker
éxito *m.* success
experiencia *f.* experience
explicar *v.* to explain **1.2**
explorar *v.* to explore
expresión *f.* expression
extinción *f.* extinction **3.1**
extranjero/a *adj.* foreign **3.5**
extrañar *v.* to miss **3.4**
extraño/a *adj.* strange **3.1**

F

fábrica *f.* factory **3.1**
fabuloso/a *adj.* fabulous **1.5**
fácil *adj.* easy **1.3**
falda *f.* skirt **1.6**
faltar *v.* to lack; to need **2.1**
familia *f.* family **1.3**
famoso/a *adj.* famous
farmacia *f.* pharmacy **2.4**
fascinar *v.* to fascinate **2.1**
favorito/a *adj.* favorite **1.4**
fax *m.* fax (machine)
febrero *m.* February **1.5**
fecha *f.* date **1.5**
¡Felicidades! Congratulations! **2.3**
¡Felicitaciones! Congratulations! **2.3**
feliz *adj.* happy **2.3**
  ¡Feliz cumpleaños! Happy birthday! **2.3**
fenomenal *adj.* great, phenomenal **1.5**
feo/a *adj.* ugly **1.3**
festival *m.* festival **3.5**
fiebre *f.* fever **2.4**
fiesta *f.* party **2.3**
fijo/a *adj.* fixed, set **1.6**
fin *m.* end **1.4**
  fin de semana weekend **1.4**
finalmente *adv.* finally
firmar *v.* to sign (*a document*) **3.2**
física *f.* physics **1.2**
flan (de caramelo) *m.* baked (caramel) custard **2.3**

flexible *adj.* flexible **3.3**
flor *f.* flower **3.1**
folclórico/a *adj.* folk; folkloric **3.5**
folleto *m.* brochure
forma *f.* shape **3.3**
formulario *m.* form **3.2**
foto(grafía) *f.* photograph **1.1**
francés, francesa *adj. m., f.* French **1.3**
frecuentemente *adv.* frequently
frenos *m., pl.* brakes
frente (frío) *m.* (cold) front **1.5**
fresco/a *adj.* cool
frijoles *m., pl.* beans **2.2**
frío/a *adj.* cold
frito/a *adj.* fried **2.2**
fruta *f.* fruit **2.2**
frutería *f.* fruit store **3.2**
fuera *adv.* outside
fuerte *adj. m., f.* strong **3.3**
fumar *v.* to smoke **3.3**
  (no) fumar *v.* (not) to smoke **3.3**
funcionar *v.* to work **2.5**; to function
fútbol *m.* soccer **1.4**
fútbol americano *m.* football **1.4**
futuro/a *adj.* future
  en el futuro in the future

G

gafas (de sol) *f., pl.* (sun)glasses **1.6**
gafas (oscuras) *f., pl.* (sun)glasses
galleta *f.* cookie **2.3**
ganar *v.* to win **1.4**; to earn (money) **3.4**
ganga *f.* bargain **1.6**
garaje *m.* garage; (mechanic's) repair shop **2.5**; garage (*in a house*) **2.6**
garganta *f.* throat **2.4**
gasolina *f.* gasoline **2.5**
gasolinera *f.* gas station **2.5**
gastar *v.* to spend (money) **1.6**
gato *m.* cat **3.1**
gemelo/a *m., f.* twin **1.3**
genial *adj.* great **3.4**
gente *f.* people **1.3**
geografía *f.* geography **1.2**
gerente *m., f.* manager **2.2, 3.4**
gimnasio *m.* gymnasium **1.4**
gobierno *m.* government **3.1**
golf *m.* golf **1.4**
gordo/a *adj.* fat **1.3**
grabar *v.* to record **2.5**
gracias *f., pl.* thank you; thanks **1.1**
  Gracias por invitarme. Thanks for inviting me. **2.3**
graduarse (de/en) *v.* to graduate (from/in) **2.3**
grande *adj.* big; large **1.3**
grasa *f.* fat **3.3**
gratis *adj. m., f.* free of charge **3.2**
grave *adj.* grave; serious **2.4**
gripe *f.* flu **2.4**
gris *adj. m., f.* gray **1.6**

gritar *v.* to scream, to shout
grito *m.* scream 1.5
guantes *m., pl.* gloves 1.6
guapo/a *adj.* handsome; good-looking 1.3
guardar *v.* to save (on a computer) 2.5
guerra *f.* war 3.6
guía *m., f.* guide
gustar *v.* to be pleasing to; to like 1.2
  Me gustaría... I would like...
gusto *m.* pleasure 1.1
  El gusto es mío. The pleasure is mine. 1.1
  Mucho gusto. Pleased to meet you. 1.1
  ¡Qué gusto verlo/la! *(form.)* How nice to see you! 3.6
  ¡Qué gusto verte! *(fam.)* How nice to see you! 3.6

H

haber *(auxiliar) v.* to have (done something) 3.3
habitación *f.* room 1.5
  habitación doble double room 1.5
  habitación individual single room 1.5
hablar *v.* to talk; to speak 1.2
hacer *v.* to do; to make 1.4
  Hace buen tiempo. The weather is good. 1.5
  Hace (mucho) calor. It's (very) hot. *(weather)* 1.5
  Hace fresco. It's cool. *(weather)* 1.5
  Hace (mucho) frío. It's (very) cold. *(weather)* 1.5
  Hace mal tiempo. The weather is bad. 1.5
  Hace (mucho) sol. It's (very) sunny. *(weather)* 1.5
  Hace (mucho) viento. It's (very) windy. *(weather)* 1.5
  hacer cola to stand in line 3.2
  hacer diligencias to run errands 3.2
  hacer ejercicio to exercise 3.3
  hacer ejercicios aeróbicos to do aerobics 3.3
  hacer ejercicios de estiramiento to do stretching exercises 3.3
  hacer el papel (de) to play the role (of) 3.5
  hacer gimnasia to work out 3.3
  hacer juego (con) to match (with) 1.6
  hacer la cama to make the bed 2.6
  hacer las maletas to pack (one's) suitcases 1.5
  hacer quehaceres domésticos to do household chores 2.6

  hacer (wind)surf to (wind)surf 1.5
  hacer turismo to go sightseeing
  hacer un viaje to take a trip 1.5
¿Me harías el honor de casarte conmigo? Would you do me the honor of marrying me? 3.5
hacia *prep.* toward 3.2
hambre *f.* hunger
hamburguesa *f.* hamburger 2.2
hasta *prep.* until 1.6; toward
  Hasta la vista. See you later. 1.1
  Hasta luego. See you later. 1.1
  Hasta mañana. See you tomorrow. 1.1
  Hasta pronto. See you soon. 1.1
  hasta que *conj.* until 3.1
hay there is; there are 1.1
  Hay (mucha) contaminación. It's (very) smoggy.
  Hay (mucha) niebla. It's (very) foggy.
  Hay que It is necessary that
  No hay de qué. You're welcome. 1.1
  No hay duda de There's no doubt 3.1
hecho/a *p.p.* done 3.2
heladería *f.* ice cream shop 3.2
helado/a *adj.* iced 2.2
helado *m.* ice cream 2.3
hermanastro/a *m., f.* stepbrother/stepsister 1.3
hermano/a *m., f.* brother/sister 1.3
hermano/a mayor/menor *m., f.* older/younger brother/sister 1.3
hermanos *m., pl.* siblings (brothers and sisters) 1.3
hermoso/a *adj.* beautiful 1.6
hierba *f.* grass 3.1
hijastro/a *m., f.* stepson/stepdaughter 1.3
hijo/a *m., f.* son/daughter 1.3
  hijo/a único/a *m., f.* only child 1.3
  hijos *m., pl.* children 1.3
híjole *interj.* wow 1.6
historia *f.* history 1.2; story 3.5
hockey *m.* hockey 1.4
hola *interj.* hello; hi 1.1
hombre *m.* man 1.1
  hombre de negocios *m.* businessman 3.4
hora *f.* hour 1.1; the time
horario *m.* schedule 1.2
horno *m.* oven 2.6
  horno de microondas *m.* microwave oven 2.6
horror *m.* horror 3.5
  de horror horror (genre) 3.5
hospital *m.* hospital 2.4
hotel *m.* hotel 1.5
hoy *adv.* today 1.2
  hoy día *adv.* nowadays

  Hoy es... Today is... 1.2
hueco *m.* hole 1.4
huelga *f.* strike *(labor)* 3.6
hueso *m.* bone 2.4
huésped *m., f.* guest 1.5
huevo *m.* egg 2.2
humanidades *f., pl.* humanities 1.2
huracán *m.* hurricane 3.6

I

ida *f.* one way *(travel)*
idea *f.* idea 3.6
iglesia *f.* church 1.4
igualdad *f.* equality 3.6
igualmente *adv.* likewise 1.1
impermeable *m.* raincoat 1.6
importante *adj. m., f.* important 1.3
importar *v.* to be important to; to matter 2.1
imposible *adj. m., f.* impossible 3.1
impresora *f.* printer 2.5
imprimir *v.* to print 2.5
improbable *adj. m., f.* improbable 3.1
impuesto *m.* tax 3.6
incendio *m.* fire 3.6
increíble *adj. m., f.* incredible 1.5
indicar cómo llegar *v.* to give directions 3.2
individual *adj.* single *(room)* 1.5
infección *f.* infection 2.4
informar *v.* to inform 3.6
informe *m.* report; paper *(written work)* 3.6
ingeniero/a *m., f.* engineer 1.3
inglés *m.* English *(language)* 1.2
inglés, inglesa *adj.* English 1.3
inodoro *m.* toilet 2.1
insistir (en) *v.* to insist (on) 2.6
inspector(a) de aduanas *m., f.* customs inspector 1.5
inteligente *adj. m., f.* intelligent 1.3
intento *m.* attempt 2.5
intercambiar *v.* to exchange
interesante *adj. m., f.* interesting 1.3
interesar *v.* to be interesting to; to interest 2.1
internacional *adj. m., f.* international 3.6
Internet Internet 2.5
inundación *f.* flood 3.6
invertir (e:ie) *v.* to invest 3.4
invierno *m.* winter 1.5
invitado/a *m., f.* guest 2.3
invitar *v.* to invite 2.3
inyección *f.* injection 2.4
ir *v.* to go 1.4
  ir a (+ inf.) to be going to do something 1.4
  ir de compras to go shopping 1.5
  ir de excursión (a las montañas) to go on a hike (in the mountains) 1.4
  ir de pesca to go fishing

ir de vacaciones to go on vacation 1.5
ir en autobús to go by bus 1.5
ir en auto(móvil) to go by auto(mobile); to go by car 1.5
ir en avión to go by plane 1.5
ir en barco to go by boat 1.5
ir en metro to go by subway 1.5
ir en moto(cicleta) to go by motorcycle 1.5
ir en taxi to go by taxi 1.5
ir en tren to go by train 1.5
irse v. to go away; to leave 2.1
italiano/a adj. Italian 1.3
izquierda f. left 1.2
   a la izquierda de to the left of 1.2

J

jabón m. soap 2.1
jamás adv. never; not ever 2.1
jamón m. ham 2.2
japonés, japonesa adj. Japanese 1.3
jardín m. garden; yard 2.6
jefe, jefa m., f. boss 3.4
jengibre m. ginger 2.4
joven adj. m., f., sing. (**jóvenes** pl.) young 1.3
   joven m., f., sing. (**jóvenes** pl.) young person 1.1
joyería f. jewelry store 3.2
jubilarse v. to retire (from work) 2.3
juego m. game
jueves m., sing. Thursday 1.2
jugador(a) m., f. player 1.4
jugar (u:ue) v. to play 1.4
   jugar a las cartas f., pl. to play cards 1.5
jugo m. juice 2.2
   jugo de fruta m. fruit juice 2.2
julio m. July 1.5
jungla f. jungle 3.1
junio m. June 1.5
juntos/as adj. together 2.3
juventud f. youth 2.3

K

kilómetro m. kilometer 2.5

L

la f., sing., def. art. the 1.1; f., sing., d.o. pron. her, it, form. you 1.5
laboratorio m. laboratory 1.2
lago m. lake 3.1
lámpara f. lamp 2.6
lana f. wool 1.6
langosta f. lobster 2.2
lápiz m. pencil 1.1
largo/a adj. long 1.6
las f., pl., def. art. the 1.1; f., pl., d.o. pron. them; you 1.5

lástima f. shame 3.1
lastimarse v. to injure oneself 2.4
   lastimarse el pie to injure one's foot 2.4
lata f. (tin) can 3.1
lavabo m. sink 2.1
lavadora f. washing machine 2.6
lavandería f. laundromat 3.2
lavaplatos m., sing. dishwasher 2.6
lavar v. to wash 2.6
   lavar (el suelo, los platos) to wash (the floor, the dishes) 2.6
lavarse v. to wash oneself 2.1
   lavarse la cara to wash one's face 2.1
   lavarse las manos to wash one's hands 2.1
le sing., i.o. pron. to/for him, her, form. you 1.6
   Le presento a... form. I would like to introduce you to (name). 1.1
lección f. lesson 1.1
leche f. milk 2.2
lechuga f. lettuce 2.2
leer v. to read 1.3
   leer el correo electrónico to read e-mail 1.4
   leer un periódico to read a newspaper 1.4
   leer una revista to read a magazine 1.4
leído/a p.p. read 3.2
lejos de prep. far from 1.2
lengua f. language 1.2
   lenguas extranjeras f., pl. foreign languages 1.2
lentes de contacto m., pl. contact lenses
   lentes (de sol) (sun)glasses 1.6
lento/a adj. slow 2.5
les pl., i.o. pron. to/for them, you 1.6
letrero m. sign 3.2
levantar v. to lift 3.3
   levantar pesas to lift weights 3.3
levantarse v. to get up 2.1
ley f. law 3.1
libertad f. liberty; freedom 3.6
libre adj. m., f. free 1.4
librería f. bookstore 1.2
libro m. book 1.2
licencia de conducir f. driver's license 2.5
limón m. lemon 2.2
limpiar v. to clean 2.6
   limpiar la casa v. to clean the house 2.6
limpio/a adj. clean 1.5
línea f. line 1.4
listo/a adj. ready; smart 1.5
literatura f. literature 1.2
llamar v. to call 2.5
   llamar por teléfono to call on the phone

llamarse v. to be called; to be named 2.1
llanta f. tire 2.5
llave f. key 1.5; wrench 2.5
llegada f. arrival 1.5
llegar v. to arrive 1.2
llenar v. to fill 2.5, 3.2
   llenar el tanque to fill the tank 2.5
   llenar (un formulario) to fill out (a form) 3.2
lleno/a adj. full 2.5
llevar v. to carry 1.2; to wear; to take 1.6
   llevar una vida sana to lead a healthy lifestyle 3.3
   llevarse bien/mal (con) to get along well/badly (with) 2.3
llorar v. to cry 3.3
llover (o:ue) v. to rain 1.5
   Llueve. It's raining. 1.5
lluvia f. rain
lo m., sing. d.o. pron. him, it, form. you 1.5
   ¡Lo he pasado de película! I've had a fantastic time! 3.6
   lo mejor the best (thing)
   lo que that which; what 2.6
   Lo siento. I'm sorry. 1.1
loco/a adj. crazy 1.6
locutor(a) m., f. (TV or radio) announcer 3.6
lodo m. mud
los m., pl., def. art. the 1.1; m. pl., d.o. pron. them, you 1.5
luchar (contra/por) v. to fight; to struggle (against/for) 3.6
luego adv. then 2.1; later 1.1
lugar m. place 1.2, 1.4
luna f. moon 3.1
lunares m. polka dots
lunes m., sing. Monday 1.2
luz f. light; electricity 2.6

M

madrastra f. stepmother 1.3
madre f. mother 1.3
madurez f. maturity; middle age 2.3
maestro/a m., f. teacher 3.4
magnífico/a adj. magnificent 1.5
maíz m. corn 2.2
mal, malo/a adj. bad 1.3
maleta f. suitcase 1.1
mamá f. mom
mandar v. to order 2.6; to send; to mail 3.2
manejar v. to drive 2.5
manera f. way
mano f. hand 1.1
manta f. blanket 2.6
mantener v. to maintain 3.3
   mantenerse en forma to stay in shape 3.3
mantequilla f. butter 2.2
manzana f. apple 2.2

mañana *f.* morning, a.m. 1.1; tomorrow 1.1
mapa *m.* map 1.1, 1.2
maquillaje *m.* makeup 2.1
maquillarse *v.* to put on makeup 2.1
mar *m.* sea 1.5
maravilloso/a *adj.* marvelous 1.5
mareado/a *adj.* dizzy; nauseated 2.4
margarina *f.* margarine 2.2
mariscos *m., pl.* shellfish 2.2
marrón *adj. m., f.* brown 1.6
martes *m., sing.* Tuesday 1.2
marzo *m.* March 1.5
más *adv.* more 1.2
   más de (+ *number*) more than 2.2
   más tarde later (on) 2.1
   más... que more... than 2.2
masaje *m.* massage 3.3
matemáticas *f., pl.* mathematics 1.2
materia *f.* course 1.2
matrimonio *m.* marriage 2.3
máximo/a *adj.* maximum 2.5
mayo *m.* May 1.5
mayonesa *f.* mayonnaise 2.2
mayor *adj.* older 1.3
   el/la mayor *adj.* oldest 2.2
me *sing., d.o. pron.* me 1.5; *sing. i.o. pron.* to/for me 1.6
   Me gusta... I like... 1.2
   Me gustaría(n)... I would like... 3.3
   Me llamo... My name is... 1.1
   Me muero por... I'm dying to (for)...
mecánico/a *m., f.* mechanic 2.5
mediano/a *adj.* medium
medianoche *f.* midnight 1.1
medias *f., pl.* pantyhose, stockings 1.6
medicamento *m.* medication 2.4
medicina *f.* medicine 2.4
médico/a *m., f.* doctor 1.3; *adj.* medical 2.4
medio/a *adj.* half 1.3
   medio ambiente *m.* environment 3.1
   medio/a hermano/a *m., f.* half-brother/half-sister 1.3
   mediodía *m.* noon 1.1
   medios de comunicación *m., pl.* means of communication; media 3.6
   y media thirty minutes past the hour (time) 1.1
mejor *adj.* better 2.2
   el/la mejor *m., f.* the best 2.2
mejorar *v.* to improve 3.1
melocotón *m.* peach 2.2
menor *adj.* younger 1.3
   el/la menor *m., f.* youngest 2.2
menos *adv.* less 2.4
   menos cuarto..., menos

quince... quarter to... (*time*) 1.1
menos de (+ *number*) fewer than 2.2
menos... que less... than 2.2
mensaje *m.* **de texto** text message 2.5
mensaje electrónico *m.* e-mail message 1.4
mentira *f.* lie 1.4
menú *m.* menu 2.2
mercado *m.* market 1.6
   mercado al aire libre open-air market 1.6
merendar (e:ie) *v.* to snack 2.2; to have an afternoon snack
merienda *f.* afternoon snack 3.3
mes *m.* month 1.5
mesa *f.* table 1.2
mesita *f.* end table 2.6
   mesita de noche night stand 2.6
meterse en problemas *v.* to get into trouble 3.1
metro *m.* subway 1.5
mexicano/a *adj.* Mexican 1.3
mí *pron., obj. of prep.* me 2.3
mi(s) *poss. adj.* my 1.3
microonda *f.* microwave 2.6
   horno de microondas *m.* microwave oven 2.6
miedo *m.* fear
miel *f.* honey 2.4
mientras *conj.* while 2.4
miércoles *m., sing.* Wednesday 1.2
mil *m.* one thousand 1.2
   mil millones billion
milla *f.* mile
millón *m.* million 1.2
millones (de) *m.* millions (of)
mineral *m.* mineral 3.3
minuto *m.* minute
mío(s)/a(s) *poss.* my; (of) mine 2.5
mirar *v.* to look (at); to watch 1.2
   mirar (la) televisión to watch television 1.2
mismo/a *adj.* same 1.3
mochila *f.* backpack 1.2
moda *f.* fashion 1.6
moderno/a *adj.* modern 3.5
molestar *v.* to bother; to annoy 2.1
monitor *m.* (computer) monitor 2.5
   monitor(a) *m., f.* trainer
mono *m.* monkey 3.1
montaña *f.* mountain 1.4
montar *v.* **a caballo** to ride a horse 1.5
montón: un montón de a lot of 1.4
monumento *m.* monument 1.4
morado/a *adj.* purple 1.6
moreno/a *adj.* brunet(te) 1.3
morir (o:ue) *v.* to die 2.2
mostrar (o:ue) *v.* to show 1.4
moto(cicleta) *f.* motorcycle 1.5

motor *m.* motor
muchacho/a *m., f.* boy/girl 1.3
mucho/a *adj.,* a lot of; much; many 1.3
   (Muchas) gracias. Thank you (very much); Thanks (a lot). 1.1
   muchas veces *adv.* a lot; many times 2.4
   Mucho gusto. Pleased to meet you. 1.1
mudarse *v.* to move (from one house to another) 2.6
muebles *m., pl.* furniture 2.6
muerte *f.* death 2.3
muerto/a *p.p.* died 3.2
mujer *f.* woman 1.1
   mujer de negocios *f.* business woman 3.4
   mujer policía *f.* female police officer
multa *f.* fine
mundial *adj. m., f.* worldwide
mundo *m.* world 2.2
muro *m.* wall 3.3
músculo *m.* muscle 3.3
museo *m.* museum 1.4
música *f.* music 1.2, 3.5
musical *adj. m., f.* musical 3.5
músico/a *m., f.* musician 3.5
muy *adv.* very 1.1
   (Muy) bien, gracias. (Very) well, thanks. 1.1

N

nacer *v.* to be born 2.3
nacimiento *m.* birth 2.3
nacional *adj. m., f.* national 3.6
nacionalidad *f.* nationality 1.1
nada nothing 1.1; not anything 2.1
   nada mal not bad at all 1.5
nadar *v.* to swim 1.4
nadie *pron.* no one, nobody, not anyone 2.1
naranja *f.* orange 2.2
nariz *f.* nose 2.4
natación *f.* swimming 1.4
natural *adj. m., f.* natural 3.1
naturaleza *f.* nature 3.1
navegador *m.* **GPS** GPS 2.5
navegar (en Internet) *v.* to surf (the Internet) 2.5
Navidad *f.* Christmas 2.3
necesario/a *adj.* necessary 2.6
necesitar (+ *inf.*) *v.* to need 1.2
negar (e:ie) *v.* to deny 3.1
   no negar (e:ie) *v.* not to deny 3.1
negocios *m., pl.* business; commerce 3.4
negro/a *adj.* black 1.6
nervioso/a *adj.* nervous 1.5
nevar (e:ie) *v.* to snow 1.5
   Nieva. It's snowing. 1.5
ni...ni neither... nor 2.1
niebla *f.* fog

nieto/a *m., f.* grandson/ granddaughter 1.3
nieve *f.* snow
ningún, ninguno/a(s) *adj.* no; none; not any 2.1
niñez *f.* childhood 2.3
niño/a *m., f.* child 1.3
no no; not 1.1
   ¿no? right? 1.1
   no cabe duda de there is no doubt 3.1
   no es seguro it's not certain 3.1
   no es verdad it's not true 3.1
   No está nada mal. It's not bad at all. 1.5
   no estar de acuerdo to disagree
   No estoy seguro. I'm not sure.
   no hay there is not; there are not 1.1
   No hay de qué. You're welcome. 1.1
   no hay duda de there is no doubt 3.1
   ¡No me diga(s)! You don't say!
   No me gustan nada. I don't like them at all. 1.2
   no muy bien not very well 1.1
   No quiero. I don't want to. 1.4
   No sé. I don't know.
   No te preocupes. *(fam.)* Don't worry. 2.1
   no tener razón to be wrong 1.3
noche *f.* night 1.1
nombre *m.* name 1.1
norte *m.* north 3.2
norteamericano/a *adj.* (North) American 1.3
nos *pl., d.o. pron.* us 1.5; *pl., i.o. pron.* to/for us 1.6
   Nos vemos. See you. 1.1
nosotros/as *sub. pron.* we 1.1; *obj. pron.* us
noticia *f.* news 2.5
noticias *f., pl.* news 3.6
noticiero *m.* newscast 3.6
novecientos/as nine hundred 1.2
noveno/a *adj.* ninth 1.5
noventa ninety 1.2
noviembre *m.* November 1.5
novio/a *m., f.* boyfriend/ girlfriend 1.3
nube *f.* cloud 3.1
nublado/a *adj.* cloudy 1.5
   Está (muy) nublado. It's very cloudy. 1.5
nuclear *adj. m. f.* nuclear 3.1
nuera *f.* daughter-in-law 1.3
nuestro(s)/a(s) *poss. adj.* our 1.3; our, (of) ours 2.5
nueve nine 1.1
nuevo/a *adj.* new 1.6
número *m.* number 1.1; (shoe) size 1.6
nunca *adv.* never; not ever 2.1

nutrición *f.* nutrition 3.3
nutricionista *m., f.* nutritionist 3.3

O

o or 2.1
o... o ; either... or 2.1
obedecer *v.* to obey 3.6
obra *f.* work (*of art, literature, music, etc.*) 3.5
   obra maestra *f.* masterpiece 3.5
obtener *v.* to obtain; to get 3.4
obvio/a *adj.* obvious 3.1
océano *m.* ocean
ochenta eighty 1.2
ocho eight 1.1
ochocientos/as eight hundred 1.2
octavo/a *adj.* eighth 1.5
octubre *m.* October 1.5
ocupación *f.* occupation 3.4
ocupado/a *adj.* busy 1.5
ocurrir *v.* to occur; to happen 3.6
odiar *v.* to hate 2.3
oeste *m.* west 3.2
oferta *f.* offer
oficina *f.* office 2.6
oficio *m.* trade 3.4
ofrecer *v.* to offer 1.6
oído *m.* (sense of) hearing; inner ear 2.4
oído/a *p.p.* heard 3.2
oír *v.* to hear 1.4
ojalá (que) *interj.* I hope (that); I wish (that) 3.1
ojo *m.* eye 2.4
olvidar *v.* to forget 2.4
once eleven 1.1
ópera *f.* opera 3.5
operación *f.* operation 2.4
ordenado/a *adj.* orderly 1.5
ordinal *adj.* ordinal (*number*)
oreja *f.* (outer) ear 2.4
organizarse *v.* to organize oneself 2.6
orquesta *f.* orchestra 3.5
ortografía *f.* spelling
ortográfico/a *adj.* spelling
os *fam., pl. d.o. pron.* you 1.5; *fam., pl. i.o. pron.* to/for you 1.6
otoño *m.* autumn 1.5
otro/a *adj.* other; another 1.6
   otra vez again

P

paciente *m., f.* patient 2.4
padrastro *m.* stepfather 1.3
padre *m.* father 1.3
padres *m., pl.* parents 1.3
pagar *v.* to pay 1.6
   pagar a plazos to pay in installments 3.2
   pagar al contado to pay in cash 3.2
   pagar en efectivo to pay in cash 3.2
   pagar la cuenta to pay the bill

página *f.* page 2.5
   página principal *f.* home page 2.5
país *m.* country 1.1
paisaje *m.* landscape 1.5
pájaro *m.* bird 3.1
palabra *f.* word 1.1
paleta helada *f.* popsicle 1.4
pálido/a *adj.* pale 3.2
pan *m.* bread 2.2
   pan tostado *m.* toasted bread 2.2
panadería *f.* bakery 3.2
pantalla *f.* screen 2.5
   pantalla táctil *f.* touch screen
pantalones *m., pl.* pants 1.6
   pantalones cortos *m., pl.* shorts 1.6
pantuflas *f.* slippers 2.1
papa *f.* potato 2.2
   papas fritas *f., pl.* fried potatoes; French fries 2.2
papá *m.* dad
   papás *m., pl.* parents
papel *m.* paper 1.2; role 3.5
papelera *f.* wastebasket 1.2
paquete *m.* package 3.2
par *m.* pair 1.6
   par de zapatos pair of shoes 1.6
para *prep.* for; in order to; by; used for; considering 2.5
   para que *conj.* so that 3.1
parabrisas *m., sing.* windshield 2.5
parar *v.* to stop 2.5
parecer *v.* to seem 1.6
pared *f.* wall 2.6
pareja *f.* (married) couple; partner 2.3
parientes *m., pl.* relatives 1.3
parque *m.* park 1.4
párrafo *m.* paragraph
parte: de parte de on behalf of 2.5
partido *m.* game; match (*sports*) 1.4
pasado/a *adj.* last; past 1.6
   pasado *p.p.* passed
pasaje *m.* ticket 1.5
   pasaje de ida y vuelta *m.* roundtrip ticket 1.5
pasajero/a *m., f.* passenger 1.1
pasaporte *m.* passport 1.5
pasar *v.* to go through
   pasar la aspiradora to vacuum 2.6
   pasar por la aduana to go through customs
   pasar tiempo to spend time
   pasarlo bien/mal to have a good/bad time 2.3
pasatiempo *m.* pastime; hobby 1.4
pasear *v.* to take a walk; to stroll 1.4
   pasear en bicicleta to ride a bicycle 1.4
   pasear por to walk around
pasillo *m.* hallway 2.6

pasta *f.* **de dientes** toothpaste 2.1
pastel *m.* cake; pie 2.3
  pastel de chocolate *m.* chocolate cake 2.3
  pastel de cumpleaños *m.* birthday cake
pastelería *f.* pastry shop 3.2
pastilla *f.* pill; tablet 2.4
patata *f.* potato 2.2
  patatas fritas *f., pl.* fried potatoes; French fries 2.2
patinar (en línea) *v.* to (inline) skate 1.4
patineta *f.* skateboard 1.4
patio *m.* patio; yard 2.6
pavo *m.* turkey 2.2
paz *f.* peace 3.6
pedir (e:i) *v.* to ask for; to request 1.4; to order (*food*) 2.2
  pedir prestado *v.* to borrow 3.2
  pedir un préstamo *v.* to apply for a loan 3.2
  Todos me dijeron que te pidiera una disculpa de su parte. They all told me to ask you to excuse them/forgive them. 3.6
peinarse *v.* to comb one's hair 2.1
película *f.* movie 1.4
peligro *m.* danger 3.1
peligroso/a *adj.* dangerous 3.6
pelirrojo/a *adj.* red-haired 1.3
pelo *m.* hair 2.1
pelota *f.* ball 1.4
peluquería *f.* beauty salon 3.2
peluquero/a *m., f.* hairdresser 3.4
penicilina *f.* penicillin
pensar (e:ie) *v.* to think 1.4
  pensar (+ inf.) *v.* to intend to; to plan to (do *something*) 1.4
  pensar en *v.* to think about 1.4
pensión *f.* boardinghouse
peor *adj.* worse 2.2
  el/la peor *adj.* the worst 2.2
pequeño/a *adj.* small 1.3
pera *f.* pear 2.2
perder (e:ie) *v.* to lose; to miss 1.4
perdido/a *adj.* lost 3.1, 3.2
Perdón. Pardon me.; Excuse me. 1.1
perezoso/a *adj.* lazy
perfecto/a *adj.* perfect 1.5
periódico *m.* newspaper 1.4
periodismo *m.* journalism 1.2
periodista *m., f.* journalist 1.3
permiso *m.* permission
pero *conj.* but 1.2
perro *m.* dog 3.1
persona *f.* person 1.3
personaje *m.* character 3.5
  personaje principal *m.* main character 3.5
pesas *f. pl.* weights 3.3
pesca *f.* fishing
pescadería *f.* fish market 3.2

pescado *m.* fish (*cooked*) 2.2
pescar *v.* to fish 1.5
peso *m.* weight 3.3
pez *m., sing.* (**peces** *pl.*) fish (*live*) 3.1
pie *m.* foot 2.4
piedra *f.* stone 3.1
pierna *f.* leg 2.4
pimienta *f.* black pepper 2.2
pintar *v.* to paint 3.5
pintor(a) *m., f.* painter 3.4
pintura *f.* painting; picture 2.6, 3.5
piña *f.* pineapple
piscina *f.* swimming pool 1.4
piso *m.* floor (*of a building*) 1.5
pizarra *f.* blackboard 1.2
placer *m.* pleasure
planchar la ropa *v.* to iron the clothes 2.6
planes *m., pl.* plans
planta *f.* plant 3.1
  planta baja *f.* ground floor 1.5
plástico *m.* plastic 3.1
plato *m.* dish (*in a meal*) 2.2; *m.* plate 2.6
  plato principal *m.* main dish 2.2
playa *f.* beach 1.5
plaza *f.* city or town square 1.4
plazos *m., pl.* periods; time 3.2
pluma *f.* pen 1.2
plumero *m.* duster 2.6
población *f.* population 3.1
pobre *adj. m., f.* poor 1.6
pobrecito/a *adj.* poor thing 1.3
pobreza *f.* poverty
poco *adv.* little 1.5, 2.4
poder (o:ue) *v.* to be able to; can 1.4
  ¿Podría pedirte algo? Could I ask you something? 3.5
  ¿Puedo dejar un recado? May I leave a message? 2.5
poema *m.* poem 3.5
poesía *f.* poetry 3.5
poeta *m., f.* poet 3.5
policía *f.* police (force) 2.5
política *f.* politics 3.6
político/a *m., f.* politician 3.4; *adj.* political 3.6
pollo *m.* chicken 2.2
  pollo asado *m.* roast chicken 2.2
poner *v.* to put; to place 1.4; to turn on (*electrical appliances*) 2.5
  poner la mesa to set the table 2.6
  poner una inyección to give an injection 2.4
  ponerle el nombre to name someone/something 2.3
ponerse (+ *adj.*) *v.* to become (+ *adj.*) 2.1; to put on 2.1
por *prep.* in exchange for; for; by; in; through; around; along; during; because of; on account of; on behalf of; in search of; by way of; by means of 2.5

por aquí around here 2.5
por ejemplo for example 2.5
por eso that's why; therefore 2.5
por favor please 1.1
por fin finally 2.5
por la mañana in the morning 2.1
por la noche at night 2.1
por la tarde in the afternoon 2.1
por lo menos *adv.* at least 2.4
¿por qué? why? 1.2
Por supuesto. Of course.
por teléfono by phone; on the phone
por último finally 2.1
porque *conj.* because 1.2
portátil *adj.* portable 2.5
portero/a *m., f.* doorman/doorwoman 1.1
porvenir *m.* future 3.4
  por el porvenir for/to the future 3.4
posesivo/a *adj.* possessive
posible *adj.* possible 3.1
  es posible it's possible 3.1
  no es posible it's not possible 3.1
postal *f.* postcard
postre *m.* dessert 2.3
practicar *v.* to practice 1.2
  practicar deportes *m., pl.* to play sports 1.4
precio (fijo) *m.* (fixed; set) price 1.6
preferir (e:ie) *v.* to prefer 1.4
pregunta *f.* question
preguntar *v.* to ask (*a question*) 1.2
premio *m.* prize; award 3.5
prender *v.* to turn on 2.5
prensa *f.* press 3.6
preocupado/a (por) *adj.* worried (about) 1.5
preocuparse (por) *v.* to worry (about) 2.1
preparar *v.* to prepare 1.2
preposición *f.* preposition
presentación *f.* introduction
presentar *v.* to introduce; to present 3.5; to put on (*a performance*) 3.5
  Le presento a... I would like to introduce you to (name). (*form.*) 1.1
  Te presento a... I would like to introduce you to (name). (*fam.*) 1.1
presiones *f., pl.* pressures 3.3
prestado/a *adj.* borrowed
préstamo *m.* loan 3.2
prestar *v.* to lend; to loan 1.6
primavera *f.* spring 1.5
primer, primero/a *adj.* first 1.5
primero *adv.* first 1.2
primo/a *m., f.* cousin 1.3
principal *adj. m., f.* main 2.2

prisa *f.* haste
  darse prisa *v.* to hurry;
    to rush **3.3**
probable *adj. m., f.* probable **3.1**
  es probable it's probable **3.1**
  no es probable it's not
    probable **3.1**
probar (o:ue) *v.* to taste; to
  try **2.2**
probarse (o:ue) *v.* to try on **2.1**
problema *m.* problem **1.1**
profesión *f.* profession **1.3; 3.4**
profesor(a) *m., f.* teacher **1.1, 1.2**
programa *m.* program **1.1**
  programa de computación
    m. software **2.5**
  programa de entrevistas *m.*
    talk show **3.5**
  programa de realidad *m.*
    reality show **3.5**
programador(a) *m., f.* computer
  programmer **1.3**
prohibir *v.* to prohibit **2.4**;
  to forbid
pronombre *m.* pronoun
pronto *adv.* soon **2.4**
propina *f.* tip **2.2**
propio/a *adj.* own
proteger *v.* to protect **3.1**
proteína *f.* protein **3.3**
próximo/a *adj.* next **1.3, 3.4**
proyecto *m.* project **2.5**
prueba *f.* test; quiz **1.2**
psicología *f.* psychology **1.2**
psicólogo/a *m., f.*
  psychologist **3.4**
publicar *v.* to publish **3.5**
público *m.* audience **3.5**
pueblo *m.* town
puerta *f.* door **1.2**
puertorriqueño/a *adj.* Puerto
  Rican **1.3**
pues *conj.* well
puesto *m.* position; job **3.4**
puesto/a *p.p.* put **3.2**
puro/a *adj.* pure **3.1**

Q

que *pron.* that; which; who **2.6**
  ¿En qué...? In which...?
  ¡Qué...! How...!
  ¡Qué dolor! What pain!
  ¡Qué ropa más bonita!
    What pretty clothes! **1.6**
  ¡Qué sorpresa! What a
    surprise!
  ¿qué? what? **1.1, 1.2**
  ¿Qué día es hoy? What day is
    it? **1.2**
  ¿Qué hay de nuevo? What's
    new? **1.1**
  ¿Qué hora es? What time
    is it? **1.1**
  ¿Qué les parece? What do
    you (*pl.*) think?
  ¿Qué onda? What's up? **3.2**

¿Qué pasa? What's happening?
  What's going on? **1.1**
¿Qué pasó? What happened?
¿Qué precio tiene? What is
  the price?
¿Qué tal...? How are you?;
  How is it going? **1.1**
¿Qué talla lleva/usa? What
  size do you wear? **1.6**
¿Qué tiempo hace? How's
  the weather? **1.5**
quedar *v.* to be left over; to fit
  (*clothing*) **2.1**; to be located **3.2**
quedarse *v.* to stay; to remain **2.1**
quehaceres domésticos *m., pl.*
  household chores **2.6**
quemar (un CD/DVD) *v.* to burn
  (a CD/DVD)
querer (e:ie) *v.* to want; to love **1.4**
queso *m.* cheese **2.2**
quien(es) *pron.* who; whom;
  that **2.6**
¿quién(es)? who?; whom? **1.1, 1.2**
  ¿Quién es...? Who is...? **1.1**
  ¿Quién habla? Who is speaking/
    calling? (*telephone*) **2.5**
química *f.* chemistry **1.2**
quince fifteen **1.1**
  menos quince quarter to
    (time) **1.1**
  y quince quarter after (time) **1.1**
quinceañera *f.* young woman
  celebrating her fifteenth
  birthday **2.3**
quinientos/as five hundred **1.2**
quinto/a *adj.* fifth **1.5**
quisiera *v.* I would like
quitar el polvo *v.* to dust **2.6**
quitar la mesa *v.* to clear the
  table **2.6**
quitarse *v.* to take off **2.1**
quizás *adv.* maybe **1.5**

R

racismo *m.* racism **3.6**
radio *f.* radio (*medium*) **1.2**;
  m. radio (set) **2.5**
radiografía *f.* X-ray **2.4**
rápido *adv.* quickly **2.4**
ratón *m.* mouse **2.5**
ratos libres *m., pl.* spare (free)
  time **1.4**
raya *f.* stripe
razón *f.* reason
rebaja *f.* sale **1.6**
receta *f.* prescription **2.4**
recetar *v.* to prescribe **2.4**
recibir *v.* to receive **1.3**
reciclaje *m.* recycling **3.1**
reciclar *v.* to recycle **3.1**
recién casado/a *m., f.* newlywed **2.3**
recoger *v.* to pick up **3.1**
recomendar (e:ie) *v.* to
  recommend **2.2, 2.6**

recordar (o:ue) *v.* to
  remember **1.4**
recorrer *v.* to tour an area
recorrido *m.* tour **3.1**
recuperar *v.* to recover **2.5**
recurso *m.* resource **3.1**
  recurso natural *m.* natural
    resource **3.1**
red *f.* network; Web **2.5**
reducir *v.* to reduce **3.1**
refresco *m.* soft drink **2.2**
refrigerador *m.* refrigerator **2.6**
regalar *v.* to give (a gift) **2.3**
regalo *m.* gift **1.6**
regatear *v.* to bargain **1.6**
región *f.* region; area
regresar *v.* to return **1.2**
regular *adv.* so-so; OK **1.1**
reído *p.p.* laughed **3.2**
reírse (e:i) *v.* to laugh **2.3**
relaciones *f., pl.* relationships
relajarse *v.* to relax **2.3**
reloj *m.* clock; watch **1.2**
renovable *adj.* renewable **3.1**
renunciar (a) *v.* to resign
  (from) **3.4**
repetir (e:i) *v.* to repeat **1.4**
reportaje *m.* report **3.6**
reportero/a *m., f.* reporter **3.4**
representante *m., f.*
  representative **3.6**
reproductor de CD *m.* CD
  player **2.5**
reproductor de DVD *m.* DVD
  player **2.5**
reproductor de MP3 *m.* MP3
  player **2.5**
resfriado *m.* cold (*illness*) **2.4**
residencia estudiantil *f.*
  dormitory **1.2**
resolver (o:ue) *v.* to resolve;
  to solve **3.1**
respirar *v.* to breathe **3.1**
responsable *adj.* responsible **2.2**
respuesta *f.* answer
restaurante *m.* restaurant **1.4**
resuelto/a *p.p.* resolved **3.2**
reunión *f.* meeting **3.4**
revisar *v.* to check **2.5**
  revisar el aceite *v.* to check
    the oil **2.5**
revista *f.* magazine **1.4**
rico/a *adj.* rich **1.6**; *adj.* tasty;
  delicious **2.2**
ridículo/a *adj.* ridiculous **3.1**
río *m.* river **3.1**
rodilla *f.* knee **2.4**
rogar (o:ue) *v.* to beg; to
  plead **2.6**
rojo/a *adj.* red **1.6**
romántico/a *adj.* romantic **3.5**
romper *v.* to break **2.4**
  romperse la pierna *v.* to break
    one's leg **2.4**
romper (con) *v.* to break up
  (with) **2.3**
ropa *f.* clothing; clothes **1.6**

ropa interior *f.* underwear 1.6
rosado/a *adj.* pink 1.6
roto/a *adj.* broken 3.2
rubio/a *adj.* blond(e) 1.3
ruso/a *adj.* Russian 1.3
rutina *f.* routine 2.1
   rutina diaria *f.* daily
     routine 2.1

S

sábado *m.* Saturday 1.2
saber *v.* to know; to know
   how 1.6
   saber a to taste like 2.2
sabrosísimo/a *adj.* extremely
   delicious 2.2
sabroso/a *adj.* tasty; delicious 2.2
sacar *v.* to take out
   sacar buenas notas to get
     good grades 1.2
   sacar fotos to take photos 1.5
   sacar la basura to take out
     the trash 2.6
   sacar(se) un diente to have a
     tooth removed 2.4
sacudir *v.* to dust 2.6
   sacudir los muebles to dust
     the furniture 2.6
sal *f.* salt 2.2
sala *f.* living room 2.6; room
   sala de emergencia(s)
     emergency room 2.4
salario *m.* salary 3.4
salchicha *f.* sausage 2.2
salida *f.* departure; exit 1.5
salir *v.* to leave 1.4; to go out
   salir con to go out with;
     to date 1.4, 2.3
   salir de to leave from 1.4
   salir para to leave for
     (*a place*) 1.4
salmón *m.* salmon 2.2
salón de belleza *m.* beauty
   salon 3.2
salud *f.* health 2.4
saludable *adj.* healthy 2.4
saludar(se) *v.* to greet (each
   other) 2.5
saludo *m.* greeting 1.1
   saludos a... greetings
     to... 1.1
sandalia *f.* sandal 1.6
sandía *f.* watermelon
sándwich *m.* sandwich 2.2
sano/a *adj.* healthy 2.4
se *ref. pron.* himself, herself, itself,
   form. yourself, themselves,
   yourselves 2.1
se *impersonal* one 2.4
   Se hizo... He/she/it became...
secadora *f.* clothes dryer 2.6
secarse *v.* to dry (oneself) 2.1
sección de (no) fumar *f.* (non)
   smoking section 2.2
secretario/a *m., f.* secretary 3.4
secuencia *f.* sequence
sed *f.* thirst

seda *f.* silk 1.6
sedentario/a *adj.* sedentary;
   related to sitting 3.3
seguir (e:i) *v.* to follow; to
   continue 1.4
según according to
segundo/a *adj.* second 1.5
seguro/a *adj.* sure; safe;
   confident 1.5
seis six 1.1
seiscientos/as six hundred 1.2
sello *m.* stamp 3.2
selva *f.* jungle 3.1
semáforo *m.* traffic light 3.2
semana *f.* week 1.2
   fin *m.* **de semana** weekend 1.4
   semana *f.* **pasada** last week 1.6
semestre *m.* semester 1.2
sendero *m.* trail; path 3.1
sentarse (e:ie) *v.* to sit down 2.1
sentir (e:ie) *v.* to be sorry; to
   regret 3.1
sentirse (e:ie) *v.* to feel 2.1
señor (Sr.); don *m.* Mr.; sir 1.1
señora (Sra.); doña *f.* Mrs.;
   ma'am 1.1
señorita (Srta.) *f.* Miss 1.1
separado/a *adj.* separated 2.3
separarse (de) *v.* to separate
   (from) 2.3
septiembre *m.* September 1.5
séptimo/a *adj.* seventh 1.5
ser *v.* to be 1.1
   ser aficionado/a (a) to be a
     fan (of)
   ser alérgico/a (a) to be allergic
     (to) 2.4
   ser gratis to be free of
     charge 3.2
serio/a *adj.* serious
servicio *m.* service 3.3
servilleta *f.* napkin 2.6
servir (e:i) *v.* to serve 2.2;
   to help 1.5
sesenta sixty 1.2
setecientos/as seven
   hundred 1.2
setenta seventy 1.2
sexismo *m.* sexism 3.6
sexto/a *adj.* sixth 1.5
sí *adv.* yes 1.1
si *conj.* if 1.4
SIDA *m.* AIDS 3.6
siempre *adv.* always 2.1
siete seven 1.1 **silla** *f.* seat 1.2
sillón *m.* armchair 2.6
similar *adj. m., f.* similar
simpático/a *adj.* nice;
   likeable 1.3
sin *prep.* without 3.1
   sin duda without a doubt
   sin embargo however
   sin que *conj.* without 3.1
sino but (rather) 2.1
síntoma *m.* symptom 2.4
sitio *m.* place 1.3
sitio *m.* **web** website 2.5

situado/a *p.p.* located
sobre *m.* envelope 3.2; *prep.*
   on; over 1.2
   sobre todo above all 3.1
(sobre)población *f.*
   (over)population 3.1
sobrino/a *m., f.* nephew/niece 1.3
sociología *f.* sociology 1.2
sofá *m.* couch; sofa 2.6
sol *m.* sun 3.1
solar *adj. m., f.* solar 3.1
soldado *m., f.* soldier 3.6
soleado/a *adj.* sunny
solicitar *v.* to apply (*for a job*) 3.4
solicitud (de trabajo) *f.* (job)
   application 3.4
sólo *adv.* only 1.6
solo/a *adj.* alone
soltero/a *adj.* single 2.3
solución *f.* solution 3.1
sombrero *m.* hat 1.6
Son las dos. It's two o'clock. 1.1
sonar (o:ue) *v.* to ring 2.5
sonreído *p.p.* smiled 3.2
sonreír (e:i) *v.* to smile 2.3
sopa *f.* soup 2.2
sorprender *v.* to surprise 2.3
sorpresa *f.* surprise 2.3
sótano *m.* basement; cellar 2.6
soy I am 1.1
   Soy de... I'm from... 1.1
su(s) *poss. adj.* his; her; its; *form.*
   your; their 1.3
subir(se) a *v.* to get on/into
   (*a vehicle*) 2.5
sucio/a *adj.* dirty 1.5
sudar *v.* to sweat 3.3
suegro/a *m., f.* father-in-law/
   mother-in-law 1.3
sueldo *m.* salary 3.4
suelo *m.* floor 2.6
sueño *m.* sleep
suerte *f.* luck
suéter *m.* sweater 1.6
sufrir *v.* to suffer 2.4
   sufrir muchas presiones to
     be under a lot of pressure 3.3
   sufrir una enfermedad to
     suffer an illness 2.4
sugerir (e:ie) *v.* to suggest 2.6
supermercado *m.*
   supermarket 3.2
suponer *v.* to suppose 1.4
sur *m.* south 3.2
sustantivo *m.* noun
suyo(s)/a(s) *poss.* (of) his/her; (of)
   hers; its; *form.* your, (of) yours,
   (of) theirs, their 2.5

T

tabla de (wind)surf *f.* surf
   board/sailboard 1.5
tal vez *adv.* maybe 1.5
talentoso/a *adj.* talented 3.5
talla *f.* size 1.6
   talla grande *f.* large

taller *m.* **mecánico** garage; mechanic's repair shop **2.5**
también *adv.* also; too **1.2; 2.1**
tampoco *adv.* neither; not either **2.1**
tan *adv.* so **1.5**
    tan... como as... as **2.2**
    tan pronto como *conj.* as soon as **3.1**
tanque *m.* tank **2.5**
tanto *adv.* so much
    tanto... como as much... as **2.2**
    tantos/as... como as many... as **2.2**
tarde *adv.* late **2.1**; *f.* afternoon; evening; P.M. **1.1**
tarea *f.* homework **1.2**
tarjeta *f.* (post) card
tarjeta de crédito *f.* credit card **1.6**
tarjeta postal *f.* postcard
taxi *m.* taxi **1.5**
taza *f.* cup **2.6**
te *sing., fam., d.o. pron.* you **1.5**; *sing., fam., i.o. pron.* to/for you **1.6**
    Te presento a... *fam.* I would like to introduce you to (name). **1.1**
    ¿Te gustaría? Would you like to?
    ¿Te gusta(n)...? Do you like...? **1.2**
té *m.* tea **2.2**
    té helado *m.* iced tea **2.2**
teatro *m.* theater **3.5**
teclado *m.* keyboard **2.5**
técnico/a *m., f.* technician **3.4**
tejido *m.* weaving **3.5**
teleadicto/a *m., f.* couch potato **3.3**
(teléfono) celular *m.* (cell) phone **2.5**
telenovela *f.* soap opera **3.5**
teletrabajo *m.* telecommuting **3.4**
televisión *f.* television **1.2**
televisión por cable *f.* cable television
televisor *m.* television set **2.5**
temer *v.* to fear; to be afraid **3.1**
temperatura *f.* temperature **2.4**
temporada *f.* period of time **1.5**
temprano *adv.* early **2.1**
tenedor *m.* fork **2.6**
tener *v.* to have **1.3**
    tener... años to be... years old **1.3**
    tener (mucho) calor to be (very) hot **1.3**
    tener (mucho) cuidado to be (very) careful **1.3**
    tener dolor to have pain **2.4**
    tener éxito to be successful **3.4**
    tener fiebre to have a fever **2.4**
    tener (mucho) frío to be (very) cold **1.3**

tener ganas de (+ *inf.*) to feel like (*doing something*) **1.3**
tener (mucha) hambre *f.* to be (very) hungry **1.3**
tener (mucho) miedo (de) to be (very) afraid (of); to be (very) scared (of) **1.3**
tener miedo (de) que to be afraid that
tener planes *m., pl.* to have plans
tener (mucha) prisa to be in a (big) hurry **1.3**
tener que (+ *inf.*) *v.* to have to (*do something*) **1.3**
tener razón *f.* to be right **1.3**
tener (mucha) sed *f.* to be (very) thirsty **1.3**
tener (mucho) sueño to be (very) sleepy **1.3**
tener (mucha) suerte to be (very) lucky **1.3**
tener tiempo to have time **3.2**
tener una cita to have a date; to have an appointment **2.3**
tenis *m.* tennis **1.4**
tensión *f.* tension **3.3**
tercer, tercero/a *adj.* third **1.5**
terco/a *adj.* stubborn **2.4**
terminar *v.* to end; to finish **1.2**
    terminar de (+ *inf.*) *v.* to finish (*doing something*)
terremoto *m.* earthquake **3.6**
terrible *adj. m., f.* terrible **3.1**
ti *obj. of prep., fam.* you **2.3**
tiempo *m.* time **3.2**; weather **1.5**
    tiempo libre free time
tienda *f.* store **1.6**
tierra *f.* land; soil **3.1**
tío/a *m., f.* uncle/aunt **1.3**
tíos *m., pl.* aunts and uncles **1.3**
título *m.* title **3.4**
tiza *f.* chalk **1.2**
toalla *f.* towel **2.1**
tobillo *m.* ankle **2.4**
tocar *v.* to play (*a musical instrument*) **3.5**; to touch **3.5**
todavía *adv.* yet; still **1.3, 1.5**
todo *m.* everything **1.5**
todo(s)/a(s) *adj.* all
todos *m., pl.* all of us; *m., pl.* everybody; everyone
todos los días *adv.* every day **2.4**
tomar *v.* to take; to drink **1.2**
    tomar clases *f., pl.* to take classes **1.2**
    tomar el sol to sunbathe **1.4**
    tomar en cuenta to take into account
    tomar fotos *f., pl.* to take photos **1.5**
    tomar la temperatura to take someone's temperature **2.4**
    tomar una decisión to make a decision **3.3**
tomate *m.* tomato **2.2**
tonto/a *adj.* foolish **1.3**

torcerse (o:ue) (el tobillo) *v.* to sprain (one's ankle) **2.4**
tormenta *f.* storm **3.6**
tornado *m.* tornado **3.6**
tortuga (marina) *f.* (sea) turtle **3.1**
tos *f., sing.* cough **2.4**
toser *v.* to cough **2.4**
tostado/a *adj.* toasted **2.2**
tostadora *f.* toaster **2.6**
trabajador(a) *adj.* hard-working **1.3**
trabajar *v.* to work **1.2**
trabajo *m.* job; work **3.4**
traducir *v.* to translate **1.6**
traer *v.* to bring **1.4**
tráfico *m.* traffic **2.5**
tragedia *f.* tragedy **3.5**
traído/a *p.p.* brought **3.2**
traje *m.* suit **1.6**
    traje de baño *m.* bathing suit **1.6**
trajinera *f.* type of barge **1.3**
tranquilo/a *adj.* calm; quiet **3.3**
    Tranquilo/a. Relax. **2.1**
    Tranquilo/a, cariño. Relax, sweetie. **2.5**
transmitir *v.* to broadcast **3.6**
tratar de (+ *inf.*) *v.* to try (*to do something*) **3.3**
trece thirteen **1.1**
treinta thirty **1.1, 1.2**
    y treinta thirty minutes past the hour (time) **1.1**
tren *m.* train **1.5**
tres three **1.1**
trescientos/as three hundred **1.2**
trimestre *m.* trimester; quarter **1.2**
triste *adj.* sad **1.5**
tú *fam. sub. pron.* you **1.1**
tu(s) *fam. poss. adj.* your **1.3**
turismo *m.* tourism
turista *m., f.* tourist **1.1**
turístico/a *adj.* touristic
tuyo(s)/a(s) *fam. poss. pron.* your; (of) yours **2.5**

U

Ud. *form. sing.* you **1.1**
Uds. *pl.* you **1.1**
último/a *adj.* last **2.1**
    la última vez the last time **2.1**
un, uno/a *indef. art.* a; one **1.1**
    a la una at one o'clock **1.1**
    una vez once **1.6**
    una vez más one more time
uno one **1.1**
único/a *adj.* only **1.3**; unique **2.3**
universidad *f.* university; college **1.2**
unos/as *m., f., pl. indef. art.* some **1.1**
urgente *adj.* urgent **2.6**
usar *v.* to wear; to use **1.6**

usted (Ud.) *form. sing.* you 1.1
ustedes (Uds.) *pl.* you 1.1
útil *adj.* useful
uva *f.* grape 2.2

V

vaca *f.* cow 3.1
vacaciones *f. pl.* vacation 1.5
valle *m.* valley 3.1
vamos let's go 1.4
vaquero *m.* cowboy 3.5
  de vaqueros *m., pl.* western
    (genre) 3.5
varios/as *adj. m. f., pl.* various;
  several
vaso *m.* glass 2.6
veces *f., pl.* times 1.6
vecino/a *m., f.* neighbor 2.6
veinte twenty 1.1
veinticinco twenty-five 1.1
veinticuatro twenty-four 1.1
veintidós twenty-two 1.1
veintinueve twenty-nine 1.1
veintiocho twenty-eight 1.1
veintiséis twenty-six 1.1
veintisiete twenty-seven 1.1
veintitrés twenty-three 1.1
veintiún, veintiuno/a *adj.*
  twenty-one 1.1
veintiuno twenty-one 1.1
vejez *f.* old age 2.3
velocidad *f.* speed 2.5
  velocidad máxima *f.* speed
    limit 2.5
vencer *v.* to expire 3.2
vendedor(a) *m., f.*
  salesperson 1.6
vender *v.* to sell 1.6

venir *v.* to come 1.3
ventana *f.* window 1.2
ver *v.* to see 1.4
  a ver *v.* let's see
  ver películas *f., pl.* to see
    movies 1.4
verano *m.* summer 1.5
verbo *m.* verb
verdad *f.* truth 1.4
  (no) es verdad it's (not)
    true 3.1
  ¿verdad? right? 1.1
verde *adj., m. f.* green 1.6
verduras *pl., f.* vegetables 2.2
vestido *m.* dress 1.6
vestirse (e:i) *v.* to get dressed 2.1
vez *f.* time 1.6
viajar *v.* to travel 1.2
viaje *m.* trip 1.5
viajero/a *m., f.* traveler 1.5
vida *f.* life 2.3
video *m.* video 1.1
videoconferencia *f.*
  videoconference 3.4
videojuego *m.* video game 1.4
vidrio *m.* glass 3.1
viejo/a *adj.* old 1.3
viento *m.* wind
viernes *m., sing.* Friday 1.2
vinagre *m.* vinegar 2.2
violencia *f.* violence 3.6
visitar *v.* to visit 1.4
  visitar monumentos *m., pl.*
    to visit monuments 1.4
visto/a *p.p.* seen 3.2
vitamina *f.* vitamin 3.3
viudo/a *adj.* widower/widow 2.3
vivienda *f.* housing 2.6
vivir *v.* to live 1.3

vivo/a *adj.* clever; living
volante *m.* steering wheel 2.5
volcán *m.* volcano 3.1
vóleibol *m.* volleyball 1.4
volver (o:ue) *v.* to return 1.4
volver a ver(te, lo, la) *v.* to see
  (you, him, her) again
vos *pron.* you
vosotros/as *fam., pl.* you 1.1
votar *v.* to vote 3.6
vuelta *f.* return trip
vuelto/a *p.p.* returned 3.2
vuestro(s)/a(s) *poss. adj.*
  your 1.3; your, (of) yours
  fam., pl. 2.5

Y

y *conj.* and 1.1
  y cuarto quarter after (time) 1.1
  y media half-past (time) 1.1
  y quince quarter after (time) 1.1
  y treinta thirty (minutes past
    the hour) 1.1
  ¿Y tú? *fam.* And you? 1.1
  ¿Y usted? *form.* And you? 1.1
ya *adv.* already 1.6
yerno *m.* son-in-law 1.3
yo *sub. pron.* I 1.1
yogur *m.* yogurt 2.2

Z

zanahoria *f.* carrot 2.2
zapatería *f.* shoe store 3.2
zapatos de tenis *m., pl.* tennis
  shoes, sneakers 1.6

English–Spanish

A

a **un/a** *m., f., sing.; indef. art.* 1.1
@ *(symbol)* **arroba** *f.* 2.5
a.m. **de la mañana** *f.* 1.1
able: be able to **poder (o:ue)** *v.* 1.4
aboard **a bordo**
above all **sobre todo** 3.1
accident **accidente** *m.* 2.4
accompany **acompañar** *v.* 3.2
account **cuenta** *f.* 3.2
    on account of **por** *prep.* 2.5
accountant **contador(a)** *m., f.* 3.4
accounting **contabilidad** *f.* 1.2
ache **dolor** *m.* 2.4
acquainted: be acquainted with
    conocer *v.* 1.6
action (genre) **de acción** *f.* 3.5
active **activo/a** *adj.* 3.3
actor **actor** *m.*, **actriz** *f.* 3.4
additional **adicional** *adj.*
address **dirección** *f.* 3.2
adjective **adjetivo** *m.*
adolescence **adolescencia** *f.* 2.3
adventure (genre) **de aventuras**
    f. 3.5
advertise **anunciar** *v.* 3.6
advertisement **anuncio** *m.* 3.4
advice **consejo** *m.*
    give advice **dar consejos** 1.6
advise **aconsejar** *v.* 2.6
advisor **consejero/a** *m., f.* 3.4
aerobic **aeróbico/a** *adj.* 3.3
    aerobics class **clase de**
        ejercicios aeróbicos 3.3
    to do aerobics **hacer ejercicios**
        aeróbicos 3.3
affected **afectado/a** *adj.* 3.1
    be affected (by) **estar** *v.*
        afectado/a (por) 3.1
affirmative **afirmativo/a** *adj.*
afraid: be (very) afraid (of) **tener**
    (mucho) miedo (de) 1.3
    be afraid that **tener miedo**
        (de) que
after **después de** *prep.* 2.1;
    después de que *conj.* 3.1
afternoon **tarde** *f.* 1.1
afterward **después** *adv.* 2.1
again **otra vez**
age **edad** *f.* 2.3
agree **concordar** *v.*
agree **estar** *v.* **de acuerdo** 3.5
    I agree. **Estoy de acuerdo.** 3.5
    I don't agree. **No estoy de**
        acuerdo. 3.5
agreement **acuerdo** *m.*
AIDS **SIDA** *m.* 3.6
air **aire** *m.* 3.1
    air pollution **contaminación**
        del aire 3.1
airplane **avión** *m.* 1.5
airport **aeropuerto** *m.* 1.5
alarm clock **despertador** *m.* 2.1
all **todo(s)/a(s)** *adj.*
    all of us **todos**

allergic **alérgico/a** *adj.* 2.4
    be allergic (to) **ser alérgico/a**
        (a) 2.4
alleviate **aliviar** *v.*
almost **casi** *adv.* 2.4
alone **solo/a** *adj.*
along **por** *prep.* 2.5
already **ya** *adv.* 1.6
also **también** *adv.* 1.2; 2.1
altar **altar** *m.* 2.3
aluminum **aluminio** *m.* 3.1
    (made) of aluminum **de**
        aluminio 3.1
always **siempre** *adv.* 2.1
American (North)
    norteamericano/a *adj.* 1.3
among **entre** *prep.* 1.2
amusement **diversión** *f.*
and **y** 1.1, **e** (*before words*
    beginning with i or hi)
    And you?**¿Y tú?** *fam.* 1.1;
        ¿Y usted? *form.* 1.1
angel **ángel** *m.* 2.3
angry **enojado/a** *adj.* 1.5
    get angry (with) **enojarse** *v.*
        (con) 2.1
animal **animal** *m.* 3.1
ankle **tobillo** *m.* 2.4
anniversary **aniversario** *m.* 2.3
    (wedding) anniversary
        aniversario *m.* **(de**
        bodas) 2.3
announce **anunciar** *v.* 3.6
announcer (TV/radio) **locutor(a)**
    m., f. 3.6
annoy **molestar** *v.* 2.1
another **otro/a** *adj.* 1.6
answer **contestar** *v.* 1.2;
    respuesta *f.*
answering machine **contestadora** *f.*
antibiotic **antibiótico** *m.* 2.4
any **algún, alguno/a(s)** *adj.* 2.1
anyone **alguien** *pron.* 2.1
anything **algo** *pron.* 2.1
apartment **apartamento** *m.* 2.6
apartment building **edificio de**
    apartamentos 2.6
app **aplicación** *f.* 2.5
appear **parecer** *v.*
appetizers **entremeses** *m., pl.* 2.2
applaud **aplaudir** *v.* 3.5
apple **manzana** *f.* 2.2
appliance (electric)
    electrodoméstico *m.* 2.6
applicant **aspirante** *m., f.* 3.4
application **solicitud** *f.* 3.4
    job application **solicitud de**
        trabajo 3.4
apply (for a job) **solicitar** *v.* 3.4
    apply for a loan **pedir (e:i)** *v.*
        un préstamo 3.2
appointment **cita** *f.* 2.3
    have an appointment **tener** *v.*
        una cita 2.3
appreciate **apreciar** *v.* 3.5
April **abril** *m.* 1.5
archeologist **arqueólogo/a**
    m., f. 3.4
archeology **arqueología** *f.* 1.2
architect **arquitecto/a** *m., f.* 3.4

area **región** *f.*
Argentine **argentino/a** *adj.* 1.3
arm **brazo** *m.* 2.4
armchair **sillón** *m.* 2.6
army **ejército** *m.* 3.6
around **por** *prep.* 2.5
    around here **por aquí** 2.5
arrange **arreglar** *v.* 2.5
arrival **llegada** *f.* 1.5
arrive **llegar** *v.* 1.2
art **arte** *m.* 1.2
    (fine) arts **bellas artes** *f.,*
        pl. 3.5
article **artículo** *m.* 3.6
artist **artista** *m., f.* 1.3
artistic **artístico/a** *adj.* 3.5
arts **artes** *f., pl.* 3.5
as **como** 2.2
    as a child **de niño/a** 2.4
    as... as **tan... como** 2.2
    as many... as **tantos/as...**
        como 2.2
    as much... as **tanto... como** 2.2
    as soon as **en cuanto** *conj.* 3.1;
        tan pronto como *conj.* 3.1
ask (a question) **preguntar** *v.* 1.2
    ask for **pedir (e:i)** *v.* 1.4
asparagus **espárragos** *m., pl.* 2.2
aspirin **aspirina** *f.* 2.4
at **a** *prep.* 1.1; **en** *prep.* 1.2
    at + time **a la(s)** + time 1.1
    at home **en casa**
    at least **por lo menos** 2.4
    at night **por la noche** 2.1
    At what time...? **¿A qué**
        hora...? 1.1
    At your service. **A sus**
        órdenes.
ATM **cajero automático** *m.* 3.2
attempt **intento** *m.* 2.5
attend **asistir (a)** *v.* 1.3
attic **altillo** *m.* 2.6
audience **público** *m.* 3.5
August **agosto** *m.* 1.5
aunt **tía** *f.* 1.3
    aunts and uncles **tíos** *m., pl.* 1.3
automobile **automóvil** *m.* 1.5;
    carro *m.*; **coche** *m.* 2.5
autumn **otoño** *m.* 1.5
avenue **avenida** *f.*
avoid **evitar** *v.* 3.1
award **premio** *m.* 3.5

B

backpack **mochila** *f.* 1.2
bad **mal, malo/a** *adj.* 1.3
    It's bad that... **Es malo**
        que... 2.6
    It's not bad at all. **No está**
        nada mal. 1.5
bag **bolsa** *f.* 1.6
bakery **panadería** *f.* 3.2
balanced **equilibrado/a** *adj.* 3.3
    to eat a balanced diet **comer**
        una dieta equilibrada 3.3
balcony **balcón** *m.* 2.6
ball **pelota** *f.* 1.4
banana **banana** *f.* 2.2

band **banda** *f.* 3.5
bank **banco** *m.* 3.2
bargain **ganga** *f.* 1.6; **regatear** *v.* 1.6
baseball (*game*) **béisbol** *m.* 1.4
basement **sótano** *m.* 2.6
basketball (*game*) **baloncesto** *m.* 1.4
bathe **bañarse** *v.* 2.1
bathing suit **traje** *m.* **de baño** 1.6
bathroom **baño** *m.* 2.1; **cuarto de baño** *m.* 2.1
be **ser** *v.* 1.1; **estar** *v.* 1.2
　be... years old **tener... años** 1.3
　be sick of... **estar harto/a de...** 3.6
beach **playa** *f.* 1.5
beans **frijoles** *m., pl.* 2.2
beautiful **hermoso/a** *adj.* 1.6
beauty **belleza** *f.* 3.2
　beauty salon **peluquería** *f.* 3.2; **salón** *m.* **de belleza** 3.2
because **porque** *conj.* 1.2
　because of **por** *prep.* 2.5
become (+ *adj.*) **ponerse (+ adj.)** 2.1; **convertirse** *v.*
bed **cama** *f.* 1.5
　go to bed **acostarse (o:ue)** *v.* 2.1
bedroom **alcoba** *f.*, **recámara** *f.*; **dormitorio** *m.* 2.6
beef **carne de res** *f.* 2.2
before **antes** *adv.* 2.1; **antes de** *prep.* 2.1; **antes (de) que** *conj.* 3.1
beg **rogar (o:ue)** *v.* 2.6
begin **comenzar (e:ie)** *v.* 1.4; **empezar (e:ie)** *v.* 1.4
behalf: on behalf of **de parte de** 2.5
behind **detrás de** *prep.* 1.2
believe (in) **creer** *v.* **(en)** 1.3; **creer** *v.* 3.1
　not to believe **no creer** 3.1
believed **creído/a** *p.p.* 3.2
bellhop **botones** *m., f. sing.* 1.5
below **debajo de** *prep.* 1.2
belt **cinturón** *m.* 1.6
benefit **beneficio** *m.* 3.4
beside **al lado de** *prep.* 1.2
besides **además (de)** *adv.* 2.4
best **mejor** *adj.*
　the best **el/la mejor** *m., f.* 2.2 **lo mejor** *neuter*
better **mejor** *adj.* 2.2
　It's better that... **Es mejor que...** 2.6
between **entre** *prep.* 1.2
beverage **bebida** *f.* 2.2
bicycle **bicicleta** *f.* 1.4
big **grande** *adj.* 1.3
bill **cuenta** *f.* 2.2
billion **mil millones**
biology **biología** *f.* 1.2
bird **ave** *f.* 3.1; **pájaro** *m.* 3.1
birth **nacimiento** *m.* 2.3
birthday **cumpleaños** *m., sing.* 2.3

have a birthday **cumplir** *v.* **años**
black **negro/a** *adj.* 1.6
blackboard **pizarra** *f.* 1.2
blanket **manta** *f.* 2.6
block (city) **cuadra** *f.* 3.2
blog **blog** *m.* 2.5
blond(e) **rubio/a** *adj.* 1.3
blouse **blusa** *f.* 1.6
blue **azul** *adj. m., f.* 1.6
boarding house **pensión** *f.*
boat **barco** *m.* 1.5
body **cuerpo** *m.* 2.4
bone **hueso** *m.* 2.4
book **libro** *m.* 1.2
bookcase **estante** *m.* 2.6
bookshelves **estante** *m.* 2.6
bookstore **librería** *f.* 1.2
boot **bota** *f.* 1.6
bore **aburrir** *v.* 2.1
bored **aburrido/a** *adj.* 1.5
　be bored **estar** *v.* **aburrido/a** 1.5
　get bored **aburrirse** *v.* 3.5
boring **aburrido/a** *adj.* 1.5
born: be born **nacer** *v.* 2.3
borrow **pedir (e:i)** *v.* **prestado** 3.2
borrowed **prestado/a** *adj.*
boss **jefe** *m.*, **jefa** *f.* 3.4
bother **molestar** *v.* 2.1
bottle **botella** *f.* 2.3
bottom **fondo** *m.*
boulevard **bulevar** *m.*
boy **chico** *m.* 1.1; **muchacho** *m.* 1.3
boyfriend **novio** *m.* 1.3
brakes **frenos** *m., pl.*
bread **pan** *m.* 2.2
break **romper** *v.* 2.4
　break (one's leg) **romperse (la pierna)** 2.4
　break down **dañar** *v.* 2.4
　break up (with) **romper** *v.* **(con)** 2.3
breakfast **desayuno** *m.* 2.2
　have breakfast **desayunar** *v.* 1.2
breathe **respirar** *v.* 3.1
bring **traer** *v.* 1.4
broadcast **transmitir** *v.* 3.6; **emitir** *v.* 3.6
brochure **folleto** *m.*
broken **roto/a** *adj.* 3.2
　be broken **estar roto/a**
brother **hermano** *m.* 1.3
brother-in-law **cuñado** *m.* 1.3
brothers and sisters **hermanos** *m., pl.* 1.3
brought **traído/a** *p.p.* 3.2
brown **café** *adj.* 1.6; **marrón** *adj.* 1.6
browser **buscador** *m.* 2.5
brunet(te) **moreno/a** *adj.* 1.3
brush **cepillar(se)** *v.* 2.1
　brush one's hair **cepillarse el pelo** 2.1

brush one's teeth **cepillarse los dientes** 2.1
bucket **balde** *m.* 1.5
build **construir** *v.*
building **edificio** *m.* 2.6
bump into (*something accidentally*) **darse con** 2.4; (*someone*) **encontrarse** *v.* 2.5
burn (a CD/DVD) **quemar** *v.* **(un CD/DVD)**
bus **autobús** *m.* 1.1
　bus station **estación** *f.* **de autobuses** 1.5
business **negocios** *m. pl.* 3.4
　business administration **administración** *f.* **de empresas** 1.2
　business-related **comercial** *adj.* 3.4
businessperson **hombre** *m.* **/ mujer** *f.* **de negocios** 3.4
busy **ocupado/a** *adj.* 1.5
but **pero** *conj.* 1.2; (*rather*) **sino** *conj.* (*in negative sentences*) 2.1
butcher shop **carnicería** *f.* 3.2
butter **mantequilla** *f.* 2.2
buy **comprar** *v.* 1.2
by **por** *prep.* 2.5; **para** *prep.* 2.5
　by means of **por** *prep.* 2.5
　by phone **por teléfono**
　by plane **en avión** 1.5
　by way of **por** *prep.* 2.5
bye **chau** *interj. fam.* 1.1

C

cable television **televisión** *f.* **por cable** *m.*
café **café** *m.* 1.4
cafeteria **cafetería** *f.* 1.2
caffeine **cafeína** *f.* 3.3
cake **pastel** *m.* 2.3
　chocolate cake **pastel de chocolate** *m.* 2.3
calculator **calculadora** *f.* 1.2
call **llamar** *v.* 2.5
　be called **llamarse** *v.* 2.1
　call on the phone **llamar por teléfono**
calm **tranquilo/a** *adj.* 3.3
calorie **caloría** *f.* 3.3
camera **cámara** *f.* 2.5
camp **acampar** *v.* 1.5
can (*tin*) **lata** *f.* 3.1
can **poder (o:ue)** *v.* 1.4
　Could I ask you something? **¿Podría pedirte algo?** 3.5
Canadian **canadiense** *adj.* 1.3
candidate **aspirante** *m., f.* 3.4; **candidato/a** *m., f.* 3.6
candy **dulces** *m., pl.* 2.3
capital city **capital** *f.*
car **coche** *m.* 2.5; **carro** *m.* 2.5; **auto(móvil)** *m.* 1.5
caramel **caramelo** *m.* 2.3
card **tarjeta** *f.*; (*playing*) **carta** *f.* 1.5

care **cuidado** *m.*
 take care of **cuidar** *v.* 3.1
career **carrera** *f.* 3.4
careful: be (very) careful **tener** *v.* **(mucho) cuidado** 1.3
caretaker **ama** *m., f.* **de casa** 2.6
carpenter **carpintero/a** *m., f.* 3.4
carpet **alfombra** *f.* 2.6
carrot **zanahoria** *f.* 2.2
carry **llevar** *v.* 1.2
cartoons **dibujos** *m, pl.* **animados** 3.5
case: in case (that) **en caso (de) que** 3.1
cash (a check) **cobrar** *v.* 3.2;
 cash **(en) efectivo** 1.6
 cash register **caja** *f.* 1.6
 pay in cash **pagar** *v.* **al contado** 3.2; **pagar en efectivo** 3.2
cashier **cajero/a** *m., f.*
cat **gato** *m.* 3.1
CD **disco compacto** *m.* 2.5
CD player **reproductor de CD** *m.* 2.5
CD-ROM **cederrón** *m.*
celebrate **celebrar** *v.* 2.3
celebration **celebración** *f.*
cellar **sótano** *m.* 2.6
(cell) phone **(teléfono) celular** *m.* 2.5
cemetery **cementerio** *m.* 2.3
cereal **cereales** *m., pl.* 2.2
certain **cierto/a** *adj.*; **seguro/a** *adj.* 3.1
 it's (not) certain **(no) es cierto/seguro** 3.1
chalk **tiza** *f.* 1.2
change **cambiar** *v.* **(de)** 2.3
change: in change **de cambio** 1.2
channel *(TV)* **canal** *m.* 2.5; 3.5
character *(fictional)* **personaje** *m.* 3.5
 (main) character *m.* **personaje (principal)** 3.5
charger **cargador** *m.* 2.5
chat **conversar** *v.* 1.2; **chatear** *v.* 2.5
cheap **barato/a** *adj.* 1.6
check **comprobar (o:ue)** *v.*; **revisar** *v.* 2.5; *(bank)* **cheque** *m.* 3.2
 check the oil **revisar el aceite** 2.5
checking account **cuenta** *f.* **corriente** 3.2
cheese **queso** *m.* 2.2
chef **cocinero/a** *m., f.* 3.4
chemistry **química** *f.* 1.2
chest of drawers **cómoda** *f.* 2.6
chicken **pollo** *m.* 2.2
child **niño/a** *m., f.* 1.3
childhood **niñez** *f.* 2.3
children **hijos** *m., pl.* 1.3
Chinese **chino/a** *adj.* 1.3
chocolate **chocolate** *m.* 2.3
 chocolate cake **pastel** *m.* **de chocolate** 2.3
cholesterol **colesterol** *m.* 3.3
choose **escoger** *v.* 2.2

chop *(food)* **chuleta** *f.* 2.2
Christmas **Navidad** *f.* 2.3
church **iglesia** *f.* 1.4
cinnamon **canela** *f.* 2.4
citizen **ciudadano/a** *m., f.* 3.6
city **ciudad** *f.*
class **clase** *f.* 1.2
 take classes **tomar clases** 1.2
classical **clásico/a** *adj.* 3.5
classmate **compañero/a** *m., f.* **de clase** 1.2
clean **limpio/a** *adj.* 1.5; **limpiar** *v.* 2.6
 clean the house *v.* **limpiar la casa** 2.6
clear *(weather)* **despejado/a** *adj.*
 clear the table **quitar la mesa** 2.6
 It's (very) clear. *(weather)* **Está (muy) despejado.**
clerk **dependiente/a** *m., f.* 1.6
climate change **cambio climático** *m.* 3.1
climb **escalar** *v.* 1.4
 climb mountains **escalar montañas** 1.4
clinic **clínica** *f.* 2.4
clock **reloj** *m.* 1.2
close **cerrar (e:ie)** *v.* 1.4
closed **cerrado/a** *adj.* 1.5
closet **armario** *m.* 2.6
clothes **ropa** *f.* 1.6
 clothes dryer **secadora** *f.* 2.6
clothing **ropa** *f.* 1.6
cloud **nube** *f.* 3.1
cloudy **nublado/a** *adj.* 1.5
 It's (very) cloudy. **Está (muy) nublado.** 1.5
coat **abrigo** *m.* 1.6
coffee **café** *m.* 2.2
 coffee maker **cafetera** *f.* 2.6
cold **frío** *m.* 1.5;
 (illness) **resfriado** *m.* 2.4
 be *(feel)* (very) cold **tener (mucho) frío** 1.3
 It's (very) cold. *(weather)* **Hace (mucho) frío.** 1.5
college **universidad** *f.* 1.2
collision **choque** *m.* 3.6
color **color** *m.* 1.6
comb one's hair **peinarse** *v.* 2.1
come **venir** *v.* 1.3
come on **ándale** *interj.* 3.2
comedy **comedia** *f.* 3.5
comfortable **cómodo/a** *adj.* 1.5
commerce **negocios** *m., pl.* 3.4
commercial **comercial** *adj.* 3.4
communicate (with) **comunicarse** *v.* **(con)** 3.6
communication **comunicación** *f.* 3.6
 means of communication **medios** *m. pl.* **de comunicación** 3.6
community **comunidad** *f.* 1.1
company **compañía** *f.* 3.4; **empresa** *f.* 3.4
comparison **comparación** *f.*
composer **compositor(a)** *m., f.* 3.5
computer **computadora** *f.* 1.1

computer disc **disco** *m.*
computer monitor **monitor** *m.* 2.5
computer programmer **programador(a)** *m., f.* 1.3
computer science **computación** *f.* 1.2
concert **concierto** *m.* 3.5
conductor *(musical)* **director(a)** *m., f.* 3.5
confident **seguro/a** *adj.* 1.5
confirm **confirmar** *v.* 1.5
 confirm a reservation **confirmar una reservación** 1.5
confused **confundido/a** *adj.* 1.5
congested **congestionado/a** *adj.* 2.4
Congratulations! **¡Felicidades!**; **¡Felicitaciones!** *f., pl.* 2.3
conservation **conservación** *f.* 3.1
conserve **conservar** *v.* 3.1
considering **para** *prep.* 2.5
consume **consumir** *v.* 3.3
container **envase** *m.* 3.1
contamination **contaminación** *f.*
content **contento/a** *adj.* 1.5
contest **concurso** *m.* 3.5
continue **seguir (e:i)** *v.* 1.4
control **control** *m.*; **controlar** *v.* 3.1
conversation **conversación** *f.* 1.1
converse **conversar** *v.* 1.2
cook **cocinar** *v.* 2.6; **cocinero/a** *m., f.* 3.4
cookie **galleta** *f.* 2.3
cool **fresco/a** *adj.* 1.5
 It's cool. *(weather)* **Hace fresco.** 1.5
corn **maíz** *m.* 2.2
corner **esquina** *f.* 3.2
cost **costar (o:ue)** *v.* 1.6
Costa Rican **costarricense** *adj.* 1.3
costume **disfraz** *m.* 2.3
cotton **algodón** *f.* 1.6
 (made of) cotton **de algodón** 1.6
couch **sofá** *m.* 2.6
couch potato **teleadicto/a** *m., f.* 3.3
cough **tos** *f.* 2.4; **toser** *v.* 2.4
counselor **consejero/a** *m., f.* 3.4
count **contar (o:ue)** *v.* 1.4
country *(nation)* **país** *m.* 1.1
countryside **campo** *m.* 1.5
(married) couple **pareja** *f.* 2.3
course **curso** *m.* 1.2; **materia** *f.* 1.2
courtesy **cortesía** *f.*
cousin **primo/a** *m., f.* 1.3
cover **cubrir** *v.*
covered **cubierto/a** *p.p.*
cow **vaca** *f.* 3.1
crafts **artesanía** *f.* 3.5
craftsmanship **artesanía** *f.* 3.5
crater **cráter** *m.* 3.1
crazy **loco/a** *adj.* 1.6
create **crear** *v.*
credit **crédito** *m.* 1.6
 credit card **tarjeta** *f.* **de crédito** 1.6
crime **crimen** *m.* 3.6
cross **cruzar** *v.* 3.2

cry **llorar** *v.* 3.3
Cuban **cubano/a** *adj.* 1.3
culture **cultura** *f.* 1.2, 3.5
cup **taza** *f.* 2.6
currency exchange **cambio** *m.* **de moneda**
current events **actualidades** *f.,* *pl.* 3.6
curtains **cortinas** *f., pl.* 2.6
custard (*baked*) **flan** *m.* 2.3
custom **costumbre** *f.*
customer **cliente/a** *m., f.* 1.6
customs **aduana** *f.*
   customs inspector **inspector(a)** *m., f.* **de aduanas** 1.5
cybercafé **cibercafé** *m.* 2.5
cycling **ciclismo** *m.* 1.4

D

dad **papá** *m.*
daily **diario/a** *adj.* 2.1
   daily routine **rutina** *f.* **diaria** 2.1
damage **dañar** *v.* 2.4
dance **bailar** *v.* 1.2; **danza** *f.* 3.5; **baile** *m.* 3.5
dancer **bailarín/bailarina** *m., f.* 3.5
danger **peligro** *m.* 3.1
dangerous **peligroso/a** *adj.* 3.6
date (*appointment*) **cita** *f.* 2.3; (*calendar*) **fecha** *f.* 1.5; (*someone*) **salir** *v.* **con (alguien)** 2.3
   have a date **tener una cita** 2.3
daughter **hija** *f.* 1.3
daughter-in-law **nuera** *f.* 1.3
day **día** *m.* 1.1
   day before yesterday **anteayer** *adv.* 1.6
death **muerte** *f.* 2.3
decaffeinated **descafeinado/a** *adj.* 3.3
December **diciembre** *m.* 1.5
decide **decidir** *v.* (+ *inf.*) 1.3
declare **declarar** *v.* 3.6
deforestation **deforestación** *f.* 3.1
delicious **delicioso/a** *adj.* 2.2; **rico/a** *adj.* 2.2; **sabroso/a** *adj.* 2.2
delighted **encantado/a** *adj.* 1.1
dentist **dentista** *m., f.* 2.4
deny **negar (e:ie)** *v.* 3.1
   not to deny **no negar** 3.1
department store **almacén** *m.* 1.6
departure **salida** *f.* 1.5
deposit **depositar** *v.* 3.2
describe **describir** *v.* 1.3
described **descrito/a** *p.p.* 3.2
desert **desierto** *m.* 3.1
design **diseño** *m.*
designer **diseñador(a)** *m., f.* 3.4
desire **desear** *v.* 1.2
desk **escritorio** *m.* 1.2
dessert **postre** *m.* 2.3
destroy **destruir** *v.* 3.1
develop **desarrollar** *v.* 3.1

diary **diario** *m.* 1.1
dictatorship **dictadura** *f.* 3.6
dictionary **diccionario** *m.* 1.1
die **morir (o:ue)** *v.* 2.2
died **muerto/a** *p.p.* 3.2
diet **dieta** *f.* 3.3; **alimentación**
   balanced diet **dieta equilibrada** 3.3
   be on a diet **estar a dieta** 3.3
difficult **difícil** *adj. m., f.* 1.3
digital camera **cámara** *f.* **digital** 2.5
dining room **comedor** *m.* 2.6
dinner **cena** *f.* 2.2
   have dinner **cenar** *v.* 1.2
direct **dirigir** *v.* 3.5
director **director(a)** *m., f.* 3.5
dirty **ensuciar** *v.*; **sucio/a** *adj.* 1.5
   get (something) dirty **ensuciar** *v.* 2.6
disagree **no estar de acuerdo**
disaster **desastre** *m.* 3.6
discover **descubrir** *v.* 3.1
discovered **descubierto/a** *p.p.* 3.2
discrimination **discriminación** *f.* 3.6
dish **plato** *m.* 2.2, 2.6
   main dish *m.* **plato principal** 2.2
dishwasher **lavaplatos** *m., sing.* 2.6
disk **disco** *m.*
disorderly **desordenado/a** *adj.* 1.5
divorce **divorcio** *m.* 2.3
divorced **divorciado/a** *adj.* 2.3
   get divorced (from) **divorciarse** *v.* **(de)** 2.3
dizzy **mareado/a** *adj.* 2.4
do **hacer** *v.* 1.4
   do aerobics **hacer ejercicios aeróbicos** 3.3
   do household chores **hacer quehaceres domésticos** 2.6
   do stretching exercises **hacer ejercicios de estiramiento** 3.3
   (I) don't want to. **No quiero.** 1.4
doctor **doctor(a)** *m., f.* 1.3; 2.4; **médico/a** *m., f.* 1.3
documentary (*film*) **documental** *m.* 3.5
dog **perro** *m.* 3.1
domestic **doméstico/a** *adj.*
   domestic appliance **electrodoméstico** *m.*
done **hecho/a** *p.p.* 3.2
door **puerta** *f.* 1.2
doorman/doorwoman **portero/a** *m., f.* 1.1
dormitory **residencia** *f.* **estudiantil** 1.2
double **doble** *adj.* 1.5
   double room **habitación** *f.* **doble** 1.5
doubt **duda** *f.* 3.1; **dudar** *v.* 3.1
   not to doubt **no dudar** 3.1
   there is no doubt that **no cabe duda de** 3.1; **no hay duda de** 3.1
download **descargar** *v.* 2.5
downtown **centro** *m.* 1.4
drama **drama** *m.* 3.5

dramatic **dramático/a** *adj.* 3.5
draw **dibujar** *v.* 1.2
drawing **dibujo** *m.*
dress **vestido** *m.* 1.6
   get dressed **vestirse (e:i)** *v.* 2.1
drink **beber** *v.* 1.3; **bebida** *f.* 2.2; **tomar** *v.* 1.2
drive **conducir** *v.* 1.6; **manejar** *v.* 2.5
driver **conductor(a)** *m., f.* 1.1
dry (oneself) **secarse** *v.* 2.1
during **durante** *prep.* 2.1; **por** *prep.* 2.5
dust **sacudir** *v.* 2.6; **quitar** *v.* **el polvo** 2.6
   dust the furniture **sacudir los muebles** 2.6
duster **plumero** *m.* 2.6
DVD player **reproductor** *m.* **de DVD** 2.5

E

each **cada** *adj.* 1.6
ear (outer) **oreja** *f.* 2.4
early **temprano** *adv.* 2.1
earn **ganar** *v.* 3.4
earring **arete** *m.* 1.6
earthquake **terremoto** *m.* 3.6
ease **aliviar** *v.*
east **este** *m.* 3.2
   to the east **al este** 3.2
easy **fácil** *adj. m., f.* 1.3
eat **comer** *v.* 1.3
ecological **ecológico/a** *adj.* 3.1
ecologist **ecologista** *m., f.* 3.1
ecology **ecología** *f.* 3.1
economics **economía** *f.* 1.2
ecotourism **ecoturismo** *m.* 3.1
Ecuadorian **ecuatoriano/a** *adj.* 1.3
effective **eficaz** *adj. m., f.*
egg **huevo** *m.* 2.2
eight **ocho** 1.1
eight hundred **ochocientos/as** 1.2
eighteen **dieciocho** 1.1
eighth **octavo/a** 1.5
eighty **ochenta** 1.2
either... or **o... o** *conj.* 2.1
elect **elegir (e:i)** *v.* 3.6
election **elecciones** *f. pl.* 3.6
electric appliance **electrodoméstico** *m.* 2.6
electrician **electricista** *m., f.* 3.4
electricity **luz** *f.* 2.6
elegant **elegante** *adj. m., f.* 1.6
elevator **ascensor** *m.* 1.5
eleven **once** 1.1
e-mail **correo** *m.* **electrónico** 1.4
   e-mail address **dirección** *f.* **electrónica** 2.5
   e-mail message **mensaje** *m.* **electrónico** 1.4
   read e-mail **leer** *v.* **el correo electrónico** 1.4
embarrassed **avergonzado/a** *adj.* 1.5
embrace (each other) **abrazar(se)** *v.* 2.5

emergency **emergencia** *f.* 2.4
   emergency room **sala** *f.* **de emergencia(s)** 2.4
employee **empleado/a** *m., f.* 1.5
employment **empleo** *m.* 3.4
end **fin** *m.* 1.4; **terminar** *v.* 1.2
   end table **mesita** *f.* 2.6
endure **aguantar** *v.* 3.2
energy **energía** *f.* 3.1
engaged: get engaged (to) **comprometerse** *v.* **(con)** 2.3
engineer **ingeniero/a** *m., f.* 1.3
English (*language*) **inglés** *m.* 1.2; **inglés, inglesa** *adj.* 1.3
enjoy **disfrutar** *v.* **(de)** 3.3
enough **bastante** *adv.* 2.4
entertainment **diversión** *f.* 1.4
entrance **entrada** *f.* 2.6
envelope **sobre** *m.* 3.2
environment **medio ambiente** *m.* 3.1
environmental science **ciencias ambientales** 1.2
equality **igualdad** *f.* 3.6
erase **borrar** *v.* 2.5
eraser **borrador** *m.* 1.2
errand **diligencia** *f.* 3.2
essay **ensayo** *m.* 1.3
establish **establecer** *v.* 3.4
evening **tarde** *f.* 1.1
event **acontecimiento** *m.* 3.6
every day **todos los días** 2.4
everything **todo** *m.* 1.5
exactly **en punto** 1.1
exam **examen** *m.* 1.2
excellent **excelente** *adj.* 1.5
excess **exceso** *m.* 3.3
   in excess **en exceso** 3.3
exchange **intercambiar** *v.*
   in exchange for **por** 2.5
exciting **emocionante** *adj. m., f.*
excursion **excursión** *f.*
excuse **disculpar** *v.*
Excuse me. (*May I?*) **Con permiso.** 1.1; (*I beg your pardon.*) **Perdón.** 1.1
exercise **ejercicio** *m.* 3.3; **hacer** *v.* **ejercicio** 3.3; (a degree/profession) **ejercer** *v.* 3.4
exit **salida** *f.* 1.5
expensive **caro/a** *adj.* 1.6
experience **experiencia** *f.*
expire **vencer** *v.* 3.2
explain **explicar** *v.* 1.2
explore **explorar** *v.*
expression **expresión** *f.*
extinction **extinción** *f.* 3.1
eye **ojo** *m.* 2.4

F

fabulous **fabuloso/a** *adj.* 1.5
face **cara** *f.* 2.1
facing **enfrente de** *prep.* 3.2
fact: in fact **de hecho**
factory **fábrica** *f.* 3.1
fall (down) **caerse** *v.* 2.4
   fall asleep **dormirse (o:ue)** *v.* 2.1

fall in love (with) **enamorarse** *v.* **(de)** 2.3
fall (season) **otoño** *m.* 1.5
fallen **caído/a** *p.p.* 3.2
family **familia** *f.* 1.3
famous **famoso/a** *adj.*
fan **aficionado/a** *m., f.* 1.4
   be a fan (of) **ser aficionado/a (a)**
far from **lejos de** *prep.* 1.2
farewell **despedida** *f.*
fascinate **fascinar** *v.* 2.1
fashion **moda** *f.* 1.6
   be in fashion **estar de moda** 1.6
fast **rápido/a** *adj.*
fat **gordo/a** *adj.* 1.3; **grasa** *f.* 3.3
father **padre** *m.* 1.3
father-in-law **suegro** *m.* 1.3
favorite **favorito/a** *adj.* 1.4
fax (machine) **fax** *m.*
fear **miedo** *m.*; **temer** *v.* 3.1
February **febrero** *m.* 1.5
feel **sentir(se) (e:ie)** *v.* 2.1
   feel like (*doing something*) **tener ganas de** (+ *inf.*) 1.3
festival **festival** *m.* 3.5
fever **fiebre** *f.* 2.4
   have a fever **tener** *v.* **fiebre** 2.4
few **pocos/as** *adj. pl.*
   fewer than **menos de** (+ *number*) 2.2
field: major field of study **especialización** *f.*
fifteen **quince** 1.1
   fifteen-year-old girl celebrating her birthday **quinceañera** *f.*
fifth **quinto/a** 1.5
fifty **cincuenta** 1.2
fight (for/against) **luchar** *v.* **(por/ contra)** 3.6
figure (*number*) **cifra** *f.*
file **archivo** *m.* 2.5
fill **llenar** *v.* 2.5
   fill out (a form) **llenar (un formulario)** 3.2
   fill the tank **llenar el tanque** 2.5
finally **finalmente** *adv.*; **por último** 2.1; **por fin** 2.5
find **encontrar (o:ue)** *v.* 1.4
   find (each other) **encontrar(se)**
   find out **enterarse** *v.* 3.4
fine **multa** *f.*
   That's fine. **Está bien.**
(fine) arts **bellas artes** *f., pl.* 3.5
finger **dedo** *m.* 2.4
finish **terminar** *v.* 1.2
   finish (*doing something*) **terminar** *v.* **de** (+ *inf.*)
fire **incendio** *m.* 3.6; **despedir (e:i)** *v.* 3.4
firefighter **bombero/a** *m., f.* 3.4
firm **compañía** *f.* 3.4; **empresa** *f.* 3.4
first **primer, primero/a** 1.2, 1.5

fish (*food*) **pescado** *m.* 2.2; **pescar** *v.* 1.5; (*live*) **pez** *m., sing.* (**peces** *pl.*) 3.1
fish market **pescadería** *f.* 3.2
fishing **pesca** *f.*
fit (*clothing*) **quedar** *v.* 2.1
five **cinco** 1.1
five hundred **quinientos/as** 1.2
fix (*put in working order*) **arreglar** *v.* 2.5; (*clothes, hair, etc. to go out*) **arreglarse** *v.* 2.1
fixed **fijo/a** *adj.* 1.6
flag **bandera** *f.*
flexible **flexible** *adj.* 3.3
flood **inundación** *f.* 3.6
floor (*of a building*) **piso** *m.* 1.5; **suelo** *m.* 2.6
   ground floor **planta baja** *f.* 1.5
   top floor **planta** *f.* **alta**
flower **flor** *f.* 3.1
flu **gripe** *f.* 2.4
fog **niebla** *f.*
folk **folclórico/a** *adj.* 3.5
follow **seguir (e:i)** *v.* 1.4
food **comida** *f.* 1.4, 2.2
foolish **tonto/a** *adj.* 1.3
foot **pie** *m.* 2.4
football **fútbol** *m.* **americano** 1.4
for **para** *prep.* 2.5; **por** *prep.* 2.5
   for example **por ejemplo** 2.5
   for me **para mí** 2.2
forbid **prohibir** *v.*
foreign **extranjero/a** *adj.* 3.5
   foreign languages **lenguas** *f., pl.* **extranjeras** 1.2
forest **bosque** *m.* 3.1
forget **olvidar** *v.* 2.4
fork **tenedor** *m.* 2.6
form **formulario** *m.* 3.2
forty **cuarenta** 1.2
four **cuatro** 1.1
four hundred **cuatrocientos/as** 1.2
fourteen **catorce** 1.1
fourth **cuarto/a** *m., f.* 1.5
free **libre** *adj. m., f.* 1.4
   be free (of charge) **ser gratis** 3.2
   free time **tiempo libre**; spare (free) time **ratos libres** 1.4
freedom **libertad** *f.* 3.6
freezer **congelador** *m.* 2.6
French **francés, francesa** *adj.* 1.3
   French fries **papas** *f., pl.* **fritas** 2.2; **patatas** *f., pl.* **fritas** 2.2
frequently **frecuentemente** *adv.*; **con frecuencia** *adv.* 2.4
Friday **viernes** *m., sing.* 1.2
fried **frito/a** *adj.* 2.2
   fried potatoes **papas** *f., pl.* **fritas** 2.2; **patatas** *f., pl.* **fritas** 2.2
friend **amigo/a** *m., f.* 1.3
friendly **amable** *adj. m., f.* 1.5

friendship **amistad** *f.* 2.3
from **de** *prep.* 1.1; **desde** *prep.* 1.6
  from the United States
    estadounidense *m., f. adj.* 1.3
  from time to time **de vez en**
    cuando 2.4
  I'm from… **Soy de…** 1.1
front: (cold) front **frente (frío)**
  m. 1.5
fruit **fruta** *f.* 2.2
  fruit juice **jugo** *m.* **de fruta** 2.2
  fruit store **frutería** *f.* 3.2
full **lleno/a** *adj.* 2.5
fun **divertido/a** *adj.*
  fun activity **diversión** *f.* 1.4
  have fun **divertirse (e:ie)** *v.* 2.3
function **funcionar** *v.*
furniture **muebles** *m., pl.* 2.6
furthermore **además (de)** *adv.* 2.4
future **porvenir** *m.* 3.4
  for/to the future **por el**
    porvenir 3.4
  in the future **en el futuro**

G

gain weight **aumentar** *v.* **de**
  peso 3.3; **engordar** *v.* 3.3
game **juego** *m.*; *(match)*
  partido *m.* 1.4
  game show **concurso** *m.* 3.5
garage *(in a house)* **garaje** *m.* 2.6;
  garaje *m.* 2.5; **taller**
  (mecánico) 2.5
garden **jardín** *m.* 2.6
garlic **ajo** *m.* 2.2
gas station **gasolinera** *f.* 2.5
gasoline **gasolina** *f.* 2.5
gentleman **caballero** *m.* 2.2
geography **geografía** *f.* 1.2
German **alemán, alemana**
  adj. 1.3
get **conseguir(e:i)** *v.* 1.4;
  obtener *v.* 3.4
  get along well/badly (with)
    llevarse bien/mal (con) 2.3
  get bigger **aumentar** *v.* 3.1
  get bored **aburrirse** *v.* 3.5
  get good grades **sacar buenas**
    notas 1.2
  get into trouble **meterse en**
    problemas *v.* 3.1
  get off of (a vehicle) **bajar(se)** *v.*
    de 2.5
  get on/into (a vehicle) **subir(se)**
    v. **a** 2.5
  get out of (a vehicle) **bajar(se)**
    v. **de** 2.5
  get ready **arreglarse** *v.* 2.1
  get up **levantarse** *v.* 2.1
gift **regalo** *m.* 1.6
ginger **jengibre** *m.* 2.4
girl **chica** *f.* 1.1; **muchacha** *f.* 1.3
girlfriend **novia** *f.* 1.3

give **dar** *v.* 1.6; *(as a gift)*
  regalar 2.3
  give directions **indicar cómo**
    llegar 3.2
glass *(drinking)* **vaso** *m.* 2.6;
  vidrio *m.* 3.1
  (made) of glass **de vidrio** 3.1
glasses **gafas** *f., pl.* 1.6
  sunglasses **gafas** *f., pl.*
    de sol 1.6
global warming **calentamiento**
  global *m.* 3.1
gloves **guantes** *m., pl.* 1.6
go **ir** *v.* 1.4
  go away **irse** 2.1
  go by boat **ir en barco** 1.5
  go by bus **ir en autobús** 1.5
  go by car **ir en auto(móvil)** 1.5
  go by motorcycle **ir en**
    moto(cicleta) 1.5
  go by plane **ir en avión** 1.5
  go by taxi **ir en taxi** 1.5
  go down **bajar(se)** *v.*
  go on a hike **ir de excursión** 1.4
  go out (with) **salir** *v.* **(con)** 2.3
  go up **subir** *v.*
  Let's go. **Vamos.** 1.4
goblet **copa** *f.* 2.6
going to: be going to (*do*
  something) **ir a (+ *inf.*)** 1.4
golf **golf** *m.* 1.4
good **buen, bueno/a** *adj.* 1.3, 1.6
  Good afternoon. **Buenas**
    tardes. 1.1
  Good evening. **Buenas**
    noches. 1.1
  Good morning. **Buenos días.** 1.1
  Good night. **Buenas noches.** 1.1
  It's good that… **Es bueno**
    que… 2.6
goodbye **adiós** *m.* 1.1
  say goodbye (to) **despedirse** *v.*
    (de) (e:i) 3.6
good-looking **guapo/a** *adj.* 1.3
government **gobierno** *m.* 3.1
GPS **navegador GPS** *m.* 2.5
graduate (from/in) **graduarse** *v.*
  (de/en) 2.3
grains **cereales** *m., pl.* 2.2
granddaughter **nieta** *f.* 1.3
grandfather **abuelo** *m.* 1.3
grandmother **abuela** *f.* 1.3
grandparents **abuelos** *m., pl.* 1.3
grandson **nieto** *m.* 1.3
grape **uva** *f.* 2.2
grass **hierba** *f.* 3.1
grave **grave** *adj.* 2.4
gray **gris** *adj. m., f.* 1.6
great **fenomenal** *adj. m., f.* 1.5;
  genial *adj.* 3.4
great-grandfather **bisabuelo** *m.* 1.3
great-grandmother **bisabuela** *f.* 1.3
green **verde** *adj. m., f.* 1.6
greet (each other) **saludar(se)**
  v. 2.5

greeting **saludo** *m.* 1.1
  Greetings to… **Saludos a…** 1.1
grilled **a la plancha** 2.2
ground floor **planta baja** *f.* 1.5
grow **aumentar** *v.* 3.1
guest (*at a house/hotel*) **huésped**
  m., f. 1.5 (*invited to a function*)
  invitado/a *m., f.* 2.3
guide **guía** *m., f.*
gymnasium **gimnasio** *m.* 1.4

H

hair **pelo** *m.* 2.1
hairdresser **peluquero/a** *m., f.* 3.4
half **medio/a** *adj.* 1.3
  half-brother **medio**
    hermano *m.* 1.3
  half-past… (*time*) **…y media** 1.1
  half-sister **media hermana** *f.* 1.3
hallway **pasillo** *m.* 2.6
ham **jamón** *m.* 2.2
hamburger **hamburguesa** *f.* 2.2
hand **mano** *f.* 1.1
hand in **entregar** *v.* 2.5
handsome **guapo/a** *adj.* 1.3
happen **ocurrir** *v.* 3.6
happiness **alegría** *v.* 2.3
Happy birthday!
  ¡Feliz cumpleaños! 2.3
happy **alegre** *adj.* 1.5; **contento/a**
  adj. 1.5; **feliz** *adj. m., f.* 1.5
  be happy **alegrarse** *v.* **(de)** 3.1
hard **difícil** *adj. m., f.* 1.3
hard-working **trabajador(a)** *adj.* 1.3
hardly **apenas** *adv.* 2.4
hat **sombrero** *m.* 1.6
hate **odiar** *v.* 2.3
have **tener** *v.* 1.3
  have time **tener tiempo** 3.2
  have to (*do something*) **tener**
    que (+ *inf.*) 1.3
  have a tooth removed **sacar(se)**
    un diente 2.4
he **él** 1.1
head **cabeza** *f.* 2.4
headache **dolor** *m.* **de cabeza** 2.4
health **salud** *f.* 2.4
healthy **saludable** *adj. m., f.* 2.4;
  sano/a *adj.* 2.4
  lead a healthy lifestyle **llevar** *v.*
    una vida sana 3.3
hear **oír** *v.* 1.4
heard **oído/a** *p.p.* 3.2
hearing: sense of hearing **oído** *m.* 2.4
heart **corazón** *m.* 2.4
heat **calor** *m.*
Hello. **Hola.** 1.1; (*on the*
  telephone) **Aló.** 2.5;
  Bueno. 2.5; **Diga.** 2.5
help **ayudar** *v.*; **servir (e:i)** *v.* 1.5
  help each other **ayudarse** *v.* 2.5
her **su(s)** *poss. adj.* 1.3; (*of*) hers
  suyo(s)/a(s) *poss.* 2.5
  her **la** *f., sing., d.o. pron.* 1.5
  to/for her **le** *f., sing., i.o. pron.* 1.6

here **aquí** *adv.* 1.1
   Here is/are... **Aquí está(n)...** 1.5
Hi. **Hola.** 1.1
highway **autopista** *f.* 2.5;
   carretera *f.* 2.5
hike **excursión** *f.* 1.4
   go on a hike **ir de**
   excursión 1.4
hiker **excursionista** *m., f.*
hiking **de excursión** 1.4
him *m., sing., d.o. pron.* **lo** 1.5;
   to/for him **le** *m., sing., i.o.*
   pron. 1.6
hire **contratar** *v.* 3.4
his **su(s)** *poss. adj.* 1.3; (of) his
   suyo(s)/a(s) *poss. pron.* 2.5
history **historia** *f.* 1.2; 3.5
hobby **pasatiempo** *m.* 1.4
hockey **hockey** *m.* 1.4
hold up **aguantar** *v.* 3.2
hole **hueco** *m.* 1.4
holiday **día** *m.* **de fiesta** 2.3
home **casa** *f.* 1.2
   home page **página** *f.*
   principal 2.5
homework **tarea** *f.* 1.2
honey **miel** *f.* 2.4
hood **capó** *m.* 2.5; **cofre** *m.* 2.5
hope **esperar** *v.* (+ *inf.*) 1.2;
   esperar *v.* 3.1
   I hope (that) **ojalá (que)** 3.1
horror (genre) **de horror** *m.* 3.5
hors d'oeuvres **entremeses** *m.,*
   pl. 2.2
horse **caballo** *m.* 1.5
hospital **hospital** *m.* 2.4
hot: be (*feel*) (very) hot **tener**
   (mucho) calor 1.3
   It's (very) hot. **Hace (mucho)**
   calor. 1.5
hotel **hotel** *m.* 1.5
hour **hora** *f.* 1.1
house **casa** *f.* 1.2
household chores **quehaceres** *m.*
   pl. **domésticos** 2.6
housekeeper **ama** *m., f.* **de casa** 2.6
housing **vivienda** *f.* 2.6
How...! **¡Qué...!**
   how **¿cómo?** *adv.* 1.1, 1.2
   How are you? **¿Qué tal?** 1.1
   How are you? **¿Cómo estás?**
   fam. 1.1
   How are you? **¿Cómo está**
   usted? *form.* 1.1
   How can I help you? **¿En qué**
   puedo servirles? 1.5
   How is it going? **¿Qué tal?** 1.1
   How is the weather? **¿Qué**
   tiempo hace? 1.5
   How much/many?
   ¿Cuánto(s)/a(s)? 1.1
   How much does... cost?
   ¿Cuánto cuesta...? 1.6
   How old are you? **¿Cuántos**
   años tienes? *fam.*
however **sin embargo**

hug (each other) **abrazar(se)** *v.* 2.5
humanities **humanidades** *f., pl.* 1.2
hundred **cien, ciento** 1.2
hunger **hambre** *f.*
hungry: be (very) hungry **tener** *v.*
   (mucha) hambre 1.3
hunt **cazar** *v.* 3.1
hurricane **huracán** *m.* 3.6
hurry **apurarse** *v.* 3.3; **darse**
   prisa *v.* 3.3
   be in a (big) hurry **tener** *v.*
   (mucha) prisa 1.3
hurt **doler (o:ue)** *v.* 2.4
husband **esposo** *m.* 1.3

I

I **yo** 1.1
   I hope (that) **Ojalá (que)**
   interj. 3.1
   I wish (that) **Ojalá (que)**
   interj. 3.1
ice cream **helado** *m.* 2.3
   ice cream shop **heladería** *f.* 3.2
iced **helado/a** *adj.* 2.2
   iced tea **té** *m.* **helado** 2.2
idea **idea** *f.* 3.6
if **si** *conj.* 1.4
illness **enfermedad** *f.* 2.4
important **importante** *adj.* 1.3
   be important to **importar** *v.* 2.1
   It's important that... **Es**
   importante que... 2.6
impossible **imposible** *adj.* 3.1
   it's impossible **es imposible** 3.1
improbable **improbable** *adj.* 3.1
   it's improbable **es**
   improbable 3.1
improve **mejorar** *v.* 3.1
in **en** *prep.* 1.2; **por** *prep.* 2.5
   in the afternoon **de la**
   tarde 1.1; **por la tarde** 2.1
   in a bad mood **de mal**
   humor 1.5
   in the direction of **para** *prep.* 2.5
   in the early evening **de la**
   tarde 1.1
   in the evening **de la noche** 1.1;
   por la tarde 2.1
   in a good mood **de buen**
   humor 1.5
   in the morning **de la mañana**
   1.1; **por la mañana** 2.1
   in love (with) **enamorado/a**
   (de) 1.5
   in search of **por** *prep.* 2.5
in front of **delante de** *prep.* 1.2
increase **aumento** *m.*
incredible **increíble** *adj.* 1.5
inequality **desigualdad** *f.* 3.6
infection **infección** *f.* 2.4
inform **informar** *v.* 3.6
injection **inyección** *f.* 2.4
   give an injection *v.* **poner una**
   inyección 2.4

injure (oneself) **lastimarse** 2.4
   injure (one's foot) **lastimarse** *v.*
   (el pie) 2.4
inner ear **oído** *m.* 2.4
inside **dentro** *adv.*
insist (on) **insistir** *v.* **(en)** 2.6
installments: pay in installments
   pagar *v.* **a plazos** 3.2
intelligent **inteligente** *adj.* 1.3
intend to **pensar** *v.* **(+ inf.)** 1.4
interest **interesar** *v.* 2.1
interesting **interesante** *adj.* 1.3
   be interesting to **interesar** *v.* 2.1
international **internacional**
   adj. m., f. 3.6
Internet **Internet** 2.5
interview **entrevista** *f.* 3.4;
   interview **entrevistar** *v.* 3.4
interviewer **entrevistador(a)** *m.,*
   f. 3.4
introduction **presentación** *f.*
   I would like to introduce you to
   (name). **Le presento a...**
   form. 1.1; **Te presento a...**
   fam. 1.1
invest **invertir (e:ie)** *v.* 3.4
invite **invitar** *v.* 2.3
iron (clothes) **planchar** *v.* **la**
   ropa 2.6
it **lo/la** *sing., d.o., pron.* 1.5
Italian **italiano/a** *adj.* 1.3
its **su(s)** *poss. adj.* 1.3;
   suyo(s)/a(s) *poss. pron.* 2.5
it's the same **es igual** 1.5

J

jacket **chaqueta** *f.* 1.6
January **enero** *m.* 1.5
Japanese **japonés, japonesa**
   adj. 1.3
jeans **(blue)jeans** *m., pl.* 1.6
jewelry store **joyería** *f.* 3.2
job **empleo** *m.* 3.4; **puesto**
   m. 3.4; **trabajo** *m.* 3.4
   job application **solicitud** *f.* **de**
   trabajo 3.4
jog **correr** *v.*
journalism **periodismo** *m.* 1.2
journalist **periodista** *m., f.* 1.3
joy **alegría** *f.* 2.3
juice **jugo** *m.* 2.2
July **julio** *m.* 1.5
June **junio** *m.* 1.5
jungle **selva, jungla** *f.* 3.1
just **apenas** *adv.*
   have just done something
   acabar de (+ inf.) 1.6

K

key **llave** *f.* 1.5
keyboard **teclado** *m.* 2.5
kilometer **kilómetro** *m.* 2.5

kiss **beso** *m.* 2.3
  kiss each other **besarse** *v.* 2.5
kitchen **cocina** *f.* 2.3, 2.6
knee **rodilla** *f.* 2.4
knife **cuchillo** *m.* 2.6
know **saber** *v.* 1.6; **conocer**
  v. 1.6
know how **saber** *v.* 1.6

L

laboratory **laboratorio** *m.* 1.2
lack **faltar** *v.* 2.1
lake **lago** *m.* 3.1
lamp **lámpara** *f.* 2.6
land **tierra** *f.* 3.1
landscape **paisaje** *m.* 1.5
language **lengua** *f.* 1.2
laptop (computer) **computadora**
  f. **portátil** 2.5
large **grande** *adj.* 1.3
large (*clothing size*) **talla grande**
last **durar** *v.* 3.6; **pasado/a**
  adj. 1.6; **último/a** *adj.* 2.1
  last name **apellido** *m.* 1.3
  last night **anoche** *adv.* 1.6
  last week **semana** *f.*
    pasada 1.6
  last year **año** *m.* **pasado** 1.6
  the last time **la última vez** 2.1
late **tarde** *adv.* 2.1
later (on) **más tarde** 2.1
  See you later. **Hasta la vista.** 1.1;
    Hasta luego. 1.1
laugh **reírse (e:i)** *v.* 2.3
laughed **reído** *p.p.* 3.2
laundromat **lavandería** *f.* 3.2
law **ley** *f.* 3.1
lawyer **abogado/a** *m., f.* 3.4
lazy **perezoso/a** *adj.*
learn **aprender** *v.* **(a + *inf.*)** 1.3
least, at **por lo menos** *adv.* 2.4
leave **salir** *v.* 1.4; **irse** *v.* 2.1
  leave a tip **dejar una**
    propina
  leave behind **dejar** *v.* 3.4
  leave for (*a place*) **salir para**
  leave from **salir de**
left **izquierda** *f.* 1.2
  be left over **quedar** *v.* 2.1
  to the left of **a la izquierda**
    de 1.2
leg **pierna** *f.* 2.4
lemon **limón** *m.* 2.2
lend **prestar** *v.* 1.6
less **menos** *adv.* 2.4
  less... than **menos... que** 2.2
  less than **menos de (+ *number*)**
lesson **lección** *f.* 1.1
let **dejar** *v.*
let's see **a ver**
letter **carta** *f.* 1.4, 3.2
lettuce **lechuga** *f.* 2.2
liberty **libertad** *f.* 3.6
library **biblioteca** *f.* 1.2
license (*driver's*) **licencia** *f.* **de**
  conducir 2.5

lie **mentira** *f.* 1.4
life **vida** *f.* 2.3
lifestyle: lead a healthy lifestyle
  llevar una vida sana 3.3
lift **levantar** *v.* 3.3
  lift weights **levantar pesas** 3.3
light **luz** *f.* 2.6
like **como** *prep.* 2.2; **gustar** *v.* 1.2
  I like... **Me gusta(n)...** 1.2
  like this **así** *adv.* 2.4
  like very much **encantar** *v.*;
    fascinar *v.* 2.1
  Do you like...? **¿Te**
    gusta(n)...? 1.2
likeable **simpático/a** *adj.* 1.3
likewise **igualmente** *adv.* 1.1
line **línea** *f.* 1.4; **cola** (*queue*)
  f. 3.2
listen (to) **escuchar** *v.* 1.2
  listen to music **escuchar**
    música 1.2
  listen to the radio **escuchar la**
    radio 1.2
literature **literatura** *f.* 1.2
little (*quantity*) **poco** *adv.* 2.4
live **vivir** *v.* 1.3; **en vivo** *adj.* 2.1
living room **sala** *f.* 2.6
loan **préstamo** *m.* 3.2; **prestar**
  v. 1.6, 3.2
lobster **langosta** *f.* 2.2
located **situado/a** *adj.*
  be located **quedar** *v.* 3.2
long **largo/a** *adj.* 1.6
look (at) **mirar** *v.* 1.2
look for **buscar** *v.* 1.2
lose **perder (e:ie)** *v.* 1.4
  lose weight **adelgazar** *v.* 3.3
lost **perdido/a** *adj.* 3.1, 3.2
  be lost **estar perdido/a** 3.2
lot, a **muchas veces** *adv.* 2.4
lot of, a **mucho/a** *adj.* 1.3;
  un montón de 1.4
love (*another person*) **querer**
  (e:ie) *v.* 1.4; (*inanimate objects*)
  encantar *v.* 2.1; **amor** *m.* 2.3
  in love **enamorado/a** *adj.* 1.5
  love at first sight **amor a**
    primera vista 2.3
luck **suerte** *f.*
lucky: be (very) lucky **tener**
  (mucha) suerte 1.3
luggage **equipaje** *m.* 1.5
lunch **almuerzo** *m.* 1.4, 2.2
  have lunch **almorzar (o:ue)**
    v. 1.4

M

ma'am **señora (Sra.)**; **doña** *f.* 1.1
mad **enojado/a** *adj.* 1.5
magazine **revista** *f.* 1.4
magnificent **magnífico/a** *adj.* 1.5
mail **correo** *m.* 3.2; **enviar** *v.*,
  mandar *v.* 3.2; **echar (una**
  carta) al buzón 3.2
  mail carrier **cartero** *m.* 3.2
mailbox **buzón** *m.* 3.2
main **principal** *adj. m., f.* 2.2

maintain **mantener** *v.* 3.3
major **especialización** *f.* 1.2
make **hacer** *v.* 1.4
  make a decision **tomar una**
    decisión 3.3
  make the bed **hacer la cama** 2.6
makeup **maquillaje** *m.* 2.1
  put on makeup **maquillarse**
    v. 2.1
man **hombre** *m.* 1.1
manager **gerente** *m., f.* 2.2, 3.4
many **mucho/a** *adj.* 1.3
  many times **muchas veces** 2.4
map **mapa** *m.* 1.1, 1.2
March **marzo** *m.* 1.5
margarine **margarina** *f.* 2.2
marinated fish **ceviche** *m.* 2.2
  lemon-marinated shrimp
    ceviche *m.* **de camarón** 2.2
marital status **estado** *m.* **civil** 2.3
market **mercado** *m.* 1.6
  open-air market **mercado al**
    aire libre 1.6
marriage **matrimonio** *m.* 2.3
married **casado/a** *adj.* 2.3
  get married (to) **casarse** *v.*
    (con) 2.3
  I'll marry you! **¡Acepto**
    casarme contigo! 3.5
marvelous **maravilloso/a** *adj.* 1.5
massage **masaje** *m.* 3.3
masterpiece **obra maestra** *f.* 3.5
match (*sports*) **partido** *m.* 1.4
match (with) **hacer** *v.*
  juego (con) 1.6
mathematics **matemáticas**
  f., pl. 1.2
matter **importar** *v.* 2.1
maturity **madurez** *f.* 2.3
maximum **máximo/a** *adj.* 2.5
May **mayo** *m.* 1.5
May I leave a message? **¿Puedo**
  dejar un recado? 2.5
maybe **tal vez** 1.5; **quizás** 1.5
mayonnaise **mayonesa** *f.* 2.2
me **me** *sing., d.o. pron.* 1.5
  to/for me **me** *sing., i.o. pron.* 1.6
meal **comida** *f.* 2.2
means of communication **medios**
  m., pl. **de comunicación** 3.6
meat **carne** *f.* 2.2
mechanic **mecánico/a** *m., f.* 2.5
  mechanic's repair shop **taller**
    mecánico 2.5
media **medios** *m., pl.* **de**
  comunicación 3.6
medical **médico/a** *adj.* 2.4
medication **medicamento** *m.* 2.4
medicine **medicina** *f.* 2.4
medium **mediano/a** *adj.*
meet (each other) **encontrar(se)**
  v. 2.5; **conocer(se)** *v.* 2.2
  meet up with **encontrarse**
    con 2.1
meeting **reunión** *f.* 3.4
menu **menú** *m.* 2.2

message **mensaje** *m.*
Mexican **mexicano/a** *adj.* 1.3
microwave **microonda** *f.* 2.6
  microwave oven **horno** *m.* **de**
    microondas 2.6
middle age **madurez** *f.* 2.3
midnight **medianoche** *f.* 1.1
mile **milla** *f.*
milk **leche** *f.* 2.2
million **millón** *m.* 1.2
  million of **millón de** 1.2
mine **mío(s)/a(s)** *poss.* 2.5
mineral **mineral** *m.* 3.3
  mineral water **agua** *f.*
    mineral 2.2
minute **minuto** *m.*
mirror **espejo** *m.* 2.1
Miss **señorita (Srta.)** *f.* 1.1
miss **perder (e:ie)** *v.* 1.4;
  extrañar *v.* 3.4
mistaken **equivocado/a** *adj.*
modern **moderno/a** *adj.* 3.5
mom **mamá** *f.*
Monday **lunes** *m., sing.* 1.2
money **dinero** *m.* 1.6
monitor **monitor** *m.* 2.5
monkey **mono** *m.* 3.1
month **mes** *m.* 1.5
monument **monumento** *m.* 1.4
moon **luna** *f.* 3.1
more **más** 1.2
  more… than **más… que** 2.2
  more than **más de (+**
    number) 2.2
morning **mañana** *f.* 1.1
mother **madre** *f.* 1.3
mother-in-law **suegra** *f.* 1.3
motor **motor** *m.*
motorcycle **moto(cicleta)** *f.* 1.5
mountain **montaña** *f.* 1.4
mouse **ratón** *m.* 2.5
mouth **boca** *f.* 2.4
move *(from one house to another)*
  mudarse *v.* 2.6
movie **película** *f.* 1.4
  movie star **estrella** *f.*
    de cine 3.5
  movie theater **cine** *m.* 1.4
MP3 player **reproductor** *m.* **de**
  MP3 2.5
Mr. **señor (Sr.); don** *m.* 1.1
Mrs. **señora (Sra.); doña** *f.* 1.1
much **mucho/a** *adj.* 1.3
mud **lodo** *m.*
murder **crimen** *m.* 3.6
muscle **músculo** *m.* 3.3
museum **museo** *m.* 1.4
mushroom **champiñón** *m.* 2.2
music **música** *f.* 1.2, 3.5
musical **musical** *adj., m., f.* 3.5
musician **músico/a** *m., f.* 3.5
must **deber** *v.* (+ *inf.*) 1.3
my **mi(s)** *poss. adj.* 1.3; **mío(s)/a(s)**
  poss. pron. 2.5

N

name **nombre** *m.* 1.1
  be named **llamarse** *v.* 2.1
  in the name of **a nombre**
    de 1.5
  last name **apellido** *m.* 1.3
  My name is… **Me llamo…** 1.1
  name someone/something
    ponerle el nombre 2.3
napkin **servilleta** *f.* 2.6
national **nacional** *adj. m., f.* 3.6
nationality **nacionalidad** *f.* 1.1
natural **natural** *adj. m., f.* 3.1
  natural disaster **desastre** *m.*
    natural 3.6
  natural resource **recurso** *m.*
    natural 3.1
nature **naturaleza** *f.* 3.1
nauseated **mareado/a** *adj.* 2.4
near **cerca de** *prep.* 1.2
neaten **arreglar** *v.* 2.6
necessary **necesario/a** *adj.* 2.6
  It is necessary that… **Es**
    necesario que… 2.6
neck **cuello** *m.* 2.4
need **faltar** *v.* 2.1; **necesitar** *v.*
  (+ *inf.*) 1.2
neighbor **vecino/a** *m., f.* 2.6
neighborhood **barrio** *m.* 2.6
neither **tampoco** *adv.* 2.1
neither… nor **ni… ni** *conj.* 2.1
nephew **sobrino** *m.* 1.3
nervous **nervioso/a** *adj.* 1.5
network **red** *f.* 2.5
never **nunca** *adj.* 2.1; **jamás** 2.1
new **nuevo/a** *adj.* 1.6
newlywed **recién casado/a**
  m., f. 2.3
news **noticias** *f., pl.* 3.6;
  actualidades *f., pl.* 3.6;
  noticia *f.* 2.5
newscast **noticiero** *m.* 3.6
newspaper **periódico** 1.4;
  diario *m.* 3.6
next **próximo/a** *adj.* 1.3, 3.4
  next to **al lado de** *prep.* 1.2
nice **simpático/a** *adj.* 1.3;
  amable *adj.* 1.5
niece **sobrina** *f.* 1.3
night **noche** *f.* 1.1
  night stand **mesita** *f.* **de**
    noche 2.6
nine **nueve** 1.1
nine hundred
  novecientos/as 1.2
nineteen **diecinueve** 1.1
ninety **noventa** 1.2
ninth **noveno/a** 1.5
no **no** 1.1; **ningún,**
  ninguno/a(s) *adj.* 2.1
  no one **nadie** *pron.* 2.1
nobody **nadie** 2.1
none **ningún, ninguno/a(s)**
  adj. 2.1

noon **mediodía** *m.* 1.1
nor **ni** *conj.* 2.1
north **norte** *m.* 3.2
  to the north **al norte** 3.2
nose **nariz** *f.* 2.4
not **no** 1.1
  not any **ningún, ninguno/a(s)**
    adj. 2.1
  not anyone **nadie** *pron.* 2.1
  not anything **nada** *pron.* 2.1
  not bad at all **nada mal** 1.5
  not either **tampoco** *adv.* 2.1
  not ever **nunca** *adv.* 2.1; **jamás**
    adv. 2.1
  not very well **no muy bien** 1.1
  not working **descompuesto/a**
    adj. 2.5
notebook **cuaderno** *m.* 1.1
nothing **nada** 1.1; 2.1
noun **sustantivo** *m.*
November **noviembre** *m.* 1.5
now **ahora** *adv.* 1.2
nowadays **hoy día** *adv.*
nuclear **nuclear** *adj. m., f.* 3.1
  nuclear energy **energía**
    nuclear 3.1
number **número** *m.* 1.1
nurse **enfermero/a** *m., f.* 2.4
nutrition **nutrición** *f.* 3.3
nutritionist **nutricionista** *m.,*
  f. 3.3

O

o'clock: It's… o'clock **Son**
  las… 1.1
  It's one o'clock. **Es la una.** 1.1
obey **obedecer** *v.* 3.6
obligation **deber** *m.* 3.6
obtain **conseguir (e:i)** *v.* 1.4;
  obtener *v.* 3.4
obvious **obvio/a** *adj.* 3.1
  it's obvious **es obvio** 3.1
occupation **ocupación** *f.* 3.4
occur **ocurrir** *v.* 3.6
October **octubre** *m.* 1.5
of **de** *prep.* 1.1
  Of course. **Claro que sí.;**
    Por supuesto.
offer **oferta** *f.*; **ofrecer (c:zc)**
  v. 1.6
office **oficina** *f.* 2.6
  doctor's office **consultorio**
    m. 2.4
often **a menudo** *adv.* 2.4
Oh! **¡Ay!**
oil **aceite** *m.* 2.2
OK **regular** *adj.* 1.1
  It's okay. **Está bien.**
old **viejo/a** *adj.* 1.3
old age **vejez** *f.* 2.3
older **mayor** *adj. m., f.* 1.3
  older brother, sister **hermano/a**
    mayor *m., f.* 1.3
oldest **el/la mayor** 2.2
on **en** *prep.* 1.2; **sobre** *prep.* 1.2

on behalf of **por** *prep.* 2.5
on the dot **en punto** 1.1
on time **a tiempo** 2.4
on top of **encima de** 1.2
once **una vez** 1.6
one **uno** 1.1
  one hundred **cien(to)** 1.2
  one million **un millón** *m.* 1.2
  one more time **una vez más**
  one thousand **mil** 1.2
  one time **una vez** 1.6
onion **cebolla** *f.* 2.2
only **sólo** *adv.* 1.6; **único/a** *adj.* 1.3
  only child **hijo/a único/a**
    m., f. 1.3
open **abierto/a** *adj.* 1.5, 3.2;
  abrir *v.* 1.3
open-air **al aire libre** 1.6
opera **ópera** *f.* 3.5
operation **operación** *f.* 2.4
opposite **enfrente de** *prep.* 3.2
or **o** *conj.* 2.1
orange **anaranjado/a** *adj.* 1.6;
  naranja *f.* 2.2
orchestra **orquesta** *f.* 3.5
order **mandar** 2.6; *(food)*
  pedir (e:i) *v.* 2.2
  in order to **para** *prep.* 2.5
orderly **ordenado/a** *adj.* 1.5
ordinal *(numbers)* **ordinal** *adj.*
organize oneself **organizarse** *v.* 2.6
other **otro/a** *adj.* 1.6
ought to **deber** *v.* *(+ inf.)* *adj.* 1.3
our **nuestro(s)/a(s)** *poss. adj.* 1.3;
  poss. pron. 2.5
out of order **descompuesto/a**
  adj. 2.5
outside **afuera** *adv.* 1.5
outskirts **afueras** *f., pl.* 2.6
oven **horno** *m.* 2.6
over **sobre** *prep.* 1.2
(over)population
  (sobre)población *f.* 3.1
over there **allá** *adv.* 1.2
own **propio/a** *adj.*
owner **dueño/a** *m., f.* 2.2

P

p.m. **de la tarde, de la noche**
  f. 1.1
pack *(one's suitcases)* **hacer** *v.* **las**
  maletas 1.5
package **paquete** *m.* 3.2
page **página** *f.* 2.5
pain **dolor** *m.* 2.4
  have pain **tener** *v.* **dolor** 2.4
paint **pintar** *v.* 3.5
painter **pintor(a)** *m., f.* 3.4
painting **pintura** *f.* 2.6, 3.5
pair **par** *m.* 1.6
  pair of shoes **par** *m.* **de**
    zapatos 1.6
pale **pálido/a** *adj.* 3.2
pants **pantalones** *m., pl.* 1.6

pantyhose **medias** *f., pl.* 1.6
paper **papel** *m.* 1.2; *(report)*
  informe *m.* 3.6
Pardon me. *(May I?)* **Con**
  permiso. 1.1; *(Excuse me.)*
  Pardon me. **Perdón.** 1.1
parents **padres** *m., pl.* 1.3;
  papás *m., pl.*
park **estacionar** *v.* 2.5; **parque**
  m. 1.4
parking lot **estacionamiento**
  m. 3.2
partner *(one of a married couple)*
  pareja *f.* 2.3
party **fiesta** *f.* 2.3
passed **pasado/a** *p.p.*
passenger **pasajero/a** *m., f.* 1.1
passport **pasaporte** *m.* 1.5
past **pasado/a** *adj.* 1.6
pastime **pasatiempo** *m.* 1.4
pastry shop **pastelería** *f.* 3.2
path **sendero** *m.* 3.1
patient **paciente** *m., f.* 2.4
patio **patio** *m.* 2.6
pay **pagar** *v.* 1.6
  pay in cash **pagar** *v.* **al contado;**
    pagar en efectivo 3.2
  pay in installments **pagar** *v.* **a**
    plazos 3.2
  pay the bill **pagar la cuenta**
pea **arveja** *m.* 2.2
peace **paz** *f.* 3.6
peach **melocotón** *m.* 2.2
peak **cima** *f.* 3.3
pear **pera** *f.* 2.2
pen **pluma** *f.* 1.2
pencil **lápiz** *m.* 1.1
penicillin **penicilina** *f.*
people **gente** *f.* 1.3
pepper *(black)* **pimienta** *f.* 2.2
per **por** *prep.* 2.5
perfect **perfecto/a** *adj.* 1.5
period of time **temporada** *f.* 1.5
person **persona** *f.* 1.3
pharmacy **farmacia** *f.* 2.4
phenomenal **fenomenal** *adj.* 1.5
photograph **foto(grafía)** *f.* 1.1
physical *(exam)* **examen** *m.*
  médico 2.4
physician **doctor(a), médico/a**
  m., f. 1.3
physics **física** *f. sing.* 1.2
pick up **recoger** *v.* 3.1
picture **cuadro** *m.* 2.6;
  pintura *f.* 2.6
pie **pastel** *m.* 2.3
pill *(tablet)* **pastilla** *f.* 2.4
pillow **almohada** *f.* 2.6
pineapple **piña** *f.*
pink **rosado/a** *adj.* 1.6
place **lugar** *m.* 1.2, 1.4; **sitio** *m.*
  1.3; **poner** *v.* 1.4
plaid **de cuadros** 1.6
plans **planes** *m., pl.*
  have plans **tener planes**
plant **planta** *f.* 3.1
plastic **plástico** *m.* 3.1
  (made) of plastic **de plástico** 3.1

plate **plato** *m.* 2.6
play **drama** *m.* 3.5; **comedia**
  f. 3.5 **jugar (u:ue)** *v.* 1.4; *(a*
  musical instrument) **tocar** *v.*
  3.5; *(a role)* **hacer el papel**
  de 3.5; *(cards)* **jugar a (las**
  cartas) 1.5; *(sports)*
  practicar deportes 1.4
player **jugador(a)** *m., f.* 1.4
playwright **dramaturgo/a**
  m., f. 3.5
plead **rogar (o:ue)** *v.* 2.6
pleasant **agradable** *adj.*
please **por favor** 1.1
Pleased to meet you. **Mucho gusto.**
  1.1; **Encantado/a.** *adj.* 1.1
pleasing: be pleasing to **gustar**
  v. 2.1
pleasure **gusto** *m.* 1.1; **placer** *m.*
  The pleasure is mine. **El gusto**
    es mío. 1.1
poem **poema** *m.* 3.5
poet **poeta** *m., f.* 3.5
poetry **poesía** *f.* 3.5
police *(force)* **policía** *f.* 2.5
political **político/a** *adj.* 3.6
politician **político/a** *m., f.* 3.4
politics **política** *f.* 3.6
polka-dotted **de lunares** 1.6
poll **encuesta** *f.* 3.6
pollute **contaminar** *v.* 3.1
polluted **contaminado/a** *m., f.* 3.1
  be polluted **estar**
    contaminado/a 3.1
pollution **contaminación** *f.* 3.1
pool **piscina** *f.* 1.4
poor **pobre** *adj., m., f.* 1.6
  poor thing **pobrecito/a** *adj.* 1.3
popsicle **paleta helada** *f.* 1.4
population **población** *f.* 3.1
pork **cerdo** *m.* 2.2
  pork chop **chuleta** *f.* **de**
    cerdo 2.2
portable **portátil** *adj.* 2.5
  portable computer
    computadora *f.*
    portátil 2.5
position **puesto** *m.* 3.4
possessive **posesivo/a** *adj.*
possible **posible** *adj.* 3.1
  it's (not) possible **(no) es**
    posible 3.1
post office **correo** *m.* 3.2
postcard **postal** *f.*
poster **cartel** *m.* 2.6
potato **papa** *f.* 2.2; **patata** *f.* 2.2
pottery **cerámica** *f.* 3.5
practice **entrenarse** *v.* 3.3;
  practicar *v.* 1.2; *(a degree/*
  profession) **ejercer** *v.* 3.4
prefer **preferir (e:ie)** *v.* 1.4
pregnant **embarazada** *adj. f.* 2.4
prepare **preparar** *v.* 1.2
preposition **preposición** *f.*
prescribe *(medicine)* **recetar** *v.* 2.4
prescription **receta** *f.* 2.4
present **regalo** *m.*; **presentar**
  v. 3.5

press **prensa** *f.* 3.6
pressure **presión** *f.*
   be under a lot of pressure **sufrir muchas presiones** 3.3
pretty **bonito/a** *adj.* 1.3
price **precio** *m.* 1.6
   (fixed, set) price **precio** *m.* **fijo** 1.6
print **imprimir** *v.* 2.5
printer **impresora** *f.* 2.5
prize **premio** *m.* 3.5
probable **probable** *adj.* 3.1
   it's (not) probable **(no) es probable** 3.1
problem **problema** *m.* 1.1
profession **profesión** *f.* 1.3; 3.4
professor **profesor(a)** *m., f.*
program **programa** *m.* 1.1
programmer **programador(a)** *m., f.* 1.3
prohibit **prohibir** *v.* 2.4
project **proyecto** *m.* 2.5
promotion (*career*) **ascenso** *m.* 3.4
pronoun **pronombre** *m.*
protect **proteger** *v.* 3.1
protein **proteína** *f.* 3.3
provided (that) **con tal (de) que** *conj.* 3.1
psychologist **psicólogo/a** *m., f.* 3.4
psychology **psicología** *f.* 1.2
publish **publicar** *v.* 3.5
Puerto Rican **puertorriqueño/a** *adj.* 1.3
purchases **compras** *f., pl.*
pure **puro/a** *adj.* 3.1
purple **morado/a** *adj.* 1.6
purse **bolsa** *f.* 1.6
put **poner** *v.* 1.4; **puesto/a** *p.p.* 3.2
   put (a letter) in the mailbox **echar (una carta) al buzón** 3.2
   put on (*a performance*) **presentar** *v.* 3.5
   put on (*clothing*) **ponerse** *v.* 2.1
   put on makeup **maquillarse** *v.* 2.1

Q

quality **calidad** *f.* 1.6
quarter (*academic*) **trimestre** *m.* 1.2
   quarter after (*time*) **y cuarto** 1.1; **y quince** 1.1
   quarter to (*time*) **menos cuarto** 1.1; **menos quince** 1.1
question **pregunta** *f.*
quickly **rápido** *adv.* 2.4
quiet **tranquilo/a** *adj.* 3.3
quit **dejar** *v.* 3.4
quiz **prueba** *f.* 1.2

R

racism **racismo** *m.* 3.6
radio (*medium*) **radio** *f.* 1.2
   radio (set) **radio** *m.* 2.5
rain **llover (o:ue)** *v.* 1.5; **lluvia** *f.*
   It's raining. **Llueve.** 1.5; **Está lloviendo.** 1.5
raincoat **impermeable** *m.* 1.6
rain forest **bosque** *m.* **tropical** 3.1
raise (*salary*) **aumento de sueldo** 3.4
rather **bastante** *adv.* 2.4
read **leer** *v.* 1.3; **leído/a** *p.p.* 3.2
   read e-mail **leer el correo electrónico** 1.4
   read a magazine **leer una revista** 1.4
   read a newspaper **leer un periódico** 1.4
ready **listo/a** *adj.* 1.5
reality show **programa de realidad** *m.* 3.5
reap the benefits (of) *v.* **disfrutar** *v.* **(de)** 3.3
receive **recibir** *v.* 1.3
recommend **recomendar (e:ie)** *v.* 2.2; 2.6
record **grabar** *v.* 2.5
recover **recuperar** *v.* 2.5
recreation **diversión** *f.* 1.4
recycle **reciclar** *v.* 3.1
recycling **reciclaje** *m.* 3.1
red **rojo/a** *adj.* 1.6
red-haired **pelirrojo/a** *adj.* 1.3
reduce **reducir** *v.* 3.1; **disminuir** *v.* 3.4
   reduce stress/tension **aliviar el estrés/la tensión** 3.3
refrigerator **refrigerador** *m.* 2.6
region **región** *f.*
regret **sentir (e:ie)** *v.* 3.1
relatives **parientes** *m., pl.* 1.3
relax **relajarse** *v.* 2.3
   Relax. **Tranquilo/a.** 2.1
   Relax, sweetie. **Tranquilo/a, cariño.** 2.5
remain **quedarse** *v.* 2.1
remember **acordarse (o:ue)** *v.* **(de)** 2.1; **recordar (o:ue)** *v.* 1.4
remote control **control remoto** *m.* 2.5
renewable **renovable** *adj.* 3.1
rent **alquilar** *v.* 2.6; (*payment*) **alquiler** *m.* 2.6
repeat **repetir (e:i)** *v.* 1.4
report **informe** *m.* 3.6; **reportaje** *m.* 3.6
reporter **reportero/a** *m., f.* 3.4
representative **representante** *m., f.* 3.6
request **pedir (e:i)** *v.* 1.4
reservation **reservación** *f.* 1.5
resign (from) **renunciar (a)** *v.* 3.4
resolve **resolver (o:ue)** *v.* 3.1

resolved **resuelto/a** *p.p.* 3.2
resource **recurso** *m.* 3.1
responsibility **deber** *m.* 3.6; **responsabilidad** *f.*
responsible **responsable** *adj.* 2.2
rest **descansar** *v.* 1.2
restaurant **restaurante** *m.* 1.4
résumé **currículum** *m.* 3.4
retire (from work) **jubilarse** *v.* 2.3
return **regresar** *v.* 1.2; **volver (o:ue)** *v.* 1.4
returned **vuelto/a** *p.p.* 3.2
rice **arroz** *m.* 2.2
rich **rico/a** *adj.* 1.6
ride a bicycle **pasear** *v.* **en bicicleta** 1.4
ride a horse **montar** *v.* **a caballo** 1.5
ridiculous **ridículo/a** *adj.* 3.1
   it's ridiculous **es ridículo** 3.1
right **derecha** *f.* 1.2
   be right **tener razón** 1.3
   right? (*question tag*) **¿no?** 1.1; **¿verdad?** 1.1
   right away **enseguida** *adv.*
   right now **ahora mismo** 1.5
   to the right of **a la derecha de** 1.2
rights **derechos** *m.* 3.6
ring **anillo** *m.* 3.5
ring (*a doorbell*) **sonar (o:ue)** *v.* 2.5
river **río** *m.* 3.1
road **carretera** *f.* 2.5; **camino** *m.*
roast **asado/a** *adj.* 2.2
roast chicken **pollo** *m.* **asado** 2.2
rollerblade **patinar en línea** *v.*
romantic **romántico/a** *adj.* 3.5
room **habitación** *f.* 1.5; **cuarto** *m.* 1.2; 2.1
   living room **sala** *f.* 2.6
roommate **compañero/a** *m., f.* **de cuarto** 1.2
roundtrip **de ida y vuelta** 1.5
   roundtrip ticket **pasaje** *m.* **de ida y vuelta** 1.5
routine **rutina** *f.* 2.1
rug **alfombra** *f.* 2.6
run **correr** *v.* 1.3
   run errands **hacer diligencias** 3.2
   run into (*have an accident*) **chocar (con)** *v.*; (*meet accidentally*) **encontrar(se) (o:ue)** *v.* 2.5; (*run into something*) **darse (con)** 2.4
   run into (each other) **encontrar(se) (o:ue)** *v.* 2.5
rush **apurarse, darse prisa** *v.* 3.3
Russian **ruso/a** *adj.* 1.3

S

sad **triste** *adj.* 1.5; 3.1
  it's sad **es triste** 3.1
safe **seguro/a** *adj.* 1.5
said **dicho/a** *p.p.* 3.2
sailboard **tabla de windsurf** *f.* 1.5
salad **ensalada** *f.* 2.2
salary **salario** *m.* 3.4; **sueldo** *m.* 3.4
sale **rebaja** *f.* 1.6
salesperson **vendedor(a)** *m.*, *f.* 1.6
salmon **salmón** *m.* 2.2
salt **sal** *f.* 2.2
same **mismo/a** *adj.* 1.3
sandal **sandalia** *f.* 1.6
sandwich **sándwich** *m.* 2.2
Saturday **sábado** *m.* 1.2
sausage **salchicha** *f.* 2.2
save (*on a computer*) **guardar** *v.* 2.5; save (money) **ahorrar** *v.* 3.2
savings **ahorros** *m.* 3.2
  savings account **cuenta** *f.* **de ahorros** 3.2
say **decir** *v.* 1.4; **declarar** *v.* 3.6
say (that) **decir (que)** *v.* 1.4
  say the answer **decir la respuesta** 1.4
scan **escanear** *v.* 2.5
scarcely **apenas** *adv.* 2.4
scared: be (very) scared (of) **tener (mucho) miedo (de)** 1.3
schedule **horario** *m.* 1.2
school **escuela** *f.* 1.1
sciences *f., pl.* **ciencias** 1.2
science fiction (genre) **de ciencia ficción** *f.* 3.5
scientist **científico/a** *m., f.* 3.4
scream **grito** *m.* 1.5; **gritar** *v.*
screen **pantalla** *f.* 2.5
scuba dive **bucear** *v.* 1.4
sculpt **esculpir** *v.* 3.5
sculptor **escultor(a)** *m., f.* 3.5
sculpture **escultura** *f.* 3.5
sea **mar** *m.* 1.5
  (sea) turtle **tortuga (marina)** *f.* 3.1
season **estación** *f.* 1.5
seat **silla** *f.* 1.2
second **segundo/a** 1.5
secretary **secretario/a** *m., f.* 3.4
sedentary **sedentario/a** *adj.* 3.3
see **ver** *v.* 1.4
  see (you, him, her) again **volver a ver(te, lo, la)**
  see movies **ver películas** 1.4
  See you. **Nos vemos.** 1.1
  See you later. **Hasta la vista.** 1.1; **Hasta luego.** 1.1
  See you soon. **Hasta pronto.** 1.1
  See you tomorrow. **Hasta mañana.** 1.1
seem **parecer** *v.* 1.6
seen **visto/a** *p.p.* 3.2
sell **vender** *v.* 1.6
semester **semestre** *m.* 1.2
send **enviar; mandar** *v.* 3.2
separate (from) **separarse** *v.* **(de)** 2.3

separated **separado/a** *adj.* 2.3
September **septiembre** *m.* 1.5
sequence **secuencia** *f.*
serious **grave** *adj.* 2.4
serve **servir (e:i)** *v.* 2.2
service **servicio** *m.* 3.3
set (*fixed*) **fijo/a** *adj.* 1.6
  set the table **poner la mesa** 2.6
seven **siete** 1.1
seven hundred **setecientos/as** 1.2
seventeen **diecisiete** 1.1
seventh **séptimo/a** 1.5
seventy **setenta** 1.2
several **varios/as** *adj. pl.*
sexism **sexismo** *m.* 3.6
shame **lástima** *f.* 3.1
  it's a shame **es una lástima** 3.1
shampoo **champú** *m.* 2.1
shape **forma** *f.* 3.3
  be in good shape **estar en buena forma** 3.3
  stay in shape **mantenerse en forma** 3.3
share **compartir** *v.* 1.3
sharp (*time*) **en punto** 1.1
shave **afeitarse** *v.* 2.1
shaving cream **crema** *f.* **de afeitar** 1.5, 2.1
she **ella** 1.1
shellfish **mariscos** *m., pl.* 2.2
ship **barco** *m.*
shirt **camisa** *f.* 1.6
shoe **zapato** *m.* 1.6
  shoe size **número** *m.* 1.6
  shoe store **zapatería** *f.* 3.2
    tennis shoes **zapatos** *m., pl.* **de tenis** 1.6
shop **tienda** *f.* 1.6
shopping, to go **ir de compras** 1.5
  shopping mall **centro comercial** *m.* 1.6
short (*in height*) **bajo/a** *adj.* 1.3; (*in length*) **corto/a** *adj.* 1.6
short story **cuento** *m.* 3.5
shorts **pantalones cortos** *m., pl.* 1.6
should (*do something*) **deber** *v.* **(+ *inf.*)** 1.3
shout **gritar** *v.*
show **espectáculo** *m.* 3.5; **mostrar (o:ue)** *v.* 1.4
  game show **concurso** *m.* 3.5
shower **ducha** *f.* 2.1; **ducharse** *v.* 2.1
shrimp **camarón** *m.* 2.2
siblings **hermanos/as** *pl.* 1.3
sick **enfermo/a** *adj.* 2.4
  be sick **estar enfermo/a** 2.4
  get sick **enfermarse** *v.* 2.4
sign **firmar** *v.* 3.2; **letrero** *m.* 3.2
silk **seda** *f.* 1.6
  (made of) silk **de seda** 1.6
since **desde** *prep.*
sing **cantar** *v.* 1.2
singer **cantante** *m., f.* 3.5
single **soltero/a** *adj.* 2.3
  single room **habitación** *f.* **individual** 1.5
sink **lavabo** *m.* 2.1
sir **señor (Sr.), don** *m.* 1.1; **caballero** *m.* 2.2

sister **hermana** *f.* 1.3
sister-in-law **cuñada** *f.* 1.3
sit down **sentarse (e:ie)** *v.* 2.1
six **seis** 1.1
six hundred **seiscientos/as** 1.2
sixteen **dieciséis** 1.1
sixth **sexto/a** 1.5
sixty **sesenta** 1.2
size **talla** *f.* 1.6
  shoe size *m.* **número** 1.6
(in-line) skate **patinar (en línea)** 1.4
skateboard **andar en patineta** *v.* 1.4
ski **esquiar** *v.* 1.4
skiing **esquí** *m.* 1.4
  water-skiing **esquí** *m.* **acuático** 1.4
skirt **falda** *f.* 1.6
skull made out of sugar **calavera de azúcar** *f.* 2.3
sky **cielo** *m.* 3.1
sleep **dormir (o:ue)** *v.* 1.4; **sueño** *m.*
  go to sleep **dormirse (o:ue)** *v.* 2.1
sleepy: be (very) sleepy **tener (mucho) sueño** 1.3
slender **delgado/a** *adj.* 1.3
slim down **adelgazar** *v.* 3.3
slippers **pantuflas** *f.* 2.1
slow **lento/a** *adj.* 2.5
slowly **despacio** *adv.* 2.4
small **pequeño/a** *adj.* 1.3
smart **listo/a** *adj.* 1.5
smile **sonreír (e:i)** *v.* 2.3
smiled **sonreído** *p.p.* 3.2
smoggy: It's (very) smoggy. **Hay (mucha) contaminación.**
smoke **fumar** *v.* 3.3
  (not) to smoke **(no) fumar** 3.3
smoking section **sección** *f.* **de fumar** 2.2
  (non) smoking section *f.* **sección de (no) fumar** 2.2
snack **merendar (e:ie)** *v.* 2.2
  afternoon snack **merienda** *f.* 3.3
  have a snack **merendar** *v.* 2.2
sneakers **los zapatos de tenis** 1.6
sneeze **estornudar** *v.* 2.4
snow **nevar (e:ie)** *v.* 1.5; **nieve** *f.*
snowing: It's snowing. **Nieva.** 1.5; **Está nevando.** 1.5
so (*in such a way*) **así** *adv.* 2.4; **tan** *adv.* 1.5
  so much **tanto** *adv.*
  so-so **regular** 1.1
  so that **para que** *conj.* 3.1
soap **jabón** *m.* 2.1
soap opera **telenovela** *f.* 3.5
soccer **fútbol** *m.* 1.4
sociology **sociología** *f.* 1.2
sock(s) **calcetín (calcetines)** *m.* 1.6
sofa **sofá** *m.* 2.6
soft drink **refresco** *m.* 2.2
software **programa** *m.* **de computación** 2.5
soil **tierra** *f.* 3.1
solar **solar** *adj., m., f.* 3.1
  solar energy **energía solar** 3.1

soldier **soldado** *m., f.* 3.6
solution **solución** *f.* 3.1
solve **resolver (o:ue)** *v.* 3.1
some **algún, alguno/a(s)**
　　adj. 2.1; **unos/as** *indef.*
　　art. 1.1
somebody **alguien** *pron.* 2.1
someone **alguien** *pron.* 2.1
something **algo** *pron.* 2.1
sometimes **a veces** *adv.* 2.4
son **hijo** *m.* 1.3
song **canción** *f.* 3.5
son-in-law **yerno** *m.* 1.3
soon **pronto** *adv.* 2.4
　　See you soon. **Hasta pronto.** 1.1
sorry: be sorry **sentir (e:ie)** *v.* 3.1
　　I'm sorry. **Lo siento.** 1.1
soul **alma** *f.* 2.3
soup **sopa** *f.* 2.2
south **sur** *m.* 3.2
　　to the south **al sur** 3.2
Spain **España** *f.*
Spanish *(language)* **español**
　　m. 1.2; **español(a)** *adj.* 1.3
spare (free) time **ratos libres** 1.4
speak **hablar** *v.* 1.2
　　Speaking. *(on the telephone)*
　　Con él/ella habla. 2.5
special: today's specials **las
　　especialidades del día** 2.2
spectacular **espectacular** *adj.*
　　m., f.
speech **discurso** *m.* 3.6
speed **velocidad** *f.* 2.5
　　speed limit **velocidad** *f.*
　　máxima 2.5
spelling **ortografía** *f.*,
　　ortográfico/a *adj.*
spend *(money)* **gastar** *v.* 1.6
spoon *(table or large)* **cuchara**
　　f. 2.6
sport **deporte** *m.* 1.4
　　sports-related **deportivo/a**
　　adj. 1.4
spouse **esposo/a** *m., f.* 1.3
sprain (one's ankle) **torcerse
　　(o:ue)** *v.* **(el tobillo)** 2.4
spring **primavera** *f.* 1.5
(city or town) square **plaza** *f.* 1.4
stadium **estadio** *m.* 1.2
stage **etapa** *f.* 2.3
stairs **escalera** *f.* 2.6
stairway **escalera** *f.* 2.6
stamp **estampilla** *f.* 3.2; **sello**
　　m. 3.2
stand in line **hacer** *v.* **cola** 3.2
star **estrella** *f.* 3.1
start *(a vehicle)* **arrancar** *v.* 2.5
station **estación** *f.* 1.5
statue **estatua** *f.* 3.5
status: marital status **estado** *m.*
　　civil 2.3
stay **quedarse** *v.* 2.1
　　stay in shape **mantenerse en
　　forma** 3.3
steak **bistec** *m.* 2.2
steering wheel **volante** *m.* 2.5
step **escalón** *m.* 3.3
stepbrother **hermanastro** *m.* 1.3

stepdaughter **hijastra** *f.* 1.3
stepfather **padrastro** *m.* 1.3
stepmother **madrastra** *f.* 1.3
stepsister **hermanastra** *f.* 1.3
stepson **hijastro** *m.* 1.3
stereo **estéreo** *m.* 2.5
still **todavía** *adv.* 1.5
stockbroker **corredor(a)** *m., f.*
　　de bolsa 3.4
stockings **medias** *f., pl.* 1.6
stomach **estómago** *m.* 2.4
stone **piedra** *f.* 3.1
stop **parar** *v.* 2.5
　　stop *(doing something)* **dejar
　　de (+ *inf.*)** 3.1
store **tienda** *f.* 1.6
storm **tormenta** *f.* 3.6
story **cuento** *m.* 3.5; **historia** *f.* 3.5
stove **cocina, estufa** *f.* 2.6
straight **derecho** *adv.* 3.2
　　straight (ahead) **derecho** 3.2
straighten up **arreglar** *v.* 2.6
strange **extraño/a** *adj.* 3.1
　　it's strange **es extraño** 3.1
street **calle** *f.* 2.5
stress **estrés** *m.* 3.3
stretching **estiramiento** *m.* 3.3
　　do stretching exercises **hacer
　　ejercicios** *m. pl.* **de
　　estiramiento** 3.3
strike *(labor)* **huelga** *f.* 3.6
striped **de rayas** 1.6
stroll **pasear** *v.* 1.4
strong **fuerte** *adj. m., f.* 3.3
struggle (for/against) **luchar** *v.*
　　(por/contra) 3.6
student **estudiante** *m., f.* 1.1; 1.2;
　　estudiantil *adj.* 1.2
study **estudiar** *v.* 1.2
stupendous **estupendo/a** *adj.* 1.5
style **estilo** *m.*
suburbs **afueras** *f., pl.* 2.6
subway **metro** *m.* 1.5
　　subway station **estación** *f.*
　　del metro 1.5
success **éxito** *m.*
successful: be successful **tener
　　éxito** 3.4
such as **tales como**
suddenly **de repente** *adv.* 1.6
suffer **sufrir** *v.* 2.4
　　suffer an illness **sufrir una
　　enfermedad** 2.4
sugar **azúcar** *m.* 2.2
suggest **sugerir (e:ie)** *v.* 2.6
suit **traje** *m.* 1.6
suitcase **maleta** *f.* 1.1
summer **verano** *m.* 1.5
sun **sol** *m.* 3.1
sunbathe **tomar** *v.* **el sol** 1.4
Sunday **domingo** *m.* 1.2
(sun)glasses **gafas** *f., pl.*
　　(de sol) 1.6
sunny: It's (very) sunny. **Hace
　　(mucho) sol.** 1.5
supermarket **supermercado**
　　m. 3.2

suppose **suponer** *v.* 1.4
sure **seguro/a** *adj.* 1.5
　　be sure **estar seguro/a** 1.5
surf **hacer** *v.* **surf** 1.5; *(the
　　Internet)* **navegar** *v.* **(en
　　Internet)** 2.5
surfboard **tabla de surf** *f.* 1.5
surprise **sorprender** *v.* 2.3;
　　sorpresa *f.* 2.3
survey **encuesta** *f.* 3.6
sweat **sudar** *v.* 3.3
sweater **suéter** *m.* 1.6
sweep the floor **barrer el
　　suelo** 2.6
sweets **dulces** *m., pl.* 2.3
swim **nadar** *v.* 1.4
swimming **natación** *f.* 1.4
　　swimming pool **piscina** *f.* 1.4
symptom **síntoma** *m.* 2.4

T

table **mesa** *f.* 1.2
tablespoon **cuchara** *f.* 2.6
tablet *(pill)* **pastilla** *f.* 2.4
take **tomar** *v.* 1.2; **llevar** *v.* 1.6
　　take care of **cuidar** *v.* 3.1
　　take someone's temperature
　　tomar *v.* **la temperatura** 2.4
　　take *(wear)* a shoe size
　　calzar *v.* 1.6
　　take a bath **bañarse** *v.* 2.1
　　take a shower **ducharse** *v.* 2.1
　　take off **quitarse** *v.* 2.1
　　take out the trash *v.* **sacar la
　　basura** 2.6
　　take photos **tomar** *v.* **fotos** 1.5;
　　sacar *v.* **fotos** 1.5
talented **talentoso/a** *adj.* 3.5
talk **hablar** *v.* 1.2
　　talk show **programa** *m.* **de
　　entrevistas** 3.5
tall **alto/a** *adj.* 1.3
tank **tanque** *m.* 2.5
taste **probar (o:ue)** *v.* 2.2
　　taste like **saber a** 2.2
tasty **rico/a** *adj.* 2.2; **sabroso/a**
　　adj. 2.2
tax **impuesto** *m.* 3.6
taxi **taxi** *m.* 1.5
tea **té** *m.* 2.2
teach **enseñar** *v.* 1.2
teacher **profesor(a)** *m., f.* 1.1, 1.2;
　　maestro/a *m., f.* 3.4
team **equipo** *m.* 1.4
technician **técnico/a** *m., f.* 3.4
telecommuting **teletrabajo** *m.* 3.4
telephone **teléfono** 2.5
television **televisión** *f.* 1.2
　　television set **televisor** *m.* 2.5
tell **contar** *v.* 1.4; **decir** *v.* 1.4
tell (that) **decir** *v.* **(que)** 1.4
　　tell lies **decir mentiras** 1.4
　　tell the truth **decir la
　　verdad** 1.4
temperature **temperatura** *f.* 2.4
ten **diez** 1.1
tennis **tenis** *m.* 1.4

tennis shoes **zapatos** *m., pl.* **de tenis** 1.6

tension **tensión** *f.* 3.3

tent **tienda** *f.* **de campaña**

tenth **décimo/a** 1.5

terrible **terrible** *adj. m., f.* 3.1
　it's terrible **es terrible** 3.1

terrific **chévere** *adj.*

test **prueba** *f.* 1.2; **examen** *m.* 1.2

text message **mensaje** *m.* **de texto** 2.5

Thank you. **Gracias.** *f., pl.* 1.1
　Thank you (very much). **(Muchas) gracias.** 1.1
　Thanks (a lot). **(Muchas) gracias.** 1.1
　Thanks for inviting me. **Gracias por invitarme.** 2.3

that **que, quien(es)** *pron.* 2.6
　that (one) **ése, ésa, eso** *pron.* 1.6; **ese, esa,** *adj.* 1.6
　that (over there) **aquél, aquélla, aquello** *pron.* 1.6; **aquel, aquella** *adj.* 1.6
　that which **lo que** 2.6
　that's why **por eso** 2.5

the **el** *m.,* **la** *f. sing.,* **los** *m.,* **las** *f., pl.* 1.1

theater **teatro** *m.* 3.5

their **su(s)** *poss. adj.* 1.3; **suyo(s)/a(s)** *poss. pron.* 2.5

them **los/las** *pl., d.o. pron.* 1.5
　to/for them **les** *pl., i.o. pron.* 1.6

then (afterward) **después** *adv.* 2.1; (as a result) **entonces** *adv.* 1.5, 2.1; (next) **luego** *adv.* 2.1

there **allí** *adv.* 1.2
　There is/are… **Hay…** 1.1
　There is/are not… **No hay…** 1.1

therefore **por eso** 2.5

these **éstos, éstas** *pron.* 1.6; **estos, estas** *adj.* 1.6

they **ellos** *m.,* **ellas** *f. pron.* 1.1
　They all told me to ask you to excuse them/forgive them. **Todos me dijeron que te pidiera una disculpa de su parte.** 3.6

thin **delgado/a** *adj.* 1.3

thing **cosa** *f.* 1.1

think **pensar (e:ie)** *v.* 1.4; (believe) **creer** *v.*
　think about **pensar en** *v.* 1.4

third **tercero/a** 1.5

thirst **sed** *f.*

thirsty: be (very) thirsty **tener (mucha) sed** 1.3

thirteen **trece** 1.1

thirty **treinta** 1.1; thirty (minutes past the hour) **y treinta; y media** 1.1

this **este, esta** *adj.;* **éste, ésta, esto** *pron.* 1.6

those **ésos, ésas** *pron.* 1.6; **esos, esas** *adj.* 1.6

those (over there) **aquéllos, aquéllas** *pron.* 1.6; **aquellos, aquellas** *adj.* 1.6

thousand **mil** *m.* 1.2

three **tres** 1.1

three hundred **trescientos/as** 1.2

throat **garganta** *f.* 2.4

through **por** *prep.* 2.5

Thursday **jueves** *m., sing.* 1.2

thus (in such a way) **así** *adv.*

ticket **boleto** *m.* 1.2, 3.5; **pasaje** *m.* 1.5

tie **corbata** *f.* 1.6

time **vez** *f.* 1.6; **tiempo** *m.* 3.2
　have a good/bad time **pasarlo bien/mal** 2.3
　I've had a fantastic time. **Lo he pasado de película.** 3.6
　What time is it? **¿Qué hora es?** 1.1
　(At) What time…? **¿A qué hora…?** 1.1

times **veces** *f., pl.* 1.6
　many times **muchas veces** 2.4
　two times **dos veces** 1.6

tip **propina** *f.* 2.2

tire **llanta** *f.* 2.5

tired **cansado/a** *adj.* 1.5
　be tired **estar cansado/a** 1.5

title **título** *m.* 3.4

to **a** *prep.* 1.1

toast (drink) **brindar** *v.* 2.3
　toast **pan** *m.* **tostado** 2.2

toasted **tostado/a** *adj.* 2.2
　toasted bread **pan tostado** *m.* 2.2

toaster **tostadora** *f.* 2.6

today **hoy** *adv.* 1.2
　Today is… **Hoy es…** 1.2

toe **dedo** *m.* **del pie** 2.4

together **juntos/as** *adj.* 2.3

toilet **inodoro** *m.* 2.1

tomato **tomate** *m.* 2.2

tomorrow **mañana** *f.* 1.1
　See you tomorrow. **Hasta mañana.** 1.1

tonight **esta noche** *adv.*

too **también** *adv.* 1.2; 2.1
　too much **demasiado** *adv.* 1.6; **en exceso** 3.3

tooth **diente** *m.* 2.1

toothpaste **pasta** *f.* **de dientes** 2.1

top **cima** *f.* 3.3

tornado **tornado** *m.* 3.6

touch **tocar** *v.* 3.5

touch screen **pantalla táctil** *f.*

tour **excursión** *f.* 1.4; **recorrido** *m.* 3.1

tour an area **recorrer** *v.*

tourism **turismo** *m.*

tourist **turista** *m., f.* 1.1; **turístico/a** *adj.*

toward **hacia** *prep.* 3.2; **para** *prep.* 2.5

towel **toalla** *f.* 2.1

town **pueblo** *m.*

trade **oficio** *m.* 3.4

traffic **circulación** *f.* 2.5; **tráfico** *m.* 2.5

traffic light **semáforo** *m.* 3.2

tragedy **tragedia** *f.* 3.5

trail **sendero** *m.* 3.1

train **entrenarse** *v.* 3.3; **tren** *m.* 1.5

train station **estación** *f.* **de tren** *m.* 1.5

trainer **entrenador(a)** *m., f.* 3.3

translate **traducir** *v.* 1.6

trash **basura** *f.* 2.6

travel **viajar** *v.* 1.2
　travel agency **agencia** f. **de viajes** 1.5
　travel agent **agente** *m., f.* **de viajes** 1.5

traveler **viajero/a** *m., f.* 1.5
　(traveler's) check **cheque (de viajero)** 3.2

treadmill **cinta caminadora** *f.* 3.3

tree **árbol** *m.* 3.1

trillion **billón** *m.*

trimester **trimestre** *m.* 1.2

trip **viaje** *m.* 1.5
　take a trip **hacer un viaje** 1.5

tropical forest **bosque** *m.* **tropical** 3.1

true: it's (not) true **(no) es verdad** 3.1

trunk **baúl** *m.* 2.5

truth **verdad** *f.* 1.4

try **intentar** *v.;* **probar (o:ue)** *v.* 2.2
　try (to do something) **tratar de (+ inf.)** 3.3
　try on **probarse (o:ue)** *v.* 2.1

t-shirt **camiseta** *f.* 1.6

Tuesday **martes** *m., sing.* 1.2

tuna **atún** *m.* 2.2

turkey **pavo** *m.* 2.2

turn **doblar** *v.* 3.2
　turn off (electricity/appliance) **apagar** *v.* 2.5
　turn on (electricity/appliance) **poner** *v.* 2.5; **prender** *v.* 2.5

twelve **doce** 1.1

twenty **veinte** 1.1

twenty-eight **veintiocho** 1.1

twenty-five **veinticinco** 1.1

twenty-four **veinticuatro** 1.1

twenty-nine **veintinueve** 1.1

twenty-one **veintiuno** 1.1; **veintiún, veintiuno/a** *adj.* 1.1

twenty-seven **veintisiete** 1.1

twenty-six **veintiséis** 1.1

twenty-three **veintitrés** 1.1

twenty-two **veintidós** 1.1

twice **dos veces** 1.6

twin **gemelo/a** *m., f.* 1.3

two **dos** 1.1
　two hundred **doscientos/as** 1.2
　two times **dos veces** 1.6

U

ugly **feo/a** *adj.* 1.3

uncle **tío** *m.* 1.3

under **debajo de** *prep.* 1.2

understand **comprender** *v.* 1.3; **entender (e:ie)** *v.* 1.4

underwear **ropa interior** 1.6

unemployment **desempleo** *m.* 3.6

unique **único/a** *adj.* 2.3
United States **Estados Unidos (EE.UU.)** *m. pl.*
university **universidad** *f.* 1.2
unless **a menos que** *conj.* 3.1
unmarried **soltero/a** *adj.* 2.3
unpleasant **antipático/a** *adj.* 1.3
until **hasta** *prep.* 1.6; **hasta que** *conj.* 3.1
urgent **urgente** *adj.* 2.6
   It's urgent that... **Es urgente que...** 2.6
us **nos** *pl., d.o. pron.* 1.5
   to/for us **nos** *pl., i.o. pron.* 1.6
use **usar** *v.* 1.6
used for **para** *prep.* 2.5
useful **útil** *adj. m., f.*

V

vacation **vacaciones** *f., pl.* 1.5
   be on vacation **estar de vacaciones** 1.5
   go on vacation **ir de vacaciones** 1.5
vacuum **pasar** *v.* **la aspiradora** 2.6
   vacuum cleaner **aspiradora** *f.* 2.6
valley **valle** *m.* 3.1
various **varios/as** *adj. m., f. pl.*
vegetables **verduras** *pl., f.* 2.2
verb **verbo** *m.*
very **muy** *adv.* 1.1
   (Very) well, thank you. **(Muy) bien, gracias.** 1.1
video **video** *m.* 1.1
   video camera **cámara** *f.* **de video** 2.5
   video game **videojuego** *m.* 1.4
videoconference **videoconferencia** *f.* 3.4
vinegar **vinagre** *m.* 2.2
violence **violencia** *f.* 3.6
visit **visitar** *v.* 1.4
   visit monuments **visitar monumentos** 1.4
vitamin **vitamina** *f.* 3.3
voice mail **correo de voz** *m.* 2.5
volcano **volcán** *m.* 3.1
volleyball **vóleibol** *m.* 1.4
vote **votar** *v.* 3.6

W

wait (for) **esperar** *v.* **(+ *inf.*)** 1.2
waiter/waitress **camarero/a** *m., f.* 2.2
wake up **despertarse (e:ie)** *v.* 2.1
walk **caminar** *v.* 1.2
   take a walk **pasear** *v.* 1.4
   walk around **pasear por** 1.4
wall **pared** *f.* 2.6; **muro** *m.* 3.3
wallet **cartera** *f.* 1.4, 1.6

want **querer (e:ie)** *v.* 1.4
war **guerra** *f.* 3.6
warm up **calentarse (e:ie)** *v.* 3.3
wash **lavar** *v.* 2.6
   wash one's face/hands **lavarse la cara/las manos** 2.1
   wash (the floor, the dishes) **lavar (el suelo, los platos)** 2.6
   wash oneself **lavarse** *v.* 2.1
washing machine **lavadora** *f.* 2.6
wastebasket **papelera** *f.* 1.2
watch **mirar** *v.* 1.2; **reloj** *m.* 1.2
   watch television **mirar (la) televisión** 1.2
water **agua** *f.* 2.2
   water pollution **contaminación del agua** 3.1
   water-skiing **esquí** *m.* **acuático** 1.4
way **manera** *f.*
we **nosotros(as)** *m., f.* 1.1
weak **débil** *adj. m., f.* 3.3
wear **llevar** *v.* 1.6; **usar** *v.* 1.6
weather **tiempo** *m.*
   The weather is bad. **Hace mal tiempo.** 1.5
   The weather is good. **Hace buen tiempo.** 1.5
weaving **tejido** *m.* 3.5
Web **red** *f.* 2.5
website **sitio** *m.* **web** 2.5
wedding **boda** *f.* 2.3
Wednesday **miércoles** *m., sing.* 1.2
week **semana** *f.* 1.2
weekend **fin** *m.* **de semana** 1.4
weight **peso** *m.* 3.3
   lift weights **levantar** *v.* **pesas** *f., pl.* 3.3
welcome **bienvenido(s)/a(s)** *adj.* 1.1
well: (Very) well, thanks. **(Muy) bien, gracias.** 1.1
well-being **bienestar** *m.* 3.3
well organized **ordenado/a** *adj.* 1.5
west **oeste** *m.* 3.2
   to the west **al oeste** 3.2
western (*genre*) **de vaqueros** 3.5
whale **ballena** *f.* 3.1
what **lo que** *pron.* 2.6
what? **¿qué?** 1.1
   At what time...? **¿A qué hora...?** 1.1
   What a pleasure to...! **¡Qué gusto (+ *inf.*)...!** 3.6
   What day is it? **¿Qué día es hoy?** 1.2
   What do you guys think? **¿Qué les parece?**
   What happened? **¿Qué pasó?**
   What is today's date? **¿Cuál es la fecha de hoy?** 1.5
   What nice clothes! **¡Qué ropa más bonita!** 1.6
   What size do you wear? **¿Qué talla lleva (usa)?** 1.6

What time is it? **¿Qué hora es?** 1.1
What's going on? **¿Qué pasa?** 1.1
What's happening? **¿Qué pasa?** 1.1
What's... like? **¿Cómo es...?**
What's new? **¿Qué hay de nuevo?** 1.1
What's the weather like? **¿Qué tiempo hace?** 1.5
What's up? **¿Qué onda?** 3.2
What's wrong? **¿Qué pasó?**
What's your name? **¿Cómo se llama usted?** *form.* 1.1; **¿Cómo te llamas (tú)?** *fam.* 1.1
when **cuando** *conj.* 2.1; 3.1
When? **¿Cuándo?** 1.2
where **donde**
where (to)? (*destination*) **¿adónde?** 1.2; (*location*) **¿dónde?** 1.1, 1.2
   Where are you from? **¿De dónde eres (tú)?** (*fam.*) 1.1; **¿De dónde es (usted)?** (*form.*) 1.1
   Where is...? **¿Dónde está...?** 1.2
which **que** *pron.*, **lo que** *pron.* 2.6
which? **¿cuál?** 1.2; **¿qué?** 1.2
   In which...? **¿En qué...?**
   which one(s)? **¿cuál(es)?** 1.2
while **mientras** *conj.* 2.4
who **que** *pron.* 2.6; **quien(es)** *pron.* 2.6
who? **¿quién(es)?** 1.1, 1.2
   Who is...? **¿Quién es...?** 1.1
   Who is speaking/calling? (*on telephone*) **¿De parte de quién?** 2.5
   Who is speaking? (*on telephone*) **¿Quién habla?** 2.5
whole **todo/a** *adj.*
whom **quien(es)** *pron.* 2.6
whose? **¿de quién(es)?** 1.1
why? **¿por qué?** 1.2
widower/widow **viudo/a** *adj.* 2.3
wife **esposa** *f.* 1.3
win **ganar** *v.* 1.4
wind **viento** *m.*
window **ventana** *f.* 1.2
windshield **parabrisas** *m., sing.* 2.5
windsurf **hacer** *v.* **windsurf** 1.5
windy: It's (very) windy. **Hace (mucho) viento.** 1.5
winter **invierno** *m.* 1.5
wireless connection **conexión inalámbrica** *f.* 2.5
wish **desear** *v.* 1.2; **esperar** *v.* 3.1
   I wish (that) **ojalá (que)** 3.1
with **con** *prep.* 1.2
   with me **conmigo** 1.4; 2.3
   with you **contigo** *fam.* 1.5, 2.3
within (ten years) **dentro de (diez años)** *prep.* 3.4
without **sin** *prep.* 1.2; **sin que** *conj.* 3.1
woman **mujer** *f.* 1.1

wool **lana** *f.* 1.6
  (made of) wool **de lana** 1.6
word **palabra** *f.* 1.1
work **trabajar** *v.* 1.2; **funcionar**
  v. 2.5; **trabajo** *m.* 3.4
  work (*of art, literature, music,*
    etc.) **obra** *f.* 3.5
  work out **hacer gimnasia** 3.3
world **mundo** *m.* 2.2
worldwide **mundial** *adj. m., f.*
worried (about) **preocupado/a**
  (por) *adj.* 1.5
worry (about) **preocuparse** *v.*
  (por) 2.1
  Don't worry. **No te preocupes.**
    fam. 2.1
worse **peor** *adj. m., f.* 2.2
worst **el/la peor** 2.2
Would you like to...? **¿Te**
  gustaría...? *fam.*
Would you do me the honor of
  marrying me? **¿Me harías**
  el honor de casarte
  conmigo? 3.5
wow **híjole** *interj.* 1.6
wrench **llave** *f.* 2.5
write **escribir** *v.* 1.3
  write a letter/an e-mail
  escribir una carta/un
  mensaje electrónico 1.4

writer **escritor(a)** *m., f* 3.5
written **escrito/a** *p.p.* 3.2
wrong **equivocado/a** *adj.* 1.5
  be wrong **no tener razón** 1.3

X

X-ray **radiografía** *f.* 2.4

Y

yard **jardín** *m.* 2.6; **patio** *m.* 2.6
year **año** *m.* 1.5
  be... years old **tener...**
    años 1.3
yellow **amarillo/a** *adj.* 1.6
yes **sí** *interj.* 1.1
yesterday **ayer** *adv.* 1.6
yet **todavía** *adv.* 1.5
yogurt **yogur** *m.* 2.2
you **tú** *fam.* **usted (Ud.)** *form.*
  sing. **vosotros/as** *m., f. fam.*
  pl. **ustedes (Uds.)** *pl.* 1.1; (to,
  for) you *fam. sing.* **te** *pl.* **os** 1.6;
  form. sing. **le** *pl.* **les** 1.6
  you **te** *fam., sing.,* **lo/la** *form.,*
  sing., **os** *fam., pl.,* **los/las**
  pl, d.o. pron. 1.5

You don't say! **¡No me digas!**
  fam.; **¡No me diga!** *form.*
You're welcome. **De nada.** 1.1;
  No hay de qué. 1.1
young **joven** *adj., sing.* (**jóvenes**
  pl.) 1.3
  young person **joven** *m., f., sing.*
    (**jóvenes** *pl.*) 1.1
  young woman **señorita (Srta.)** *f.*
younger **menor** *adj. m., f.* 1.3
younger: younger brother, sister *m.,*
  f. **hermano/a menor** 1.3
youngest **el/la menor** *m., f.* 2.2
your **su(s)** *poss. adj. form.* 1.3;
  tu(s) *poss. adj. fam. sing.* 1.3;
  vuestro/a(s) *poss. adj. fam.*
  pl. 1.3
your(s) *form.* **suyo(s)/a(s)** *poss.*
  pron. form. 2.5; **tuyo(s)/a(s)**
  poss. fam. sing. 2.5; **vuestro(s)**
  /a(s) *poss. fam.* 2.5
youth *f.* **juventud** 2.3

Z

zero **cero** *m.* 1.1

MATERIAS	ACADEMIC SUBJECTS	LOS ANIMALES	ANIMALS
la administración de empresas	business administration	la abeja	bee
la agronomía	agriculture	la araña	spider
el alemán	German	la ardilla	squirrel
el álgebra	algebra	el ave (f.), el pájaro	bird
la antropología	anthropology	la ballena	whale
la arqueología	archaeology	el burro	donkey
la arquitectura	architecture	la cabra	goat
el arte	art	el caimán	alligator
la astronomía	astronomy	el camello	camel
la biología	biology	la cebra	zebra
la bioquímica	biochemistry	el ciervo, el venado	deer
la botánica	botany	el cochino, el cerdo, el puerco	pig
el cálculo	calculus	el cocodrilo	crocodile
el chino	Chinese	el conejo	rabbit
las ciencias políticas	political science	el coyote	coyote
la computación	computer science	la culebra, la serpiente, la víbora	snake
las comunicaciones	communications	el elefante	elephant
la contabilidad	accounting	la foca	seal
la danza	dance	la gallina	hen
el derecho	law	el gallo	rooster
la economía	economics	el gato	cat
la educación	education	el gorila	gorilla
la educación física	physical education	el hipopótamo	hippopotamus
la enfermería	nursing	la hormiga	ant
el español	Spanish	el insecto	insect
la filosofía	philosophy	la jirafa	giraffe
la física	physics	el lagarto	lizard
el francés	French	el león	lion
la geografía	geography	el lobo	wolf
la geología	geology	el loro, la cotorra, el papagayo, el perico	parrot
el griego	Greek	la mariposa	butterfly
el hebreo	Hebrew	el mono	monkey
la historia	history	la mosca	fly
la informática	computer science	el mosquito	mosquito
la ingeniería	engineering	el oso	bear
el inglés	English	la oveja	sheep
el italiano	Italian	el pato	duck
el japonés	Japanese	el perro	dog
el latín	Latin	el pez	fish
las lenguas clásicas	classical languages	la rana	frog
las lenguas romances	Romance languages	el ratón	mouse
la lingüística	linguistics	el rinoceronte	rhinoceros
la literatura	literature	el saltamontes, el chapulín	grasshopper
las matemáticas	mathematics	el tiburón	shark
la medicina	medicine	el tigre	tiger
el mercadeo/ la mercadotecnia	marketing	el toro	bull
la música	music	la tortuga	turtle
los negocios	business	la vaca	cow
el periodismo	journalism	el zorro	fox
el portugués	Portuguese		
la psicología	psychology		
la química	chemistry		
el ruso	Russian		
los servicios sociales	social services		
la sociología	sociology		
el teatro	theater		
la trigonometría	trigonometry		

EL CUERPO HUMANO Y LA SALUD

THE HUMAN BODY AND HEALTH

El cuerpo humano — The human body

la barba	beard
el bigote	mustache
la boca	mouth
el brazo	arm
la cabeza	head
la cadera	hip
la ceja	eyebrow
el cerebro	brain
la cintura	waist
el codo	elbow
el corazón	heart
la costilla	rib
el cráneo	skull
el cuello	neck
el dedo	finger
el dedo del pie	toe
la espalda	back
el estómago	stomach
la frente	forehead
la garganta	throat
el hombro	shoulder
el hueso	bone
el labio	lip
la lengua	tongue
la mandíbula	jaw
la mejilla	cheek
el mentón, la barba, la barbilla	chin
la muñeca	wrist
el músculo	muscle
el muslo	thigh
las nalgas, el trasero, las asentaderas	buttocks
la nariz	nose
el nervio	nerve
el oído	(inner) ear
el ojo	eye
el ombligo	navel, belly button
la oreja	(outer) ear
la pantorrilla	calf
el párpado	eyelid
el pecho	chest
la pestaña	eyelash
el pie	foot
la piel	skin
la pierna	leg
el pulgar	thumb
el pulmón	lung
la rodilla	knee
la sangre	blood
el talón	heel
el tobillo	ankle
el tronco	torso, trunk
la uña	fingernail
la uña del dedo del pie	toenail
la vena	vein

Los cinco sentidos — The five senses

el gusto	taste
el oído	hearing
el olfato	smell
el tacto	touch
la vista	sight

La salud — Health

el accidente	accident
alérgico/a	allergic
el antibiótico	antibiotic
la aspirina	aspirin
el ataque cardiaco, el ataque al corazón	heart attack
el cáncer	cancer
la cápsula	capsule
la clínica	clinic
congestionado/a	congested
el consultorio	doctor's office
la curita	adhesive bandage
el/la dentista	dentist
el/la doctor(a), el/la médico/a	doctor
el dolor (de cabeza)	(head)ache, pain
embarazada	pregnant
la enfermedad	illness, disease
el/la enfermero/a	nurse
enfermo/a	ill, sick
la erupción	rash
el examen médico	physical exam
la farmacia	pharmacy
la fiebre	fever
la fractura	fracture
la gripe	flu
la herida	wound
el hospital	hospital
la infección	infection
el insomnio	insomnia
la inyección	injection
el jarabe	(cough) syrup
mareado/a	dizzy, nauseated
el medicamento	medication
la medicina	medicine
las muletas	crutches
la operación	operation
el/la paciente	patient
el/la paramédico/a	paramedic
la pastilla, la píldora	pill, tablet
los primeros auxilios	first aid
la pulmonía	pneumonia
los puntos	stitches
la quemadura	burn
el quirófano	operating room
la radiografía	x-ray
la receta	prescription
el resfriado	cold (illness)
la sala de emergencia(s)	emergency room
saludable	healthy, healthful
sano/a	healthy
el seguro médico	medical insurance
la silla de ruedas	wheelchair
el síntoma	symptom
el termómetro	thermometer
la tos	cough
la transfusión	transfusion

la vacuna	vaccination
la venda	bandage
el virus	virus

cortar(se)	to cut (oneself)
curar	to cure, to treat
desmayar(se)	to faint
enfermarse	to get sick
enyesar	to put in a cast
estornudar	to sneeze
guardar cama	to stay in bed
hinchar(se)	to swell
internar(se) en el hospital	to check into the hospital
lastimarse (el pie)	to hurt (one's foot)
mejorar(se)	to get better; to improve
operar	to operate
quemar(se)	to burn
respirar (hondo)	to breathe (deeply)
romperse (la pierna)	to break (one's leg)
sangrar	to bleed
sufrir	to suffer
tomarle la presión a alguien	to take someone's blood pressure
tomarle el pulso a alguien	to take someone's pulse
torcerse (el tobillo)	to sprain (one's ankle)
vendar	to bandage

EXPRESIONES ÚTILES PARA LA CLASE
USEFUL CLASSROOM EXPRESSIONS

Palabras útiles / Useful words

ausente	absent
el departamento	department
el dictado	dictation
la conversación, las conversaciones	conversation(s)
la expresión, las expresiones	expression(s)
el examen, los exámenes	test(s), exam(s)
la frase	sentence

la hoja de actividades	activity sheet
el horario de clases	class schedule
la oración, las oraciones	sentence(s)
el párrafo	paragraph
la persona	person
presente	present
la prueba	test, quiz
siguiente	following
la tarea	homework

Expresiones útiles / Useful expressions

Abra(n) su(s) libro(s).	Open your book(s).
Cambien de papel.	Change roles.
Cierre(n) su(s) libro(s).	Close your book(s).
¿Cómo se dice ___ en español?	How do you say ___ in Spanish?
¿Cómo se escribe ___ en español?	How do you write ___ in Spanish?
¿Comprende(n)?	Do you understand?
(No) comprendo.	I (don't) understand.
Conteste(n) las preguntas.	Answer the questions.
Continúe(n), por favor.	Continue, please.
Escriba(n) su nombre.	Write your name.
Escuche(n) el audio.	Listen to the audio.
Estudie(n) la Lección tres.	Study Lesson three.
Haga(n) la actividad (el ejercicio) número cuatro.	Do activity (exercise) number four.
Lea(n) la oración en voz alta.	Read the sentence aloud.
Levante(n) la mano.	Raise your hand(s).
Más despacio, por favor.	Slower, please.
No sé.	I don't know.
Páse(n)me los exámenes.	Pass me the tests.
¿Qué significa ___?	What does ___ mean?
Repita(n), por favor.	Repeat, please.
Siénte(n)se, por favor.	Sit down, please.
Siga(n) las instrucciones.	Follow the instructions.
¿Tiene(n) alguna pregunta?	Do you have any questions?
Vaya(n) a la página dos.	Go to page two.

COUNTRIES & NATIONALITIES
PAÍSES Y NACIONALIDADES

North America / Norteamérica

Canada	Canadá	canadiense
Mexico	México	mexicano/a
United States	Estados Unidos	estadounidense

Central America / Centroamérica

Belize	Belice	beliceño/a
Costa Rica	Costa Rica	costarricense
El Salvador	El Salvador	salvadoreño/a
Guatemala	Guatemala	guatemalteco/a
Honduras	Honduras	hondureño/a
Nicaragua	Nicaragua	nicaragüense
Panama	Panamá	panameño/a

The Caribbean	El Caribe	
Cuba	**Cuba**	*cubano/a*
Dominican Republic	**República Dominicana**	*dominicano/a*
Haiti	**Haití**	*haitiano/a*
Puerto Rico	**Puerto Rico**	*puertorriqueño/a*

South America	Suramérica	
Argentina	**Argentina**	*argentino/a*
Bolivia	**Bolivia**	*boliviano/a*
Brazil	**Brasil**	*brasileño/a*
Chile	**Chile**	*chileno/a*
Colombia	**Colombia**	*colombiano/a*
Ecuador	**Ecuador**	*ecuatoriano/a*
Paraguay	**Paraguay**	*paraguayo/a*
Peru	**Perú**	*peruano/a*
Uruguay	**Uruguay**	*uruguayo/a*
Venezuela	**Venezuela**	*venezolano/a*

Europe	Europa	
Armenia	**Armenia**	*armenio/a*
Austria	**Austria**	*austríaco/a*
Belgium	**Bélgica**	*belga*
Bosnia	**Bosnia**	*bosnio/a*
Bulgaria	**Bulgaria**	*búlgaro/a*
Croatia	**Croacia**	*croata*
Czech Republic	**República Checa**	*checo/a*
Denmark	**Dinamarca**	*danés, danesa*
England	**Inglaterra**	*inglés, inglesa*
Estonia	**Estonia**	*estonio/a*
Finland	**Finlandia**	*finlandés, finlandesa*
France	**Francia**	*francés, francesa*
Germany	**Alemania**	*alemán, alemana*
Great Britain (United Kingdom)	**Gran Bretaña (Reino Unido)**	*británico/a*
Greece	**Grecia**	*griego/a*
Hungary	**Hungría**	*húngaro/a*
Iceland	**Islandia**	*islandés, islandesa*
Ireland	**Irlanda**	*irlandés, irlandesa*
Italy	**Italia**	*italiano/a*
Latvia	**Letonia**	*letón, letona*
Lithuania	**Lituania**	*lituano/a*
Netherlands (Holland)	**Países Bajos (Holanda)**	*holandés, holandesa*
Norway	**Noruega**	*noruego/a*
Poland	**Polonia**	*polaco/a*
Portugal	**Portugal**	*portugués, portuguesa*
Romania	**Rumania**	*rumano/a*
Russia	**Rusia**	*ruso/a*
Scotland	**Escocia**	*escocés, escocesa*
Serbia	**Serbia**	*serbio/a*
Slovakia	**Eslovaquia**	*eslovaco/a*
Slovenia	**Eslovenia**	*esloveno/a*
Spain	**España**	*español(a)*
Sweden	**Suecia**	*sueco/a*
Switzerland	**Suiza**	*suizo/a*
Ukraine	**Ucrania**	*ucraniano/a*
Wales	**Gales**	*galés, galesa*

Asia	Asia	
Bangladesh	**Bangladés**	*bangladesí*
Cambodia	**Camboya**	*camboyano/a*
China	**China**	*chino/a*
India	**India**	*indio/a*
Indonesia	**Indonesia**	*indonesio/a*
Iran	**Irán**	*iraní*
Iraq	**Iraq, Irak**	*iraquí*

Israel	**Israel**	*israelí*
Japan	**Japón**	*japonés, japonesa*
Jordan	**Jordania**	*jordano/a*
Korea	**Corea**	*coreano/a*
Kuwait	**Kuwait**	*kuwaití*
Lebanon	**Líbano**	*libanés, libanesa*
Malaysia	**Malasia**	*malasio/a*
Pakistan	**Pakistán**	*pakistaní*
Russia	**Rusia**	*ruso/a*
Saudi Arabia	**Arabia Saudí**	*saudí*
Singapore	**Singapur**	*singapurés, singapuresa*
Syria	**Siria**	*sirio/a*
Taiwan	**Taiwán**	*taiwanés, taiwanesa*
Thailand	**Tailandia**	*tailandés, tailandesa*
Turkey	**Turquía**	*turco/a*
Vietnam	**Vietnam**	*vietnamita*

Africa / **África**

Algeria	**Argelia**	*argelino/a*
Angola	**Angola**	*angoleño/a*
Cameroon	**Camerún**	*camerunés, camerunesa*
Congo	**Congo**	*congolés, congolesa*
Egypt	**Egipto**	*egipcio/a*
Equatorial Guinea	**Guinea Ecuatorial**	*ecuatoguineano/a*
Ethiopia	**Etiopía**	*etíope*
Ivory Coast	**Costa de Marfil**	*marfileño/a*
Kenya	**Kenia, Kenya**	*keniano/a, keniata*
Libya	**Libia**	*libio/a*
Mali	**Malí**	*maliense*
Morocco	**Marruecos**	*marroquí*
Mozambique	**Mozambique**	*mozambiqueño/a*
Nigeria	**Nigeria**	*nigeriano/a*
Rwanda	**Ruanda**	*ruandés, ruandesa*
Somalia	**Somalia**	*somalí*
South Africa	**Sudáfrica**	*sudafricano/a*
Sudan	**Sudán**	*sudanés, sudanesa*
Tunisia	**Tunicia, Túnez**	*tunecino/a*
Uganda	**Uganda**	*ugandés, ugandesa*
Zambia	**Zambia**	*zambiano/a*
Zimbabwe	**Zimbabue**	*zimbabuense*

Australia and the Pacific / **Australia y el Pacífico**

Australia	**Australia**	*australiano/a*
New Zealand	**Nueva Zelanda**	*neozelandés, neozelandesa*
Philippines	**Filipinas**	*filipino/a*

MONEDAS DE LOS PAÍSES HISPANOS
CURRENCIES OF HISPANIC COUNTRIES

País / Country	Moneda / Currency
Argentina	el peso
Bolivia	el boliviano
Chile	el peso
Colombia	el peso
Costa Rica	el colón
Cuba	el peso
Ecuador	el dólar estadounidense
El Salvador	el dólar estadounidense
España	el euro
Guatemala	el quetzal
Guinea Ecuatorial	el franco
Honduras	el lempira
México	el peso
Nicaragua	el córdoba
Panamá	el balboa, el dólar estadounidense
Paraguay	el guaraní
Perú	el nuevo sol
Puerto Rico	el dólar estadounidense
República Dominicana	el peso
Uruguay	el peso
Venezuela	el bolívar

EXPRESIONES Y REFRANES

EXPRESSIONS AND SAYINGS

Expresiones y refranes con partes del cuerpo

Expressions and sayings with parts of the body

A cara o cruz	Heads or tails
A corazón abierto	Open heart
A ojos vistas	Clearly, visibly
Al dedillo	Like the back of one's hand
¡Choca/Vengan esos cinco!	Put it there!/Give me five!
Codo con codo	Side by side
Con las manos en la masa	Red-handed
Costar un ojo de la cara	To cost an arm and a leg
Darle a la lengua	To chatter/To gab
De rodillas	On one's knees
Duro de oído	Hard of hearing
En cuerpo y alma	In body and soul
En la punta de la lengua	On the tip of one's tongue
En un abrir y cerrar de ojos	In a blink of the eye
Entrar por un oído y salir por otro	In one ear and out the other
Estar con el agua al cuello	To be up to one's neck with/in
Estar para chuparse los dedos	To be delicious/To be finger-licking good
Hablar entre dientes	To mutter/To speak under one's breath
Hablar por los codos	To talk a lot/To be a chatterbox
Hacer la vista gorda	To turn a blind eye on something
Hombro con hombro	Shoulder to shoulder
Llorar a lágrima viva	To sob/To cry one's eyes out
Metérsele (a alguien) algo entre ceja y ceja	To get an idea in your head
No pegar ojo	Not to sleep a wink
No tener corazón	Not to have a heart
No tener dos dedos de frente	Not to have an ounce of common sense
Ojos que no ven, corazón que no siente	Out of sight, out of mind
Perder la cabeza	To lose one's head
Quedarse con la boca abierta	To be thunderstruck
Romper el corazón	To break someone's heart
Tener buen/mal corazón	Have a good/bad heart
Tener un nudo en la garganta	Have a knot in your throat
Tomarse algo a pecho	To take something too seriously
Venir como anillo al dedo	To fit like a charm/To suit perfectly

Expresiones y refranes con animales

Expressions and sayings with animals

A caballo regalado no le mires el diente.	Don't look a gift horse in the mouth.
Comer como un cerdo	To eat like a pig
Cuando menos se piensa, salta la liebre.	Things happen when you least expect it.
Llevarse como el perro y el gato	To fight like cats and dogs
Perro ladrador, poco mordedor./Perro que ladra no muerde.	His/her bark is worse than his/her bite.
Por la boca muere el pez.	Talking too much can be dangerous.
Poner el cascabel al gato	To stick one's neck out
Ser una tortuga	To be a slowpoke

Expresiones y refranes con alimentos

Expressions and sayings with food

Agua que no has de beber, déjala correr.	If you're not interested, don't ruin it for everybody else.
Con pan y vino se anda el camino.	Things never seem as bad after a good meal.
Contigo pan y cebolla.	You are all I need.
Dame pan y dime tonto.	I don't care what you say, as long as I get what I want.
Descubrir el pastel	To let the cat out of the bag
Dulce como la miel	Sweet as honey
Estar como agua para chocolate	To furious/To be at the boiling point
Estar en el ajo	To be in the know
Estar en la higuera	To have one's head in the clouds
Estar más claro que el agua	To be clear as a bell
Ganarse el pan	To earn a living/To earn one's daily bread
Llamar al pan, pan y al vino, vino.	Not to mince words.
No hay miel sin hiel.	Every rose has its thorn./There's always a catch.
No sólo de pan vive el hombre.	Man doesn't live by bread alone.
Pan con pan, comida de tontos.	Variety is the spice of life.
Ser agua pasada	To be water under the bridge
Ser más bueno que el pan	To be kindness itself
Temblar como un flan	To shake/tremble like a leaf

Expresiones y refranes con colores

Expressions and sayings with colors

Estar verde	To be inexperienced/wet behind the ears
Poner los ojos en blanco	To roll one's eyes
Ponerle a alguien un ojo morado	To give someone a black eye
Ponerse rojo	To turn red/To blush
Ponerse rojo de ira	To turn red with anger
Ponerse verde de envidia	To be green with envy
Quedarse en blanco	To go blank
Verlo todo de color de rosa	To see the world through rose-colored glasses

Refranes	Sayings		
A buen entendedor, pocas palabras bastan.	A word to the wise is enough.	**Lo que es moda no incomoda.**	You have to suffer in the name of fashion.
Ande o no ande, caballo grande.	Bigger is always better.	**Más vale maña que fuerza.**	Brains are better than brawn.
A quien madruga, Dios le ayuda.	The early bird catches the worm.	**Más vale prevenir que curar.**	Prevention is better than cure.
Cuídate, que te cuidaré.	Take care of yourself, and then I'll take care of you.	**Más vale solo que mal acompañado.**	Better alone than with people you don't like.
De tal palo tal astilla.	A chip off the old block.	**Más vale tarde que nunca.**	Better late than never.
Del dicho al hecho hay mucho trecho.	Easier said than done.	**No es oro todo lo que reluce.**	All that glitters is not gold.
Dime con quién andas y te diré quién eres.	A man is known by the company he keeps.	**Poderoso caballero es don Dinero.**	Money talks.
El saber no ocupa lugar.	One never knows too much.		

COMMON FALSE FRIENDS

False friends are Spanish words that look similar to English words but have very different meanings. While recognizing the English relatives of unfamiliar Spanish words you encounter is an important way of constructing meaning, there are some Spanish words whose similarity to English words is deceptive. Here is a list of some of the most common Spanish false friends.

actualmente ≠ actually
actualmente = nowadays, currently
actually = **de hecho, en realidad, en efecto**

argumento ≠ argument
argumento = plot
argument = **discusión, pelea**

armada ≠ army
armada = navy
army = **ejército**

balde ≠ bald
balde = pail, bucket
bald = **calvo/a**

batería ≠ battery
batería = drum set
battery = **pila**

bravo ≠ brave
bravo = wild; fierce
brave = **valiente**

cándido/a ≠ candid
cándido/a = innocent
candid = **sincero/a**

carbón ≠ carbon
carbón = coal
carbon = **carbono**

casual ≠ casual
casual = accidental, chance
casual = **informal, despreocupado/a**

casualidad ≠ casualty
casualidad = chance, coincidence
casualty = **víctima**

colegio ≠ college
colegio = school
college = **universidad**

collar ≠ collar (of a shirt)
collar = necklace
collar = **cuello (de camisa)**

comprensivo/a ≠ comprehensive
comprensivo/a = understanding
comprehensive = **completo, extensivo**

constipado ≠ constipated
estar constipado/a = to have a cold
to be constipated = **estar estreñido/a**

crudo/a ≠ crude
crudo/a = raw, undercooked
crude = **burdo/a, grosero/a**

divertir ≠ to divert
divertirse = to enjoy oneself
to divert = **desviar**

educado/a ≠ educated
educado/a = well-mannered
educated = **culto/a, instruido/a**

embarazada ≠ embarrassed
estar embarazada = to be pregnant
to be embarrassed = **estar avergonzado/a; dar/tener vergüenza**

eventualmente ≠ eventually
eventualmente = possibly
eventually = **finalmente, al final**

éxito ≠ exit
éxito = success
exit = **salida**

físico/a ≠ physician
físico/a = physicist
physician = **médico/a**

fútbol ≠ football
fútbol = soccer
football = **fútbol americano**

lectura ≠ lecture
lectura = reading
lecture = **conferencia**

librería ≠ library
librería = bookstore
library = **biblioteca**

máscara ≠ mascara
máscara = mask
mascara = **rímel**

molestar ≠ to molest
molestar = to bother, to annoy
to molest = **abusar**

oficio ≠ office
oficio = trade, occupation
office = **oficina**

rato ≠ rat
rato = while, time
rat = **rata**

realizar ≠ to realize
realizar = to carry out; to fulfill
to realize = **darse cuenta de**

red ≠ red
red = net
red = **rojo/a**

revolver ≠ revolver
revolver = to stir, to rummage through
revolver = **revólver**

sensible ≠ sensible
sensible = sensitive
sensible = **sensato/a, razonable**

suceso ≠ success
suceso = event
success = **éxito**

sujeto ≠ subject (topic)
sujeto = fellow; individual
subject = **tema, asunto**

LOS ALIMENTOS / FOODS

Frutas / Fruits

la aceituna	olive
el aguacate	avocado
el albaricoque, el damasco	apricot
la banana, el plátano	banana
la cereza	cherry
la ciruela	plum
el dátil	date
la frambuesa	raspberry
la fresa, la frutilla	strawberry
el higo	fig
el limón	lemon; lime
el melocotón, el durazno	peach
la mandarina	tangerine
el mango	mango
la manzana	apple
la naranja	orange
la papaya	papaya
la pera	pear
la piña	pineapple
el pomelo, la toronja	grapefruit
la sandía	watermelon
las uvas	grapes

Vegetales / Vegetables

la alcachofa	artichoke
el apio	celery
la arveja, el guisante	pea
la berenjena	eggplant
el brócoli	broccoli
la calabaza	squash; pumpkin
la cebolla	onion
el champiñón, la seta	mushroom
la col, el repollo	cabbage
la coliflor	cauliflower
los espárragos	asparagus
las espinacas	spinach
los frijoles, las habichuelas	beans
las habas	fava beans
las judías verdes, los ejotes	string beans, green beans
la lechuga	lettuce
el maíz, el choclo, el elote	corn
la papa, la patata	potato
el pepino	cucumber
el pimentón	bell pepper
el rábano	radish
la remolacha	beet
el tomate, el jitomate	tomato
la zanahoria	carrot

El pescado y los mariscos / Fish and shellfish

la almeja	clam
el atún	tuna
el bacalao	cod
el calamar	squid
el cangrejo	crab
el camarón, la gamba	shrimp
la langosta	lobster
el langostino	prawn
el lenguado	sole; flounder
el mejillón	mussel
la ostra	oyster
el pulpo	octopus
el salmón	salmon
la sardina	sardine
la vieira	scallop

La carne / Meat

la albóndiga	meatball
el bistec	steak
la carne de res	beef
el chorizo	hard pork sausage
la chuleta de cerdo	pork chop
el cordero	lamb
los fiambres	cold cuts, food served cold
el filete	fillet
la hamburguesa	hamburger
el hígado	liver
el jamón	ham
el lechón	suckling pig, roasted pig
el pavo	turkey
el pollo	chicken
el cerdo	pork
la salchicha	sausage
la ternera	veal
el tocino	bacon

Otras comidas / Other foods

el ajo	garlic
el arroz	rice
el azúcar	sugar
el batido	milkshake
el budín	pudding
el cacahuete, el maní	peanut
el café	coffee
los fideos	noodles, pasta
la harina	flour
el huevo	egg
el jugo, el zumo	juice
la leche	milk
la mermelada	marmalade, jam
la miel	honey
el pan	bread
el queso	cheese
la sal	salt
la sopa	soup
el té	tea
la tortilla	omelet (Spain), tortilla (Mexico)
el yogur	yogurt

Cómo describir la comida / Ways to describe food

a la plancha, a la parrilla	grilled
ácido/a	sour
al horno	baked
amargo/a	bitter
caliente	hot
dulce	sweet
duro/a	tough
frío/a	cold
frito/a	fried
fuerte	strong, heavy
ligero/a	light
picante	spicy
sabroso/a	tasty
salado/a	salty

DÍAS FESTIVOS / HOLIDAYS

enero — January
Año Nuevo (1) — New Year's Day
Día de los Reyes Magos (6) — Three Kings Day (Epiphany)
Día de Martin Luther King, Jr. — Martin Luther King, Jr. Day

febrero — February
Día de San Blas (Paraguay) (3) — St. Blas Day (Paraguay)
Día de San Valentín, Día de los Enamorados (14) — Valentine's Day
Día de los Presidentes — Presidents' Day
Carnaval — Carnival (Mardi Gras)

marzo — March
Día de San Patricio (17) — St. Patrick's Day
Nacimiento de Benito Juárez (México) (21) — Benito Juárez's Birthday (Mexico)

abril — April
Semana Santa — Holy Week
Pésaj — Passover
Pascua — Easter
Declaración de la Independencia de Venezuela (19) — Declaration of Independence of Venezuela
Día de la Tierra (22) — Earth Day

mayo — May
Día del Trabajo (1) — Labor Day
Cinco de Mayo (5) (México) — Cinco de Mayo (May 5th) (Mexico)
Día de las Madres — Mother's Day
Independencia Patria (Paraguay) (15) — Independence Day (Paraguay)
Día Conmemorativo — Memorial Day

junio — June
Día de los Padres — Father's Day
Día de la Bandera (14) — Flag Day
Día del Indio (Perú) (24) — Native People's Day (Peru)

julio — July
Día de la Independencia de los Estados Unidos (4) — Independence Day (United States)
Día de la Independencia de Venezuela (5) — Independence Day (Venezuela)
Día de la Independencia de la Argentina (9) — Independence Day (Argentina)
Día de la Independencia de Colombia (20) — Independence Day (Colombia)
Nacimiento de Simón Bolívar (24) — Simón Bolívar's Birthday
Día de la Revolución (Cuba) (26) — Revolution Day (Cuba)
Día de la Independencia del Perú (28) — Independence Day (Peru)

agosto — August
Día de la Independencia de Bolivia (6) — Independence Day (Bolivia)
Día de la Independencia del Ecuador (10) — Independence Day (Ecuador)
Día de San Martín (Argentina) (17) — San Martín Day (anniversary of his death) (Argentina)
Día de la Independencia del Uruguay (25) — Independence Day (Uruguay)

septiembre — September
Día del Trabajo (EE. UU.) — Labor Day (U.S.)
Día de la Independencia de Costa Rica, El Salvador, Guatemala, Honduras y Nicaragua (15) — Independence Day (Costa Rica, El Salvador, Guatemala, Honduras, Nicaragua)
Día de la Independencia de México (16) — Independence Day (Mexico)
Día de la Independencia de Chile (18) — Independence Day (Chile)
Año Nuevo Judío — Jewish New Year
Día de la Virgen de las Mercedes (Perú) (24) — Day of the Virgin of Mercedes (Peru)

octubre — October
Día de la Raza (12) — Columbus Day
Noche de Brujas (31) — Halloween

noviembre — November
Día de los Muertos (2) — All Souls Day
Día de los Veteranos (11) — Veterans' Day
Día de la Revolución Mexicana (20) — Mexican Revolution Day
Día de Acción de Gracias — Thanksgiving
Día de la Independencia de Panamá (28) — Independence Day (Panama)

diciembre — December
Día de la Virgen (8) — Day of the Virgin
Día de la Virgen de Guadalupe (México) (12) — Day of the Virgin of Guadalupe (Mexico)
Januká — Chanukah
Nochebuena (24) — Christmas Eve
Navidad (25) — Christmas
Año Viejo (31) — New Year's Eve

NOTE: In Spanish, dates are written with the day first, then the month. Christmas Day is **el 25 de diciembre**. In Latin America and in Europe, abbreviated dates also follow this pattern. Halloween, for example, falls on 31/10. You may also see the numbers in dates separated by periods: 27.4.16. When referring to centuries, roman numerals are always used. The 16th century, therefore, is **el siglo XVI**.

PESOS Y MEDIDAS

WEIGHTS AND MEASURES

Longitud
El sistema métrico
Metric system

Length
El equivalente estadounidense
U.S. equivalent

milímetro = 0,001 metro
millimeter = 0.001 meter | = 0.039 inch
centímetro = 0,01 metro
centimeter = 0.01 meter | = 0.39 inch
decímetro = 0,1 metro
decimeter = 0.1 meter | = 3.94 inches
metro
meter | = 39.4 inches
decámetro = 10 metros
dekameter = 10 meters | = 32.8 feet
hectómetro = 100 metros
hectometer = 100 meters | = 328 feet
kilómetro = 1.000 metros
kilometer = 1,000 meters | = .62 mile
U.S. system
El sistema estadounidense
inch | = 2.54 centimeters
pulgada | **= 2,54 centímetros**
foot = 12 inches | = 30.48 centimeters
pie = 12 pulgadas | **= 30,48 centímetros**
yard = 3 feet | = 0.914 meter
yarda = 3 pies | **= 0,914 metro**
mile = 5,280 feet | = 1.609 kilometers
milla = 5.280 pies | **= 1,609 kilómetros**

Metric equivalent
El equivalente métrico

Superficie
El sistema métrico
Metric system

Surface Area
El equivalente estadounidense
U.S. equivalent

metro cuadrado
square meter | = 10.764 square feet
área = 100 metros cuadrados
area = 100 square meters | = 0.025 acre
hectárea = 100 áreas
hectare = 100 ares | = 2.471 acres
U.S. system
El sistema estadounidense

Metric equivalent
El equivalente métrico

yarda cuadrada = 9 pies cuadrados = 0,836 metros cuadrados
square yard = 9 square feet = 0.836 square meters
acre = 4.840 yardas cuadradas = 0,405 hectáreas
acre = 4,840 square yards = 0.405 hectares

Capacidad
El sistema métrico
Metric system

Capacity
El equivalente estadounidense
U.S. equivalent

mililitro = 0,001 litro
milliliter = 0.001 liter | = 0.034 ounces

centilitro = 0,01 litro
centiliter = 0.01 liter | = 0.34 ounces
decilitro = 0,1 litro
deciliter = 0.1 liter | = 3.4 ounces
litro
liter | = 1.06 quarts
decalitro = 10 litros
dekaliter = 10 liters | = 2.64 gallons
hectolitro = 100 litros
hectoliter = 100 liters | = 26.4 gallons
kilolitro = 1.000 litros
kiloliter = 1,000 liters | = 264 gallons
U.S. system
El sistema estadounidense
ounce
onza
cup = 8 ounces
taza = 8 onzas
pint = 2 cups
pinta = 2 tazas
quart = 2 pints
cuarto = 2 pintas
gallon = 4 quarts
galón = 4 cuartos

Metric equivalent
El equivalente métrico
= 29.6 milliliters
= 29,6 mililitros
= 236 milliliters
= 236 mililitros
= 0.47 liters
= 0,47 litros
= 0.95 liters
= 0,95 litros
= 3.79 liters
= 3,79 litros

Peso
El sistema métrico
Metric system

Weight
El equivalente estadounidense
U.S. equivalent

miligramo = 0,001 gramo
milligram = 0.001 gram
gramo
gram | = 0.035 ounce
decagramo = 10 gramos
dekagram = 10 grams | = 0.35 ounces
hectogramo = 100 gramos
hectogram = 100 grams | = 3.5 ounces
kilogramo = 1.000 gramos
kilogram = 1,000 grams | = 2.2 pounds
tonelada (métrica) = 1.000 kilogramos
metric ton = 1,000 kilograms | = 1.1 tons

U.S. system
El sistema estadounidense
ounce
onza
pound = 16 ounces
libra = 16 onzas
ton = 2,000 pounds
tonelada = 2.000 libras

Metric equivalent
El equivalente métrico
= 28.35 grams
= 28,35 gramos
= 0.45 kilograms
= 0,45 kilogramos
= 0.9 metric tons
= 0,9 toneladas métricas

Temperatura
Grados centígrados
Degrees Celsius
To convert from Celsius to Fahrenheit, multiply by $\frac{9}{5}$ and add 32.

Temperature
Grados Fahrenheit
Degrees Fahrenheit
To convert from Fahrenheit to Celsius, subtract 32 and multiply by $\frac{5}{9}$.

NÚMEROS

Números ordinales

primer, primero/a	1o/1a
segundo/a	2o/2a
tercer, tercero/a	3o/3a
cuarto/a	4o/4a
quinto/a	5o/5a
sexto/a	6o/6a
séptimo/a	7o/7a
octavo/a	8o/8a
noveno/a	9o/9a
décimo/a	10o/10a

Fracciones

$\frac{1}{2}$	un medio, la mitad	
$\frac{1}{3}$	un tercio	
$\frac{1}{4}$	un cuarto	
$\frac{1}{5}$	un quinto	
$\frac{1}{6}$	un sexto	
$\frac{1}{7}$	un séptimo	
$\frac{1}{8}$	un octavo	
$\frac{1}{9}$	un noveno	
$\frac{1}{10}$	un décimo	
$\frac{2}{3}$	dos tercios	
$\frac{3}{4}$	tres cuartos	
$\frac{5}{8}$	cinco octavos	

Decimales

un décimo	0,1
un centésimo	0,01
un milésimo	0,001

NUMBERS

Ordinal numbers

first	1st
second	2nd
third	3rd
fourth	4th
fifth	5th
sixth	6th
seventh	7th
eighth	8th
ninth	9th
tenth	10th

Fractions

one half
one third
one fourth (quarter)
one fifth
one sixth
one seventh
one eighth
one ninth
one tenth
two thirds
three fourths (quarters)
five eighths

Decimals

one tenth	0.1
one hundredth	0.01
one thousandth	0.001

OCUPACIONES / OCCUPATIONS

el/la abogado/a	lawyer
el actor, la actriz	actor
el/la administrador(a) de empresas	business administrator
el/la agente de bienes raíces	real estate agent
el/la agente de seguros	insurance agent
el/la agricultor(a)	farmer
el/la arqueólogo/a	archaeologist
el/la arquitecto/a	architect
el/la artesano/a	artisan
el/la auxiliar de vuelo	flight attendant
el/la basurero/a	garbage collector
el/la bibliotecario/a	librarian
el/la bombero/a	firefighter
el/la cajero/a	bank teller, cashier
el/la camionero/a	truck driver
el/la carnicero/a	butcher
el/la carpintero/a	carpenter
el/la científico/a	scientist
el/la cirujano/a	surgeon
el/la cobrador(a)	bill collector
el/la cocinero/a	cook, chef
el/la consejero/a	counselor, advisor
el/la contador(a)	accountant
el/la corredor(a) de bolsa	stockbroker
el/la diplomático/a	diplomat
el/la diseñador(a) (gráfico/a)	(graphic) designer
el/la electricista	electrician
el/la fisioterapeuta	physical therapist
el/la fotógrafo/a	photographer
el hombre/la mujer de negocios	businessperson
el/la ingeniero/a en computación	computer engineer
el/la intérprete	interpreter
el/la juez(a)	judge
el/la maestro/a	elementary school teacher
el/la marinero/a	sailor
el/la obrero/a	manual laborer
el/la optometrista	optometrist
el/la panadero/a	baker
el/la paramédico/a	paramedic
el/la peluquero/a	hairdresser
el/la piloto	pilot
el/la pintor(a)	painter
el/la plomero/a	plumber
el/la político/a	politician
el/la programador(a)	computer programer
el/la psicólogo/a	psychologist
el/la reportero/a	reporter
el/la sastre	tailor
el/la secretario/a	secretary
el/la técnico/a (en computación)	(computer) technician
el/la vendedor(a)	sales representative
el/la veterinario/a	veterinarian

About the Author

José A. Blanco founded Vista Higher Learning in 1998. A native of Barranquilla, Colombia, Mr. Blanco holds degrees in Literature and Hispanic Studies from Brown University and the University of California, Santa Cruz. He has worked as a writer, editor, and translator for Houghton Mifflin and D.C. Heath and Company, and has taught Spanish at the secondary and university levels. Mr. Blanco is also the co-author of several other Vista Higher Learning programs: Vistas, Panorama, Aventuras, and ¡Viva! at the introductory level; Ventanas, Facetas, Enfoques, Imagina, and Sueña at the intermediate level; and Revista at the advanced conversation level.

About the Illustrators

Yayo, an internationally acclaimed illustrator, was born in Colombia. He has illustrated children's books, newspapers, and magazines, and has been exhibited around the world. He currently lives in Montreal, Canada.

Pere Virgili lives and works in Barcelona, Spain. His illustrations have appeared in textbooks, newspapers, and magazines throughout Spain and Europe.

Born in Caracas, Venezuela, **Hermann Mejía** studied illustration at the Instituto de Diseño de Caracas. Hermann currently lives and works in the United States.

Credits

TV Clip Credits

page 56   Courtesy of ContentLine.
page 94   Courtesy of Santander Chile.
page 130   Courtesy of Juguettos.

Photography Credits

Cover: Grandriver/iStockphoto.

Front matter (SE): xii: (l) Bettmann/Getty Images; (r) Florian Biamm/**123RF**; **xiii:** (l) Lawrence Manning/Corbis; (r) Design Pics Inc/Alamy; **xiv:** Jose Blanco, **xv:** (l) Digital Vision/Getty Images; (r) Andres/Big Stock Photo; **xvi:** Fotolia IV/Fotolia; **xvii:** (l) Goodshoot/Corbis; (r) Tyler Olson/Shutterstock; **xviii:** Shelly Wall/Shutterstock; **xix:** (t) Colorblind/Corbis; (b) Moodboard/Fotolia; **xx:** (t) Digital Vision/Getty Images; (b) Purestock/Getty Images.

Front matter (TE): T4: Teodor Cucu/500PX; **T14:** Asiseeit/iStockphoto; **T37:** Corbis Photography/Veer; (inset) Fancy Photography/Veer; **T48:** Braun S/iStockphoto.

Preliminary Lesson
1: Teodor Cucu/500PX; **2:** (t) Asiseeit/iStockphoto; (bl) Mediaphotos/iStockphoto; (br) DGLimages/iStockphoto; **2-3:** Gts/Shutterstock; **4:** Pressmaster/iStockphoto; **8:** (t) John Feingersh/Media Bakery; (b) Michael Simons/**123RF**; Zeeker2526/Shutterstock; **8-9:** Pla2na/Shutterstock; Jurisam/Deposit Photos; **10:** Cathy Yeulet/**123RF**; **12:** (all) Carolina Zapata; **13:** Carolina Zapata; **14:** Gallo Gallina/Bridgeman Art Library/Getty Images; **15:** Craig Lowell/Eagle Visions Photography/Alamy; **16:** (tl) Sorbis/Shutterstock; (tr) Vanessa Bertozzi; (ml) Ververidis Vasilis/Shutterstock; (mm) Olivier Tabary/Shutterstock; (mr) ValeStock/Shutterstock; (bl) AGE Fotostock RF; (bm) Gudrun Hommel; (br) Marc Printer/Alamy; Park Jinman/Shutterstock; **16-17:** Robbi/Shutterstock; Madredus/Shutterstock; **17:** (l) Sergey Nivens/Shutterstock; (r) Lmgorthand/iStockphoto; **19:** (t) Andresr/iStockphoto; (ml) Andres Rodriguez/Fotolia; (mr) Skynesher/iStockphoto; (bl) VHL; (br) Nicole Winchell; **20:** Davidf/iStockphoto; **24:** (all)Carolina Zapata.

Lesson 4
25: Franz Faltermaier/AGE Fotostock; **27:** George Shelley/Getty Images; **34:** (l) Javier Soriano/AFP/Getty Images; (r) Fernando Bustamante/AP Images; **35:** (t) Photo Works/Shutterstock; (r) Zuma Press/Alamy; **38:** Jacek Chabraszewski/Fotolia; **49:** Mat Hayward/Fotolia; **52:** Martín Bernetti; **53:** Fernando Llano/AP Images; **54:** JGI/Jamie Grill/Media Bakery; **55:** Rick Gomez/Getty Images; **58:** (tl) Sorincolac/Fotolia; (tr) Albright Knox Art Gallery/Art Resource; (ml) Ruben Varela; (mr) Carolina Zapata; (b) Brian Overcast/Alamy; **59:** (t) Radius Images/Alamy; (mt) Bettmann/Getty Images; (mb) Corel/Corbis; (b) David R. Frazier Photolibrary/Alamy.

Lesson 5
61: Gavin Hellier/Getty Images; **67:** Jeff Greenberg/Alamy; **72:** Gary Cook/Alamy; **73:** (t) AFP/Getty Images; (b) Pierre-Yves Babelon/**123RF**; **77:** Ronnie Kaufman/Getty Images; **87:** Blend Images/Fotolia; **90:** Carlos Gaudier; **91:** (tl) Corel/Corbis; (tr) Carlos Gaudier; (m) Carlos Gaudier; (b) Carlos Gaudier; **92:** Carolina Zapata; **96:** (tl) Bryan Mullennix/Alamy; (tr) José Blanco; (ml) Carlos Gaudier; (mr) Capricornis Photographic/Shutterstock; (b) Dave G. Houser/Getty Images; **97:** (t) Carlos Gaudier; (mt) Lawrence Manning/Getty Images; (mb) Stocktrek/Getty Images; (b) Carlos Gaudier.

Lesson 6
99: Asiapix RF/Inmagine; **108:** (l) Jose Caballero Digital Press Photos/Newscom; (r) Janet Dracksdorf; **109:** (t) Carlos Alvarez/Getty Images; (bl) Guiseppe Carace/Getty Images; (br) Mark Mainz/Getty Images; **114:** (all) Pascal Pernix; **119:** (all) Martín Bernetti; **120:** (all) Paula Díez; **121:** Paula Díez; **126-127:** Paula Díez and Shutterstock; **128:** Chris Schmidt/iStockphoto; **129:** John Henley/Media Bakery; **132:** (tl) Pascal Pernix; (tr) Pascal Pernix; (mt) Pascal Pernix; (mb) Pascal Pernix; (b) PhotoLink/Getty Images; **133:** (tl) Don Emmert/AFP/Getty Images; (tr) Pascal Pernix; (bl) Pascal Pernix; (br) Movie Prods/REX/Shutterstock.